Steep Slopes

Music and change in the Highlands of Papua New Guinea

KIRSTY GILLESPIE

Steep Slopes

Music and change in the Highlands of Papua New Guinea

KIRSTY GILLESPIE

ANU

THE AUSTRALIAN NATIONAL UNIVERSITY

E PRESS

ANU

E PRESS

Published by ANU E Press
The Australian National University
Canberra ACT 0200, Australia
Email: anuepress@anu.edu.au
This title is also available online at: http://epress.anu.edu.au/steepslopes_citation.html

---

National Library of Australia
Cataloguing-in-Publication entry

Author: Gillespie, Kirsty.

Title: Steep slopes : music and change in the highlands of Papua New Guinea /
               Kirsty Gillespie.

ISBN: 9781921666421 (pbk.) 9781921666438 (eBook : pdf)

Notes: Includes bibliographical references.

Subjects: Duna (Papua New Guinean people)--Music.
               Duna (Papua New Guinean people)--Social life and customs.
               Papua New Guinea--Music.

Dewey Number: 780.956

Cover design and layout by Epress

Contents

This book is dedicated to the memory of

Wakili Akuri (1985 – 2005)

Sane Noma (early 1900s – 2006)

&

Richard Alo (1969 – 2007)

Acknowledgments

A cross-cultural, cross-disciplinary publication such as this requires a great many colleagues and collaborators. First, I must thank Dr Alan Rumsey for starting me on my research journey in Papua New Guinea by inviting me to join the Australian Research Council-funded project 'Chanted Tales from Highland New Guinea' on which he was the chief investigator, and for encouraging me to pursue research on the music of the Highlands of Papua New Guinea as my doctoral research topic, on which this publication is based. Colleagues on the Chanted Tales project—Dr Nicole Haley, Don Niles and Dr Lila San Roque— have all played integral parts in the research, which will become evident as the book unfolds. Several people were very generous with their own materials: I was able to access not only recordings and photographs of my colleagues, but materials from Dr Nicholas Modjeska, Dr Chris Ballard, David Hook, Georgina San Roque and Tim Scott.

In Papua New Guinea, I have a great many people to thank. Jim Robins at the National Research Institute in Port Moresby assisted in the prompt processing of my visa applications. The exceptional staff of the Mission Aviation Fellowship (MAF) based at Mount Hagen not only provided the only form of transport to Kopiago for me, they brought the post and continue to relay my letters and parcels to Duna friends. MAF pilot Pierre Fasnacht and his wife, Esther, provided invaluable support during the 2005 trip to Kopiago; Pierre's tragic passing in a plane accident at Tari in the Southern Highlands Province on 23 March 2006 continues to be deeply felt by all who knew him. Kevin Murphy very kindly hosted me at his home in Mount Hagen on a number of occasions throughout 2005–07. When 'Guesthouse Kevin' was booked out, I stayed at the Mount Hagen Missionary Home, with value accommodation, enormous meals and kind staff, who were willing to answer calls, receive post, relay messages, provide airport pick-ups and welcome my daily Duna visitors.

I am of course indebted to the people of Kopiago for welcoming me into their lives. Kenny Kendoli and Kipo Piero and their family were good enough to host me at their hamlet in the parish of Hirane during my 2004 and 2005 visits to Kopiago. Not only did they provide me with a place to stay, they assisted me greatly in my day-to-day activities and contributed significantly to my understanding of Duna music and culture. It is a great responsibility and a considerable inconvenience to host foreigners in any community and I am grateful for their efforts in making me feel welcome. In 2007, I was hosted by Petros Kilapa and his wife, Julinda Yoke, in the parish of Mbara. I thank them too for their kindness.

I thank all the Duna people who ever allowed me to record or interview them. They are too many to name here, but those whose songs have been incorporated into the publication have been duly acknowledged in the list of examples (Appendix 1) and in many cases in the text as well. Without those people who patiently explained and translated concepts for me—in particular, Richard Alo, Kenny Kendoli, Petros Kilapa and Sane Noma—my research project would have been impossible.

This research was funded by an Australian Postgraduate Award, with fieldwork funding provided by the ANU Research School of Humanities and the Australian Research Council. The manuscript was finalised during a period as a Visiting Fellow in the Division of Pacific and Asian History, Research School of Pacific and Asian Studies, The Australian National University. Thank you to my colleagues and to the reviewers of the manuscript for their close reading and comments on it; any errors that remain, however, are my own.

List of figures

All photographs taken by the author unless otherwise indicated.

Table of examples

Audio samples relating to this work are available online at:
http://epress.anu.edu.au/steepslopes/media.html

ITEM	AUDIO
Example 2.1: Basic pitch structure of stylised *heya* or ancestral *khene ipakana*	
Example 2.2: Basic pitch structure of *mindimindi kāo*	
Example 2.3: Basic pitch structure of a *pikono* 'verse'	
Example 2.4: Basic pitch structure of *selepa*	
Example 2.5: Basic pitch structure of *yekia*	
Example 2.6: *Alima*	1
Example 2.7: *Kuluparapu*	2
Example 2.8: *Pilipe*	3
Example 2.9: *Luna*	4
Example 2.10: Basic pitch structure of *mali mapu* based on Chenoweth's notation	
Example 2.11: *Kēiyaka* sequence	
Example 3.1: 'Lotu' *yekia*	5
Example 3.2: *Ten Little Indians*	6
Example 3.3: Excerpt of Pugh-Kitingan's Transcription 74	
Example 3.3b: *Ega Emene*	
Example 3.4: '*Nane* laip senis n*ganda waya keina*'	7
Example 3.5: 'Memba *pi nakaya*' *(campaign song)*	8
Example 3.6: 'Memba *pi nakaya*' (Ben Peri)	9
Example 3.7: 'Memba *pi nakaya*' (Pita Pex)	10
Example 3.8: 'Memba *pi nakaya*' (Apa Ngote)	11
Example 4.1: Alo's descent	12
Example 4.2: Pokole's *khene ipakana yakaya*	13
Example 4.3: Kipu's k*hene ipakana yakaya*	14
Example 4.4: Soti's *khene ipakana yakaya*	
Example 4.5: Kepo's *khene ipakana yakaya*	15
Example 4.6: Kepo's *khene ipakana yakaya* as a duet	15
Example 4.7: Kipu's *khene ipakana* (with guitar accompaniment)	16

1. Introduction

> From time to time, when luck is on their side, ethnographers stumble
> onto culturally given ideas whose striking novelty and evident scope
> seem to cry out for thoughtful consideration beyond their accustomed
> boundaries. (Basso 1996:58)

This is the study of the musical practices of the Duna—a remote, rural
community in the Highlands of Papua New Guinea. Inspired by the frequency
and popularity of Western-style songs composed by the Duna people
themselves, I began to research these compositions alongside the pre-contact
genres that I had arrived in the region to study. Not long thereafter, I began to
realise the similarities between this pre and post-contact music. This book aims
to reveal those similarities, arguing for the existence of continuity in the Duna's
seemingly disparate musical practices.

In this introductory chapter, I set out the aims of this book, the location and
circumstance of the research and the need for such research due to the nature
of the existing literature. I explain my theoretical orientation regarding the
material I present and outline the methodology used to obtain and present this
material. Finally, I give an outline of the structure of the book in its entirety,
opening the door to the argument that follows.

Aims

It is important to state at the outset that this research does not take a salvage
approach that would concern itself with the preservation of Duna musical
forms perceived as 'dying out'. This view might be popular, particularly in
non-academic discourse, however, it is far more valuable for research into a
culture's musical practices to examine processes of change (Shiner 2003:155);
indeed, the study of cultural change as a result of social change has become
a demand of some disciplines, particularly anthropology (cf. Rumsey 2006a).
In his groundbreaking monograph on ethnomusicology, Merriam (1964:9–10)
wrote with much foresight that 'energy which is poured into lament for the
inevitability of change is energy wasted…The preservation of contemporary
music is undeniably important, but given the inevitability of change, it cannot
be the only aim of ethnomusicology'. In accordance with these views, this book
is concerned with processes of change surrounding musical practices.

The research was driven by several research questions. First, what aspects of Duna indigenous musical forms allow (or do not allow, as the case may be) the incorporation of new aspects arising from social change? Second, what forms of indigenous agency might be in place to maintain indigenous music alongside foreign music that exists in the Duna community? Third, what have been the reasons behind that community's embrace of non-indigenous music? To answer these questions, I needed to examine the music associated with both the pre-contact and the post-contact periods of history. This book does just that. Separating musical practices into these two halves, while seemingly easy, is, however, unnatural and defeats the argument for continuity before it has begun. An imperative for this book is therefore to deconstruct this dichotomy. Ultimately, this study aims to contribute to the knowledge of Duna culture more generally. After a Duna man, Richard Alo, co-presented with me at the twenty-ninth National Conference of the Musicological Society of Australia in September 2006, I asked him what he thought of the work of music researchers, this being his first formal exposure to such work. His response was very positive; with music, he said, 'you can learn very quickly about a culture. Everyone is happy to play and wants to share their music' (Richard Alo, Personal communication, 1 October 2006). This view is most optimistic, but the core belief remains: music is a very transparent and valuable way in which to understand a culture's world view. I maintain this belief throughout this book.

The geographical setting

> Kopiago is a lake of unsurpassed beauty…It has pine-clad peninsulas, grass islands drifting with the breeze, clear water which on still days mirrors the hills around, ducks and other waterbirds, and an outlet waterfall which disappears into a hillside cave. The people['s]…houses perched on hills but their gardens came to the shore, and they trenched and dyked swamps to the north as well. (Gammage 1998:135)

The Duna are an ethno-linguistic group living in the remote north-western corner of the Southern Highlands Province of Papua New Guinea.[1] They do not live in villages but in hamlets dispersed across the area, and their livelihood is based on subsistence farming, with a very low average annual income of K20 (approximately A$9) (Hanson et al. 2001:93). At present, the number of Duna speakers totals about 25 000 (Haley 2002a:11).

---

1   The Duna originally called themselves 'Yuna'; however, the term Duna, used by the neighbouring Huli people, was adopted in official documents and has now become a common term used by both Duna and non-Duna alike. I continue to use 'Duna' here to be consistent with other academic texts.

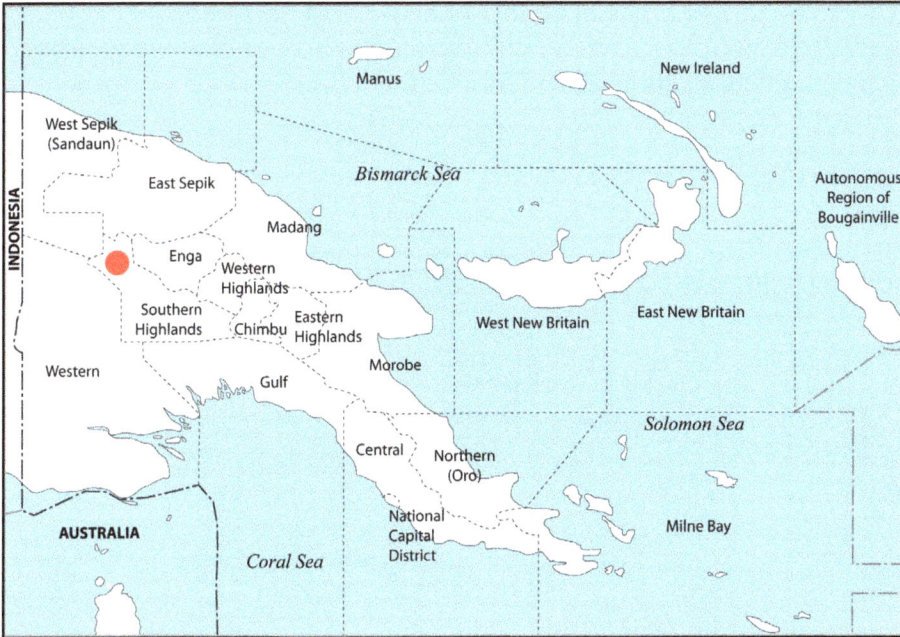

Figure 1.1 Map of Papua New Guinea, with circle indicating approximately the Duna-speaking area.

Courtesy of Don Niles

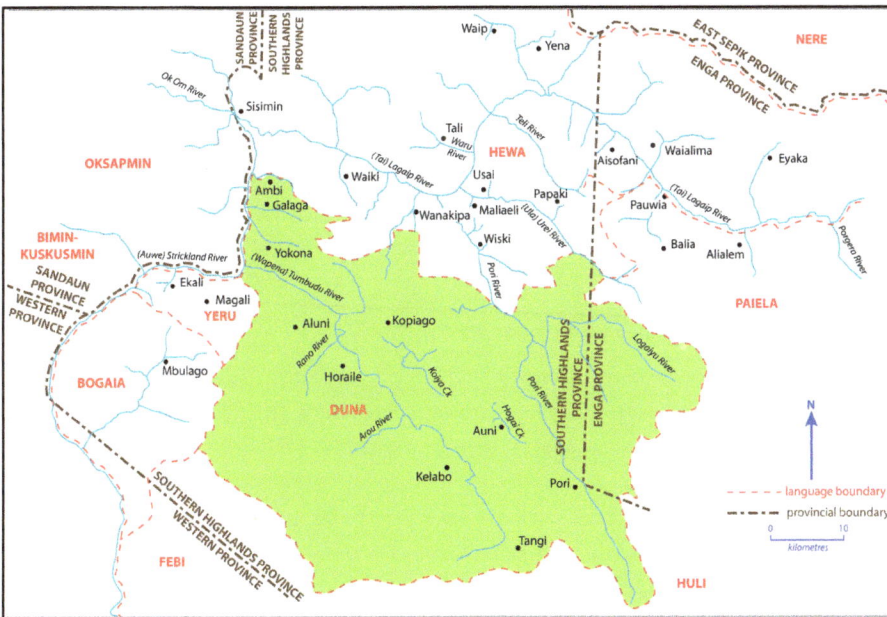

Figure 1.2 Map of Duna and neighbouring language areas.

Courtesy of Don Niles. Based on Haley (2002a:21)

The Strickland River is both a physical and a cultural border for the Duna, resulting in 'sporran people east, penis gourd people west' (Gammage 1998:95). The administrative centre of the Duna-speaking area is Lake Kopiago and it is around this centre where I have conducted my research.

The Duna people's first encounter with the outside world occurred in 1934 when an Australian patrol led by Tom and Jack Fox travelled through the area prospecting for gold. This patrol was the first into the densely populated Highlands region, which had never before been known to the rest of the world (nor was the rest of the world known to it). First contact was acrimonious; while the Foxes themselves did not document any conflict and even went so far as to deny causing any deaths or violence, the indigenous people of the Highlands report otherwise (Allen and Frankel 1991:97–9). A subsequent patrol, in 1938–39, was led by Jim Taylor and funded by the Australian government. The aim was to map the area and to bring pacification—a *'pax Australiana'*—to relations with indigenous communities ahead of the arrival of an anticipated high number of prospectors lured by gold (Gammage 1998:11). On this second patrol, chaos and conflict were reported to have occurred (possibly exacerbated by the Duna's memory of the Fox patrol), which led the Duna to believe that 'the world was falling apart' (Gammage 1998:136)—a response typical in the region at this point of first contact (Schieffelin 1991:3; Stewart and Strathern 2002b:12–13).

The colonisation of the area by the Australian government in the late 1950s and the subsequent missionisation in the early 1960s led to major social changes for the Duna, indeed for the whole Highlands region, whose people have been described as experiencing 'a crash-course in modernity' (O'Hanlon 1993:10). Nicholas Modjeska (1982:50), one of the first anthropologists to work with the Duna, writes that '[b]y 1969 the pre-colonial superstructure of cultural and social relations was nearly unrecognisable after a decade of post-contact changes. Warfare had ceased and mission activities had effected a rapid replacement of tribal beliefs and rituals by Christian practices' (see also Strathern and Stewart 2004:128).

Independence for Papua New Guinea followed soon after, in 1975, and after this was granted, the colonisers began to depart. Similarly, the colonial missionaries also departed, after training Duna people to carry on their legacy. With the departure of these visitors came also a decline in some of the key services the Duna had begun to accept as part of the new order in their community, such as policing, education, medical services, food imports and road infrastructure. As a result, there is currently a strong sense of colonial nostalgia among many Duna, especially the older generations.

The Duna today on the whole describe their place as disadvantaged. Robinson writes (2002:148): 'Duna people feel that Kopiago lacks development, and that nothing constructive has happened since independence.' The handbooks on the area claim the same: 'Overall, people in the Koroba-Lake Kopiago District are extremely disadvantaged relative to people in other districts of PNG' (Hanson et al. 2001:102). Allen (2005) argues that 'there have always been poor places in PNG' and 'the places poor now were poor before colonisation, before the state, before the monetary economy'; such 'poor places' are marked by isolation/lack of accessibility, severe environmental constraints, poor education and political 'invisibility'. These factors must be considered in an understanding of the Duna's current circumstances.

The very recent and dramatic history of colonisation and missionisation of the Duna-speaking area provides an exciting setting for a study of musical change. A number of people are still alive who can comment on their experience of encountering Western culture and its people for the first time and their impressions of learning new kinds of music alongside their indigenous ones. They can also comment first hand on the restrictions placed on their indigenous culture by the foreigners. Such primary research fuels this book—the first comprehensive study of the music of the Duna.

Review of the literature

Currently there are no substantial ethnomusicological accounts of Duna music. A doctoral thesis has been completed on the music of the Huli (Pugh-Kitingan 1981), one of the neighbouring language groups, who have been described as Duna's 'cultural kin' (Gammage 1998:91), and further work from this body of research has been published (Pugh-Kitingan 1977, 1982, 1984, 1998). Vida Chenoweth is the only ethnomusicologist to have written on the Duna; however, her observations are few and taken solely from the experience and recordings made by others (Chenoweth 1969, 2000; Chenoweth and Bee 1971).

Scholars with firsthand knowledge of Duna society have made important observations of Duna performance genres, however, these are anthropological in their approach so do not attempt to describe or analyse musical structures (see, for example, Haley 2002a; Stewart and Strathern 2002a). The same can be said of most anthropological studies of musical genres, with the 'technical requirements imposed by musical analysis' perceived as being 'so separate and severe' (Said 1991:xii).

Although these existing sources describe Duna ancestral music, none of them has addressed in any detail the vibrant and important music composed in introduced styles—a more recent development in Duna music history. One of the aims of this book is to go some way in filling this gap in the literature. Alice Moyle (1961) prophetically wrote many years ago of non-indigenous or 'contact music' that '[a]s a rule, this kind of material is passed over. But as time goes on its value will become more clearly apparent.' This has indeed happened and such material has become a focus for music research, as indicated by Denis Crowdy (1998:14): 'The ways in which non-western countries such as PNG have incorporated the music of western cultures in the development of contemporary indigenous styles has been a significant field of discussion in ethnomusicology.'

Within ethnomusicology more generally, the literature on music and change is various and includes the earlier theoretical work by scholars such as Blacking (1977) and Kartomi (1981). A number of case studies support and develop this theoretical work, by scholars such as Kubik (1986), Waterman (1990), Manuel (1994) and Kidula (1995, 1999), to name just a few. Studies undertaken within the Pacific region have been most influential to this research. Examples include Lawson (1989), Linkels (1992), Ammann (1998), Goldsworthy (1998), Alexeyeff (2004) and Neuenfeldt and Costigan (2004), and the collected volumes edited by Moyle (1992) and Lawrence and Niles (2001). Particularly influential to my research have been the comprehensive studies of Indigenous Australian music and change by Ellis (1994, 1995), Magowan (1994a, 1994b, 2007), Corn (2002) and Toner (2003). A number of parallels between music and change in Australia and Papua New Guinea can be drawn. Ellis (1994:742) observes of Indigenous Australian music: 'In contemporary Westernised music, many of the old concepts are maintained. Although compositions are no longer tied to tracts of land or to traditional technology, the sense of identity sought through musical expression by modern Aboriginal people is similar.' Observations such as this parallel my own research.

Recent works of ethnomusicology in Papua New Guinea by Webb (1993) and Crowdy (2005) detail newly introduced musical practices on a national level. With this book, I intend to build on this literature on music and change by profiling a single Papua New Guinean language group. Although there already are some studies on music and change in Papua New Guinea, particularly by Feld (1988, 2001), Webb (1995) and Suwa (2001a, 2001b), these have been conducted primarily in areas of the country quite different to Kopiago and—in the case of Webb and Suwa's research areas, which are coastal—that have a much earlier and very different history of European contact. Therefore, this book is a significant contribution to Papua New Guinean ethnomusicology. It is also timely in view of Crowdy's (2001:153) observation:

> There is…little doubt that the kinds of musical diversity [in Papua New Guinea], and their relative isolation from each other that existed even fifty years ago have changed dramatically. More importantly, the realisation that musical change has been, and will most likely continue to be the norm must be considered as a primary research perspective as the pace of change continues.

Theoretical orientation

Scholarship in the discipline of anthropology has been very influential to the formation of the theoretical framework of this research. In particular, it has shaped my thinking regarding perceived dichotomies of the 'traditional' and the 'modern'—an area extensively theorised within anthropology.

Shils (1971:123) writes, '"Tradition" and "traditional" are among the most commonly used terms in the whole vocabulary of the study of culture and society.' The polarisation of the 'traditional' and 'modern', 'ancestral' and 'contemporary' or indeed 'black' and 'white' music is common across the board, but also in many Pacific societies, and is applied not only to music but to their societies as a whole. This is, however, largely an imposed rhetoric (see also Strathern and Stewart 2004:136–7). Zagala explains it thus:

> The distinction between the 'traditional' and the 'contemporary' is not only difficult to spot within the dynamic cultures of the Pacific archipelagoes, but it is largely meaningless to Islanders themselves. They can certainly speak about this opposition, because they have learnt it from outsiders, but, in practice, tradition is not imbued with the same values of authenticity or purity that curators and ethnographers have projected onto these societies. Instead, cultural forms are generated within the rhythmic repetitions of life's cycles, simultaneously harnessing the weight of history and reverberating into the imaginative possibilities of the future. (Zagala 2003:57)

The term 'tradition' can have currency in some respects. It can be used as a point of reference to a historical period. Hau'ofa (1993:3) writes: 'In a number of Pacific societies people still divide their history into two parts: the era of darkness associated with savagery and barbarism; and the era of light and civilisation, ushered in by Christianity.' Appadurai et al. (1991:22) write that 'tradition is an ever-receding point of social reference. Tradition is about "pastness".'

In terms of performance genres, the term 'tradition' can in some contexts be used appropriately, as Kubik (1986:53) points out: 'That which is handed down from one generation to the next may be called a "tradition". A new type of music invented by someone now cannot be a tradition yet. But it may become one as time passes.' The most important thing, though, when discussing tradition in regards to performance genres is to recognise that the connotation of stasis is problematic (see, for example, Neuenfeldt and Costigan 2004:118; Dunbar-Hall and Gibson 2004:17). Change occurs within the realm of the 'traditional' as well as the modern: 'tradition is dynamic, just as is culture and the people who form and transform it. It is a human construct and configuration, altered through time to create meaning for its adherents and in their world' (Kidula 1999).

Jolly discusses the perceived dichotomy of true tradition versus inauthenticity and asks, in the case of Vanuatu cultural practice,

> why shouldn't church hymns, the mass, and *Bislama* [Vanuatu's pidgin language] be seen as part of Pacific tradition, alongside pagan songs and indigenous languages[2]...Perhaps it is not so much that Pacific peoples are glossing over differences in an undiscriminating valorization of precolonial and colonial stata of their past as that Pacific peoples are more accepting of both indigenous and exogenous elements as constituting *their* culture...it is Western commentators who are more compelled to rigidly compartmentalize indigenous and exogenous, precolonial and colonial, because they retain an exoticized and dehistoricized view of Pacific cultures. (Jolly 1992:53)

Although maintaining the dichotomy of the traditional and the modern could in some respects be considered useful—for example, it is said that the people of Papua New Guinea themselves wish to recognise a dichotomous distinction between the traditional and the modern so as to serve in the preservation of music (Niles 2001:128)—I consider this division artificial and detrimental to understanding Duna musical practices, particularly those of exogenous inspiration. Duna people do differentiate between 'traditional' and 'modern' music to a degree, as I explain below; however, this distinction is not overtly politicised as it is in other parts of Papua New Guinea (particularly the coastal areas) and island Melanesia, which have longer histories of colonisation.

Tradition, known as 'kastom' in Tok Pisin (the lingua franca spoken most widely in Papua New Guinea), has become associated with 'reinvention' in many Melanesian cultures (Keesing 1982). In this context, there is a sense that custom 'cannot afford to be invariant' (Hobsbawm and Ranger 1983:2). This notion has affected the way in which change is discussed in music scholarship. On this, Crowdy (2001:138) writes: 'Although the idea of an unbroken musical tradition passed down through many generations has been shown to be somewhat inaccurate its characterisation in relation to non-Melanesian influence is significant in defining the extent and type of musical change.'

There has, however, always been change in tradition. Even in pre-colonial times, Pacific peoples borrowed from other sources (Jolly 1992:58–9). In music there is 'deliberateness of musical change and exchange' (Myers 1993:240). The Duna are no exception, importing and exporting rituals, dancing and music from and to the neighbouring Huli and Obena language groups (Pugh-Kitingan 1998:537). Even the term 'Duna', which they are now known by, comes from the

---

2 In the case of Papua New Guinea, it has already been acknowledged by some that Christianity has become 'traditional' for a large number of the population (Denoon 2005:14).

Huli term for them (the Duna term for themselves being 'Yuna'). Such cultural relatedness is not seen as 'inauthenticising' Duna—in fact, it is an important element of their origin history (see the story of Mburulu Pango in Chapter 2).

I am not arguing here along the lines of Bhabha's (1994) notion of 'third space' or hybrid.[3] It seems inaccurate to apply a concept of hybridity here, especially if we accept Sahlins' (1999:411) argument that 'all cultures are hybrid' and that the 'dialectic of similarity and difference, of convergence of contents and divergence of schemes, is a normal mode of cultural production'. Of course, Sahlins is not alone in this opinion; Schneider (2003:217) observes too that 'there is no "original" after all...There is, so to say, nothing *before* hybridity, in fact, the term is probably misleading, as it presupposes a transition from pure elements which, through a blending process, become impure, or hybrid... syncretism, like hybridity, presupposes an earlier non-syncretic state'. Similar views have also been stated in ethnomusicology (cf. Kartomi 1981:230). Rather than engaging with the notion of hybridity, I argue in terms of convergent traditions, traditions that are recognised as originating from certain points in time in Duna history—namely, pre-contact and contact periods.

I have chosen to label the musical styles that originate from these periods 'ancestral' and 'introduced', rather than 'traditional' and 'modern', as the former pair of terms is a more appropriate translation of the Duna terms of *awenene* and *khao*.[4] Literally, these Duna terms refer to people: ancestors (*awenene* is related to the term *awa*, meaning 'grandmother', and can best be translated as 'of the grandmother kind')[5] and whites (*khao*).[6] So in my use of the terms 'ancestral' and 'introduced', abstract concepts are not invoked, but points of reference in time

---

3 I also do not argue within a framework of globalisation, Papua New Guinea being 'so far at the periphery of globalization' (Crowdy 2001:153).

4 When these qualifying terms are used, they precede the Duna terms '*ipakana*' (song) and '*alima*' (instrument). In Tok Pisin, these terms can be translated as 'tumbuna' and 'wait' (white). Webb (1993:95) notes that in Papua New Guinea, '[s]*ingsing tumbuna* (TP: ancestral songs) is a preferable term to the more ambiguous "traditional song," and is also widely understood throughout Papua New Guinea to denote both pre-contact song forms and those more recently composed in pre-contact styles'. It should be noted, however, that these Duna terms, '*awenene*' and '*khao*', are not readily used for identification of musical items; rather, genre titles are used, as the next chapter explains, and these by definition indicate the period from whence the forms originate.

5 The Duna term for 'grandmother' is similar to the term for 'father' (*awa*). Haley (2002a:97) differentiates between the two by using an apostrophe between the two syllables for grandmother: *au'wa*. The two meanings are distinguished by pitch: *awa*, when meaning 'father', has a falling tone, whereas *awa*, meaning 'grandmother', has a rising tone (Lila San Roque, Personal communication, 5 December 2007). From the current evidence, including 'u' is redundant in the spelling of this word (as it is phonetically predictable), so it has not been used here. For more information on the sound system of Duna, see Cochrane and Cochrane (1966); Giles (n.d.); Summer Institute of Linguistics et. al. (2006); and San Roque (2008).

6 The word '*khao*' can also be translated as 'redskin'; it is thought that *khao* was originally used to refer to indigenous people with lighter skin but was then adapted to refer almost exclusively to white people as a cultural/ethnic group (Lila San Roque, Personal communication, 4 December 2007).

(just as I discussed earlier regarding the temporal use of the term 'tradition') and certain places/people of origin (inside and out). Conceived of in this way, these referents are hopefully less likely to duplicate a false dichotomy.

In this book, I initially set up an opposition of the indigenous and the exogenous in Duna musical practice as I detail their music history more or less chronologically. This opposition is systematically broken down in later chapters as I argue for continuity of Duna musical practice across the spectrum of history. As Sahlins (2000:9–10) notes, 'in all change there is continuity', and indigenous peoples are active agents in the process of cultural change who 'struggle to encompass what is happening to them in the terms of their own world system' (cf. Robbins 2005:5). O'Hanlon (1993:11) too advises not to 'overlook the capacity of cultures creatively to select, adapt and re-contextualise external forms'. Ultimately, as Said declared:

> [W]hat is impressive about musical practice in all its variety is that it takes place in many different places, for different purposes, for different constituencies and practitioners, and of course at many different times. To assemble all that, to herd it under one dialectical temporal model is—no matter how compelling or dramatic the formulation—simply an untrue and therefore insufficient account of what happens. (Said 1991:xv)

By discussing Duna songs whose styles originate from recognisably distinct historical eras alongside each other, comparing aspects of composition, content and function, I aim to reveal a striking continuity in musical practice and, in doing so, draw attention to the creativity and agency of the Duna people in harnessing their own creative expression.

Methodology

There continues to be a tension in ethnomusicology between an anthropological approach to research and a musicological one (cf. Sewald 2005; Flora 2006). Flora (2006:13) advises that researchers must 'carefully think through where we are in a specific research project with respect to this bi-polarity—or, with respect to the continuum that naturally exists between the two poles'. This methodological approach—finding a position of convergence between two disciplines rather than adopting one over the other—embodies my theoretical orientation in relation to the study of Duna music.

In this section, I present important points regarding my research process, in more or less chronological order, beginning with the fieldwork experience and its issues, such as my gender, and certain methods of data collection, such as photography and recording; processes undertaken during this experience, such as song translation; and processes undertaken mostly after the fieldwork experience, including song notation and writing style.

Fieldwork

> Mulling over imperfect field notes, sorting through conflicting intuitions, and beset by a host of unanswered questions, the ethnographer must somehow fashion a written account that adequately conveys his or her understanding of other people's understandings…It is, to be sure, a discomforting business in which loose ends abound and little is ever certain. But with ample time, a dollop of patience, and steady guidance from able native instructors, one does make measurable progress. (Basso 1996:57–8)

For this research, I undertook five research trips—encompassing a variety of locations in Papua New Guinea—to work with the Duna people. These trips were conducted during the years 2004–07, adding up to a period of nine months in total. In addition, I have worked with Duna people visiting Canberra on a number of occasions over these years. Although my fieldwork at Kopiago was truncated due to social and political instability in the area,[7] I was able to make the most of these multiple field sites, both away and at home (see Gillespie 2007b), which has had the unexpected but welcome consequence of enriching my research, particularly in the area of the Duna diaspora. The existing anthropological and linguistic material made by other scholars, which included their recordings of Duna music genres, contributed significantly to my own data.

Fieldwork as a methodology has come under scrutiny in the recent past, with some scholars keen to point out the flaws of the practice. Sewald (2005:11) writes of fieldwork as 'a token of identity', which 'assures researchers and students of ethnomusicology that if they avoid the use of others' recordings and perform fieldwork they will have, on the one hand, escaped both the clutches of colonialist attitudes and comparative/historical musicology and, on the other, avoided calling into question their status as ethnomusicologists'.

She goes on to say that

> there is nothing to prevent one from drawing conclusions that are unsupported by what one actually observed in the field. One could even

---

7   Of course, interruption to fieldwork due to instability in the location of research is not uncommon; many well-known ethnographies document such events and the researcher's efforts to work around such obstacles (see, for example, Keil 1979; Shelemay 1991).

> argue that there is a far longer history of imperialistic and ethnocentric theories based on firsthand observation of other cultures than there is based on the analysis of others' sound recordings. (Sewald 2005:12)

Sewald's argument is concerned with promoting the use of archival material in ethnographic research, and as such has reiterated to me the value of examining others' recordings and written resources alongside my own. I have used the recordings of Peter White in my background research, as well as the recordings made by my colleagues on the research project 'Chanted Tales from Highland New Guinea: A comparative study of oral performance traditions and their role in contemporary land politics', funded by the Australian Research Council from 2003 to 2006.[8] I have incorporated one of Modjeska's recordings into this publication (see Chapter 6, Example 6.1). These recordings have complemented and enriched my own resources.

Despite such attacks on the fieldwork method of research, it remains a key practice in ethnomusicology, as Titon writes:

> [M]ost have not abandoned ethnographic fieldwork, even in the face of challenges from scholars in cultural studies and anthropology who critique its colonialist heritage and challenge the very concept of 'the field' and 'the other'. Rather, we have attempted to reform the cultural study of music based upon changing ideas of subject/object, self/other, inside/outside, field/fieldwork, author/authority, and the application of ethnomusicology in the public interest. (Titon 2003:173)

As emphasised in the few field manuals of the discipline of ethnomusicology (Herndon and McLeod 1983; Society for Ethnomusicology 1994; Barz and Cooley 1997), fieldwork is for the researcher a deeply personal process, 'an individual experience' (Noll 1997:163). My initial fieldwork at Kopiago was conducted alongside anthropologist Nicole Haley and my second visit there (which represented the bulk of my time 'on location') was in the company of linguist and fellow postgraduate student Lila San Roque. These extra-disciplinary influences in part account for the emphasis on song texts in my own research and for some of the techniques in gathering data—in particular, conducting interviews and undertaking translation work—which I developed from working with them as well.

The recording of musical practices was the fundamental building block for my field research. To this end, I used born-digital media: a Marantz PM670 solid-state recorder with Rode NT4 stereo microphone. Sound files were created as uncompressed Pulse Code Modulation (PCM) and stored as .wav files. Ideally, these were made at the higher end of available sampling rates (usually 44.1

---

8   Information on this project can be found at <http://rspas.anu.edu.au/anthropology/chantedtales>

kHz), providing the highest quality. As Feld (in Feld and Brenneis 2004:470–1) points out, it is very important for researchers working in sound to pay the utmost attention to the quality of their sound creations. Such high settings proved problematic in the field, however, when the ability to download the digital files was compromised; I had taken a laptop computer into the field on which to download these files and free up space for more recordings, however, it was soon discovered that the existing solar panel facility with which to charge electronic equipment was not compatible with that computer. Some sound files were therefore recorded at a lesser quality in order to minimise the digital storage space they would occupy, ensuring that opportunities to record and store other performances were not missed. Regarding recording quality, it should be noted too that although a high standard of recording was always the goal, the many and varied recording situations brought with them equally as many varied recording conditions, indoors and outdoors, with sometimes unexpected levels of performer participation, which affected some of the recordings. In order to have as many examples as possible represented in sound, I have included all recordings of the songs I discuss on the corresponding website (*http://epress. anu.edu.au/steepslopes/media.html*), despite this varying quality.

Recording as a method of data collection is not without its problems; Knopoff (2004) points out that recordings can be intrusive and can affect the understanding and perceptions of music. I have endeavoured to work around this by contextualising most of the performances/recordings as I discuss them individually. On several occasions, the performances I recorded were out of their typical context: sometimes I elicited performances, but far more frequently people would approach me and offer to sing or play certain things. This was not surprising, as the precedence of gain (in-kind or monetary) for performances or other collaborative efforts with researchers was well established. I was not selective with material presented for recording, but recorded all that was offered. On occasion, I recorded moments without the performer's knowledge of it, as seeking permission during such times (for example, at a time of mourning) would have been inappropriate. On these few occasions, I always consulted afterwards with the performers, making it known to them that I had recorded them, and later working with them on the translations.

In my field research, I aimed to obtain a translation of Duna song texts into Tok Pisin (the language in which I conducted most of my research) as soon after a recording as possible, with the performer, in a playback of the recording. The extent to which this could be undertaken depended largely on the performer's ability in Tok Pisin: sometimes it would consist only of a straightforward reciting of the text.[9] Often a second person would be employed to assist in the

---

9   Tok Pisin is spoken by the majority, but with fluency by those Duna who worked with or were educated by the colonial administration in the period from the early 1960s to the late 1970s or those who have travelled

translation, usually a person who was present during the recording and one who had experience in translating for other researchers previously. The people who are the best performers are not necessarily best at translation or explanation, as Barwick recognises in regard to Indigenous Australian song:

> Even for performers, it may be difficult to decipher, translate or explain the song texts, which are at best cryptic references to particular events in the ancestral journey, and often use archaic language, or even words from neighbouring or distant languages that may not normally be spoken by the performers…[song owners] may reveal different aspects and levels of meaning about a text to different people. The explanations given may depend on the perceived level of understanding of the person being instructed as well as on the knowledge of the person doing the explaining…It is not appropriate to postulate a single fixed 'meaning' of the song text; it is rather a matter for negotiation and even contestation. (Barwick 1990:64–5)

It was a practice of mine to photograph each of the performers whom I had recorded. Photographing in the field, as in recording and other more general fieldwork activities, requires one to consciously operate in another cultural framework. This was most apparent during times of death and grieving for the Duna—a prominent part of my fieldwork experience at Kopiago (see Chapter 4). At funerals in my own cultural context, photography would be considered inappropriate; however, it is accepted—even encouraged—to take photographs at Duna funerals. Even photographs of the corpse are sometimes requested, especially if the surviving family does not have a photograph of the deceased. Lawrence (1995) recounts an experience of attending a funeral in the Cook Islands where locals reprimanded her for not taking photographs during the service. Her story clearly illustrates the need to step outside one's cultural framework and contribute to the community on their own terms.

Toner (2003:71) writes that 'ethnomusicological research methods must be driven in large part by what our interlocutors tell us is important about their music'. As Hannerz (1997:15) observes, however: 'It could hardly be that if people do not think of [their] culture as "flowing"…they should be allowed to veto those of our analytical, or at least proto-analytical, notions which suggest otherwise.' A happy medium should therefore be the goal:

> In the ethnomusicological investigation of any musical phenomenon, we should strive for a dialogue between two discourses: the one derived from our analyses of the music in question; and the other derived from

---

outside the Duna-speaking area. Generally, those fluent in Tok Pisin are in the age bracket from twenty to sixty years and predominantly are male (women are not generally encouraged to work outside their home community, be educated very highly or travel very far).

what our interlocutors in the field tell us about the music in question. Neither discourse taken on its own is entirely satisfactory…Like all good ethnography, ethnomusicological investigation should be a kind of hermeneutic circle: our analyses of musical structure allow us to develop a certain kind of knowledge about the music; that knowledge leads us to ask our interlocutors certain kinds of questions about musical meaning; that knowledge of musical meaning then leads to further analyses of musical structure; and so on. (Toner 2003:73)

The Duna language is spoken in about 90 parishes (Haley 2002a:15),[10] but this book will focus on the music of the parish of Hirane, where I lived during my fieldwork at Kopiago. On arrival at Kopiago, I had planned to travel widely in the Duna-speaking area; however, the opportunity did not arise (travelling alone in the area would have been inappropriate and unsafe and engaging escorts a considerable disruption to the lives of my Duna friends). Although this was initially disappointing, Kopiago is a relatively major hub for the Duna, with one of the few airstrips in the area and the semblance of a road, so the limitation on my own movement was somewhat mitigated by the movements of others to and from other Duna locales and beyond. What was most beneficial, though, was that my very local existence at Kopiago meant that I developed a very local perspective for my research into musical practices, and my relationships with the Duna people I lived and worked with were the richer for this. The individuals with whom I spent the most time are foregrounded in this book and the manner in which I do this is discussed later in this chapter.

Schieffelin and Crittenden (1991:viii) observe: 'It is in the nature of field research that ethnographers become emotionally involved with the people they study, become their advocates, and establish a certain moral solidarity with them.' This involvement can in fact be beneficial to the research process; as Cesara (1982:9), the pseudonym for Karla Poewe, writes: 'being objective, emotional, personal, and cultural all at once is not dangerous nor detrimental to social analysis… instead, it may be a potent combination adding to an enriched understanding of self and other.' As researchers and human beings, we are subjective and it is best that this subjectivity be made as transparent as possible in the research we make available to others. This has been one of the more recent goals of ethnomusicological fieldwork: fostering empathy, which 'not only thickens the description through dialogue, it also introduces the subjectivities of emotion and reflexivity…empathy does not mean standing in the other person's shoes (feeling his pain) as much as it means engagement' (Titon 2003:177).

A particular kind of engagement has come about through my gender as a female researcher. Kaeppler (1998:241) has written that 'studies of music in Oceania

---

10   The concept of a parish is defined and discussed in Chapter 5.

have mostly been carried out by male researchers, who have had access mainly to male rituals and interpretations. Recent studies by female researchers have added missing pieces.' These missing pieces are essential if the discipline is to successfully achieve the aim of placing music 'within the social matrix of the people who create and produce it…[and] document the totality of that social matrix' (Herndon and Ziegler 1990:9).

I have been able to access both male and female spheres of Duna musical performance. Gender in the Highlands of Papua New Guinea is significantly delineated, which will become apparent as this book progresses, and this affects all aspects of life, including musical performance. Being a female of another culture working often with Papua New Guinean males has allowed me access to men's performance practices; however, my femaleness gives me more access to women's networks than a visiting male would have. For example, when Modjeska conducted his research with the Duna in the 1960s and 1970s, he could make only the following cursory remark regarding women's performance (admittedly though, song was not his area of research): 'Except for mourning laments and tuneless ditties sung while gardening or walking home in the rain, Duna women do not really sing at all' (Modjeska 1977:332).[11] Although the musical landscape has changed somewhat in the 30 years since this statement (cf. Strathern and Stewart 2005:12), I believe women play as great a part in Duna musical practice as men, they just perform different genres, and genres that are less public, calling for less of a 'performer–audience' relationship. One could argue that my gender as a woman plays a role in ensuring a balance, and inclusivity, to my research.[12]

Writing style

Bohlman (1992:132) writes: 'Musical ethnography should represent the musical moment, the creator of that moment, and the indigenous meaning of that moment.' I aim to give individual Duna collaborators and performers the spotlight as much as possible, allowing them to tell their own stories and sing their own songs. This is to provide not so much a truer account—'[e]thnographic truths are…inherently *partial*—committed and incomplete' (Clifford 1986:7)—but space for the reader to develop their own engagement with the material. Titon (2003:178) points out that

> the ethnographic writer selects, from among the many statements by the many voices, what will be included in the ethnographic account. But

---

11   Jim Taylor made a similar observation of the women of the Huli language group, the Duna's 'cultural kin' (Gammage 1998:91), stating that '[t]hey do not sing' (Taylor in Gammage 1998:199).

12   In a recent review (Gillespie 2008) and also in a recent book chapter (Gillespie 2009), I detail the absence of, and the need for, female ethnomusicologists working in Papua New Guinea.

when the multiply voiced texts are on display, they offer the reader far more interpretative possibilities than are present when the interpretation comes through the inflection of a single voice.

The decision to present particular individuals almost as characters in this book was inspired by recent scholarship in ethnomusicology highlighting the importance of the individual (see, for example, Stock 2001)—a turn that some consider to have begun with comments made by Nettl in 1983 (Nettl 1983:283; Slawek 1993:161). Other disciplines have also drawn attention to the importance of the individual. It is important to note here that there is significant debate within Melanesian anthropology regarding the concept of the 'individual'. There is currently a feeling of strong opposition by many scholars towards applying a Western notion of 'the individual' to Melanesian societies; rather, a person should be considered a 'dividual'—that is, relationally constituted (I discuss this again in Chapter 7). In using the term 'individual' here, I claim neither opposing position but rather believe that many of the songs of the people in question reveal aspects of both: an individual person as conceived of in Western thought, but also a person who is defined largely by their relationships with others.

In my efforts to represent each Duna person, I have included their own words as much as possible. This has resulted in reasonable lengths of interview text given in Tok Pisin followed by an English translation. In the text here, I have presented Tok Pisin terms in quotation marks and Duna terms in italics. In song texts, I have differentiated between Tok Pisin and Duna in a similar way—only the Duna is in italics, while the Tok Pisin is in normal type.

Some of the process of forming song translations in the field has already been discussed. In this the final product, I have chosen to show my translations in English only, without linguistic annotations, for the sake of clarity of understanding. Some scholars in their translations show as much information on the actual indigenous terms as possible through extensive annotations—a process Leavitt (2006) calls 'thick translation', evoking Geertz's (1973) 'thick description'. Leavitt (2006:98) defines 'thickness' as 'the presence or absence of layers of information from the source text carried over into the target text'. As he points out though, 'thickening' can occur by providing information in the text surrounding the central piece of translation. This has been my approach— aiming for a literal translation and then detailing this with an explanation outside the translation, which provides the additional information and context. Translation is a process of compromise and any result, no matter how well presented, cannot be perfect.

In a similar fashion, song transcription is also unsatisfactory in terms of a stand-alone, accurate representation of a cultural product. As Knopoff (2003:39–40) accounts, 'ethnomusicologists have come to realise that our analytic tools and methods are neither objective nor value-free' and, as a result, 'a significant cross-section of ethnomusicologists has abandoned analysis as a primary means of addressing important issues about music and culture'.

The problems with Western notation for non-Western musical traditions (and even Western ones) were identified relatively early in the history of ethnomusicology (see, for example, England et al. 1964). Not only are scholars already compromised in trying to represent often oral cultures in a written form, but the conventional system of notation is recognised as being very restricted, particularly in terms of representing pitch (List 1974:353), tone quality (Seeger 1987:102) and rhythm (List 1974:368; Kartomi 1990; Spearitt 1984). This has resulted in a number of scholars designing alternative systems of notation in an attempt to better represent the music they are studying (see, for example, Toner 2003). Notations created by an ethnomusicologist should be considered not as exhaustive representations of a musical creation but as graphic representations of certain aspects of the creation of interest to the scholar themselves. When taken this way, 'a lack of total accuracy in transcription is not problematic as long as the particular features the analyst wishes to consider are rendered accurately' (Knopoff 2003:44).

Transcription is also an important analytical process for the development of a scholar's insight. Barwick (1990:60) writes that 'analysis is a process of understanding rather than a methodology for producing "truth"'. This process is a complement to any indigenous knowledge available to the scholar: 'Careful musical transcription can reveal aspects of the performance that native categories do not highlight. A good musical transcription can raise many questions. These questions may or may not lead to a greater understanding of the music, but they are usually worth asking' (Seeger 1987:102). And, as Knopoff (2003:46) put it, '[s]tatements about the music by performers or other cultural insiders are of great importance but cannot in themselves generate the most insightful analyses'.

The transcriptions in this book are only an approximation of the performance. These transcriptions are most helpful in showing phrasing and melodic contours and the relationship of these to song text. In particular, it should be pointed out that pitch is not as fixed as it appears in these transcriptions. Duna music generally features much sliding up to and down from pitches—this occurs in both ancestral and newly introduced styles of music. It is also important to note that the assigned rhythms, where used, are not entirely accurate in these transcriptions—Duna ancestral music is largely un-metered and this characteristic is often another aspect of musical continuity apparent in compositions of exogenous origin.

The musical transcriptions that have found their way into this book have done so because they are essential to the illustration of certain points. Transcriptions are not included merely as a matter of course; where songs are discussed purely for their lyrical content or structure (and there are many of those, especially in the later chapters), musical transcriptions have not been provided, as they would be superfluous to the argument. Most musical examples (indicated by the symbol ▶) discussed are, however, provided on the corresponding website (*http://epress.anu.edu.au/steepslopes/media.html*). Ideally, the reader will access these sound files as the songs are discussed.

Structure

The constraints and conventions of writing necessitate a linear structure, when often it is more beneficial to conceive of separate sections of writing as parallel texts (Morphy 1991:8). Certainly that is the case with this book. The chapters appear in terms of song topics and functions; however, as reading of the book progresses, it will become apparent how much these separate chapters connect with and feed into each other. Still, I conform to the required linear structure and, within this, aim to make these connections apparent.

This chapter has given an outline of the project at hand: its aims, the background literature informing it, the theories and methodologies employed and the presentation of the material. Chapters 2 and 3 complement each other, providing a comprehensive outline of the totality of Duna musical practice in somewhat of a chronological order. Chapter 2 defines ancestral Duna musical practice. It explains the Duna's conception of the origins of musical difference and the role of the musician in Duna society and presents essential Duna musical structures and Duna vocabulary surrounding music. We see the Duna group song as a separate category to instrumental performance and the genres within both categories are listed and described. A brief consideration is given to the category of dance, but it emerges that the priority—for the Duna and for this book—rests on the category of song (*ipakana*). The nature of Duna verbs referring to kinds of sound production is seen to reinforce these categories as distinct. Language features of Duna song are identified, these being *kēiyaka* (a specialised vocabulary here translated as 'praise names'), repetition and metaphor.

Chapter 3 looks at music introduced to the Duna through colonial and mission history. These encounters are outlined in more detail than has been done in the early pages of this chapter. We learn of past and present efforts to circumscribe performances of ancestral traditions through certain interpretations of Christianity. The musical influences of colonisation and missionisation are shown to come together in a contemporary song format and this is illustrated by the analysis of, first, a popular Christian song, and then a number of recently composed songs on secular themes relevant to the Duna, particularly those of local politics. The vocabulary for these introduced song styles is also presented here. We begin to see here how creativity is harnessed by the Duna, not only to articulate social concerns but also to effect change.

The next three chapters change in register, focusing on the ethnographic. Chapter 4 recounts the death of the young woman Wakili Akuri, and the songs resulting from it. The importance of the lament in the Duna (and Papua New Guinean) musical soundscape is emphasised in this chapter. A number of individuals and their songs are presented; however, the chapter focuses in particular on the songs of Kipu Piero—the lament she sang directly after Wakili's death and a number of guitar-based (and church-inspired) lamentations composed some time afterwards. The comparison of these songs reveals a certain continuity, particularly in the phrasing of the texts and their content.

The study of Duna laments in Chapter 4 reveals the importance of land to the Duna. Chapter 5 examines how Duna people sing about their relationship to land, continuing the focus on song text analysis. It is proposed that Duna people identify with place in a number of ways and that these can be classified into four frames: national, regional, local and parish. The focus, for the most part of the chapter, is on the permeability and multiplicity of these categories. I look more closely at the phenomena of *kēiyaka* and how that functions in Duna song of both ancestral and introduced origin. Place as a site for food production (good or poor) is discussed, and the function of the negative in song is touched on (to be explored further in Chapter 6). I then consider how Duna song can illustrate moving through a landscape, incorporating places and modes of transport associated with the modern world. This brings forward the topic of Duna diasporic communities and the songs they sing about the experience of being away and at home.

A colleague once noted from my research that all Duna songs seemed to be about food and sex (Paul Pickering, Personal communication, 23 October 2006). Chapter 6 takes in hand the subject of courting, which has appeared in so many songs of the preceding chapters. I present ancestral courting songs sung for the new contexts of social commentary and politics. I consider both new and old courting practices as illustrated, and enacted, in new song styles. The role of eliciting sympathy in song through expressions of self-denigration (as briefly visited in Chapter 5) is discussed and is shown to be one of many aspects of continuity in Duna courting songs. The connection between courting and death is also accounted for as I revisit Wakili's death and analyse another of Kipu Piero's laments.

Chapter 7 takes us both back and forward. First, the very beginnings of the creative process are examined and we see more clearly the textual and musical elements of continuity in Duna songs, at the point of composition. Authorship and ownership (or lack thereof) with regard to song are addressed, as is individual agency and the effect this might have on any preservation endeavours. The role of politics and cultural shows in efforts to present and preserve ancestral performance genres is assessed, as is the ideal of education programs, both within schools and within revived ancestral rituals. Anxieties expressed for the future, particularly by the younger generation of males, are given voice here.

Chapter 8 concludes this book, giving an overview of the theoretical position and the way that each chapter has supported the argument of musical continuity. It emphasises the creativity and agency of the Duna people in music, in response to their rapidly changing world.

2. Duna ancestral music

> In any system of language or music, the components have order and arrangement. (Chenoweth 1969:220)

In this chapter, I aim to provide an overview of Duna ancestral musical practices and the vocabulary associated with them. As discussed in Chapter 1, the term *awenene ipakana* can be used to describe ancestral song forms (Kipu Piero, Personal communication, 30 March 2005), which would be expressed in Tok Pisin as 'tumbuna singsing'. *Hapia ipakana* ('songs from before') is another way to identify the musical genres that belong to pre-contact times (Kenny Kendoli, Personal communication, 7 March 2007). This general category is distinct from *khao ipakana* or 'white songs' that will be discussed in the next chapter.

Due to the lack of ethnomusicological research into Duna music to date, it is important in this chapter to provide a comprehensive overview of Duna musical organisation. And as the Duna do not have a word for 'music', it is important to acknowledge at the outset what exactly is under discussion in this book.

In this chapter, I first consider some general points about Duna music—some reflections on its origin and the role of the 'musician'. I present observations on Duna musical structures, drawing on the work of Vida Chenoweth. Since studying the vocabulary of a language has long been recognised as a key to understanding a culture (cf., for example, Wierzbicka 1997), I examine the vocabulary used to talk about Duna ancestral music. I explore the categories for organising Duna music, giving a brief description of the genres within these categories that I will be drawing on later as examples within my argument. I then turn to consider verb usage in relation to these genres and how this reflects the music categories established. I point out important language features in Duna song texts, but leave the discussion of introduced musical forms and instruments for the next chapter.

The origins of music

> At Mburulu Pango, close to the Strickland River, there was a big house in which lived many people. There came a time when the house fell down, and the population scattered. They all went to different regions and started speaking different languages. Bogaya went and spoke their own language, Oksapmin went and spoke their own language, Hewa went and spoke their own language, Huli went and spoke their own language,

Enga went and spoke their own language, whites went and spoke their own language…All left except the Duna, who stayed put and looked after the site, which is in Duna country. When they left they all took many common things, including the *luna, alima* and *kuluparapu.* Thus, all these neighbouring language groups share [knowledge of] the same instruments. An exception though is the Hewa—whilst all the others took the small kundu drum, the group that became the Hewa took the big drum, and that is why their drum that you see now is bigger. (Sane Noma, Personal communication, translated by Petros Kilapa, 14 March 2005)

To consider the origins of musical practices is a valuable approach in the study of another culture. Seeger (1987:52) writes: 'Ideas about the origin and composition of music provide an important indication of what music is and how it relates to other aspects of the lives and the cosmos of a community.' Although my research into this aspect of Duna music history did not yield a definitive version of Duna ideas about the origin of musical practices, I was able to gather some information that has influenced my way of thinking about this topic.

The origin story (*malu*) of Mburulu Pango describes the beginning of language differentiation—and the specific cultural practices of language groups—in the Duna region.[1] Simultaneously, this story gives reasons for the common aspects of instruments in the immediate region and for their variation. It also raises the prospect of continuity between the music of Europeans and the Duna from the earliest period.[2]

According to the above telling of the story of Mburulu Pango (and consistent with stories of this kind that are found all over Melanesia), the white man once lived with the Duna and other neighbouring language groups as their brother, often described as their first (or oldest) brother. They all shared knowledge and objects and when the time came when they no longer lived together, the different brothers (including the white brother) each took particular knowledge and objects away when they left. Once away from Mburulu Pango, the white brother developed the technology he now displays, building on the skills and items he took with him when he left (for example, the sound of the engine of an aeroplane is said to originate from within the Duna bamboo jew's harp, the *luna,* shown in Figure 2.5). When first contact occurred, some people therefore saw whites as ancestors returning from the dead. The Duna coveted items the whites

---

1   Haley (1996:280–2) has documented the story of Mburulu Pango and described in brief the rituals performed there (Haley 2002a:64), labelling the site an 'ancestral dancing ground' (Haley 2002a:159). Haley (2002a:144) also provides a map showing this site in relation to surrounding parishes.
2   It is important to note that Duna stories are constantly under revision—the story of Mburulu Pango would most likely have existed in the pre-contact period without a reference to white people—and that Sane Noma is considered to be one of the most adept at such 'revisioning' of the past (Haley 1996:282).

had, but also the Duna might have considered these items as part of their own heritage, things to which they also had a right, because of the shared history between the brothers (cf. Brutti 2000).

Similar processes assimilating introduced phenomena into indigenous belief systems have been reported in other cultures. Of the Yolngu people of Indigenous Australia, Magowan writes:

> When material goods such as money, flags and ships arrived from the Macassans and balanda [seventeenth-century visitors from Asia and Europe respectively], Yolngu incorporated these into their song cosmology since they considered they must have emerged from 'inside' the Ancestral Law rather than appearing from nowhere. These things had simply not been revealed to them in dreams. In Yolngu thought, all new ideas and objects are veiled or revealed from this foundation. (Magowan 2005:68)

The tale of Mburulu Pango was told to me using musical instruments as the focus of the discussion, in order to explain why some instruments were more prominent than others in different language groups, but also why there were similarities present. We could, however, extend this belief in shared history into the realm of song. The older Duna could have, under these conditions, considered that songs introduced by white people were also rightfully theirs. This might explain the seemingly easy, or at least enthusiastic, adoption of Christian and secular songs by the Duna. Such possibilities are worth reflecting on.

The 'musician' in Duna society

There is no social classification of 'musician' in Duna society as such. The reason for this can be explained from a social standpoint. Green (2003:263) writes: 'The more highly specialized is the division of labour generally, the more likely it is that music will also become a specialized sphere of action: listened to and enjoyed by many, but practiced only by a few.' As the division of labour for the Duna is not generally highly specialised, music is created and performed by a great proportion, if not the entire proportion, of the Duna community. Having said that, there are people in the society who are recognised as being better than others at performing particular genres, though all can aspire to such skill; there does not appear to be any firm belief in inherited musical skills.

The following describes one young Duna man's journey in learning the epic storytelling tradition known as *pikono*. Teya Hiyawi, then in his early twenties, went out hunting for a few days with his friend Kenny Kendoli and others.

One night, while camping out in the bush, Kenny asked Teya to try to sing a *pikono* story for their entertainment. Teya tried but faltered and did not get very far. After the hunting trip, back in his home parish, Teya attended *pikono* performances by various performers in the men's houses in the area. He practised singing *pikono* to himself by a nearby waterfall so that no-one could hear him. When he felt accomplished enough, he sang a complete *pikono* for performance and from then he was known as one of the performers of this genre. A few years later (in 2004), Teya was invited by colleagues of mine on the Chanted Tales project to attend and perform at a workshop in Goroka in the Eastern Highlands Province of Papua New Guinea. It was his first time to leave his home community (Teya Hiyawi with Kenny Kendoli, Personal communication, 16 February 2004).

Teya's story tells us several things about Duna musical practice. First, we are reminded that Duna music is not documented and taught, as music is in the West, in a written form; it is a culture of oral dissemination. Furthermore, people learn by example; there are no instructors as such, no apprenticeship to make the transition from non-performer to performer.[3] Compositions are generally not fixed but spontaneous creations. His story tells us that gender plays an important part in the musical expressions available to Duna people (to both listen to and perform). It also suggests that the performer enjoys status through his skills, being identified as skilled in his home community and sometimes outside as well, and that such skill brings opportunities not otherwise accessible.

This kind of progressive learning through performance without rehearsal is widespread among largely non-literate societies. Perhaps not coincidentally, such societies appear to value sung text first and foremost (see, for example, Tunstill [1995:61] on the learning of songs for the Pitjantjara of Central Australia). Learning by copying (that is, without direct tuition) opens the way for a large—almost infinite—number of styles to be incorporated by the Duna. It also often makes it difficult to establish a song's origins.

Having given an outline of the role of music in Duna society, I now provide some observations of Duna musical structures. As with some other areas of study presented in this book, I first introduce key concepts that I will then draw on in later chapters, making these concepts more apparent to the reader as the pages are turned.

---

3   This is not so surprising: 'All of us who grow up in culture and acquire its traditions do so only partly as a result of direct, pedagogical intervention of the sort commonly associated with scolding parents, teaching by teachers, or informing by informants; culture and its traditions are also acquired by observing, mimicking, and embodying shared practices' (Rice 1997:108).

Duna musical structures

Chenoweth makes some astute observations on the nature of the musical structures employed in Duna music, based on recordings collected by others. She (1969:222) declares: 'A scale as such does not exist in Duna music. What is sought instead is an emic vocabulary of musical pitches, i.e. a stock of pitches relevant to the system.' Rather than identifying a scale of fixed pitches, Chenoweth (1969:219) instead focuses on the intervals between pitches and discovers that 'the unison, major seconds and minor thirds are most prevalent; minor seconds and major thirds are common; and larger intervals are infrequent'. Most pertinent is her observation that

> Duna melodies are basically what Sachs calls 'one-step'; that is, most of the melodic interplay is between two tones, in this case between tonal centre and a major second above it. When the 'one-step' adds a tone below tonal centre the melody becomes 'two-step' with both poles gravitating toward centre. (Chenoweth 1969:223)

The melodic feature that Chenoweth describes here is the key structural element to most Duna genres (and also, it seems from Pugh-Kitingan's analyses, for the Huli). This structural element will become apparent when each Duna genre is described shortly. At this point, though, it should be made clear how I am using music terminology here. In an effort to avoid Western tonal music concepts (though admitting such a task is nearly impossible in this forum), I am describing intervals by their tonal make-up, a tone being 200 cents (and accepting that a tone is an identifiable unit in Duna music, though also a Western concept). Intervals are therefore described as being, for example, a (whole) tone above the tonal centre instead of a 'major second', as Chenoweth does above; a perfect fifth (700 cents) is described as three and a half tones; an octave is six tones (1200 cents). However, to assist the reader with familiar Western musical analysis, I provide the Western equivalent to these intervals in brackets as is appropriate.

Terminology exists for the Duna, as it does for the Huli (Pugh-Kitingan 1998), which describes the registers of 'high', 'middle' and 'low'. In Duna, these terms are *yakota*, *arakota* and *sopakona* (Kenny Kendoli, Personal communication, 22 June 2006).[4] I had theorised that these could be used to label the pitch above the tonal centre, the tonal centre itself and the pitch below it, as these are such important—and often the only—pitches employed in most genres. On later examination, however, these terms appeared to relate more to actual

---

4   It should be noted that these terms consist of more than one morpheme. *Yakota* and *arakota* are composed of the locative marker *-ta* (San Roque 2008:185–9), added to the spatial nouns *yako* ('top') and *aroko* ('middle'). *Sopakona* is composed of the deictic *sopa* ('below') and *kona*, which has emphatic meaning (Lila San Roque, Personal communication, 23 February 2007). It therefore might be best to translate these terms as 'on/at the top', 'on/at the middle' and 'down below', respectively.

melodic register or range—a clear example being that in part-singing (which occurs only in introduced musical forms; there is no form of vocal harmony in Duna ancestral music): the person singing highest would be singing *yakota*, the middle register part *arakota* and the bass *sopakona* (Richard Alo, Recorded conversation, 2 July 2006).[5]

Somewhat less helpful than her comments on pitch is Chenoweth's (1969:223) description of vocal rhythm: 'Duna melodic rhythm flows in a smooth, running-style with dotted patterns almost non-existent, except in the sing-sings. Ballads are sung *legato piano* in diametric contrast to the sing-sing renditions inducing hysteria.' Italian prescriptive directions aside, what we can determine from these comments is that rhythm for purely vocal genres (what I understand Chenoweth means by 'ballads')[6] is more flexible than rhythm that features in performances that incorporate vocals, dance movements and drums ('singsings'). Much later, she more succinctly summarises this difference: 'Ballads follow speech rhythm whereas *singsings*…follow the rhythm of the dance' (Chenoweth 2000:179).

Before moving on to consider the organisation of Duna music through vocabulary, it is necessary to pause and contemplate briefly the relationship between Duna speech and song. Duna is recognised as a tonal language, using a 'word-tone' system (Donohue 1997) with three or possibly four alternative tonal contours that extend across the length of a single word, regardless of how many syllables it has. These are: a fall, a rising tone, a level tone and possibly also a convex tone (San Roque 2004). A neighbouring language to the Duna (see Figure 1.2), Huli is also a tonal language, with much the same word-tone system as in Duna. The relationship between Huli language and music is an integral part of the research of Pugh-Kitingan (1984), who presents an argument that the two spheres are related. The relationship between speech tone and musical form is not under examination here. It is fair to suggest, however, that because of the tonal nature of the language (and considering the close relationship between the languages of Duna and Huli), the relationship between speech tones and melodic contour is a close one. Michael Sollis (2010) has explored the relationship between Duna speech and song and has identified a tune-tone relationship in the genre of *pikono*. The idea that a strong relationship exists between Duna speech and song is consistent with the fact that for the Duna, speaking and singing share

---

5   Additional terms were given for *yakota* and *sopakona* by Richard Alo and these were terms that often are used to describe positions in the physical landscape: *romakona* ('above') and *rindita* ('on the ground').

6   Stewart and Strathern choose to describe one Duna genre, *pikono*, as a 'ballad' (cf., for example, Stewart and Strathern 1997); however, it is clear that Chenoweth (1969:225) is more inclusive with her use of this category, especially as she describes that the length of ballads 'differs widely' with one song 'having one long musical phrase with 4 lines of text', which is more suggestive of a courting song genre than the epic story of a *pikono*. That Chenoweth groups such diverse genres together is suggestive of the common musical structures that they share.

the same verb (*ruwa*, to be discussed below).[7] Further supporting the argument are the descriptions that at least some Duna melodies are akin to speech, as Chenoweth suggests above when discussing 'ballads'.

Vocabulary: organisation of 'music'

The Duna language does not have one overarching term that encompasses all oral performance genres English speakers would classify as 'music'. Their neighbours, the Huli, also do not have such a term (Pugh-Kitingan 1998:538). Recently, however, the Tok Pisin term 'musik' has been adopted for this purpose—pronounced *musiki* or *misiki* by some older Duna speakers such as Sane Noma.[8]

Duna musical genres are distinguished primarily by their melodic structure.[9] No two genres share the same melodic structure, though they might share some structural elements, such as descending lines or range. There are said to be 'different songs [with] different ways of singing (*ipakana angu*)' (Richard Alo, Personal communication, 18 June 2006). It follows that no two ancestral song genres share the same text structure either, as text and melody are for the Duna inseparable (Duna song genres are rarely hummed, for example), with the possible exception of some mourning songs. There is, however, one example of a genre being identified by its textual content rather than melody. The genre *pikono*, whose texts tell a story, can be either sung or spoken—either way they can be identified as *pikono* (though it is the sung *pikono* that is most prized). No such flexibility in performance style has been observed for other Duna song genres.

Duna performance genres are usually identified individually, by the name of the genre, rather than collectively, under a categorical name. Since missionisation, however, a category for song, *ipakana*, has developed and the origins of that category will be discussed next. Duna usually discuss instrumental music too using the name of the individual instrument, although a general category name, *alima*, does exist, named after one of the more prominent instruments. There does not appear to be a generic category name for performance genres that

---

7 Feld (1982:174) reports that this is also the case for the Kaluli.

8 Adding *i* to introduced words is typical of the Duna language. According to Lila San Roque, 'Duna does not allow "closed" syllables (that is, those that end in a consonant). Words borrowed from English or Tok Pisin that end in a consonant commonly have a vowel added to them…The choice of vowel is generally predictable, for example *i* is added to words that end in an alveolar consonant (for example the English/Tok Pisin 'school/skul' becomes *sukuli*) and words that have *i* in their last syllable (for example 'sick/sik' becomes *siki*)' (Lila San Roque, Personal communication, 23 February 2007; see also San Roque 2008:54–5; Cochrane and Cochrane 1966:24). Both of these rules can be seen to apply to Duna indigenisation of the Tok Pisin 'musik'.

9 This is also the case in some other (and culturally quite different) parts of Papua New Guinea—for example, southern New Ireland (Wolffram 2006:113).

incorporate bodily movements as a structural component of the performance (what in the West would be called 'dance'). Each of these categories is worth examining in more detail.

Ipakana ('song[s]')

The term *ipakana* translates to mean 'song', singular and plural. In the introductory pages of her PhD thesis, Haley (2002a:6–7) presents *ipakana* as a word made from the uniting of two separate words: *ipa* (water/fluid) and *kana* (stone/solid forms). In these pages, Haley defines *ipakana* as a verb 'to sing' and also as 'mourning songs'. She explains:

> Through these laments, the female composers seek to capture and map the lives of the dead kin by naming the places with which they were associated during their lifetime…The performance of these laments is properly referred to as *ipakana yakaiya*—'counting/naming rivers and mountains'—mapping the landscape. (Haley 2002a:7)

In my research, I have not found any evidence of *ipakana* itself being used as a verb.[10] In conjunction with *yakaya*,[11] however, as in the above comment by Haley, the phrase has a verb function: *yakaya* acting as the verb of the construction (*yakaya* being derived from the root *yaka*, meaning 'name, count/ read', and inflected with the verbal suffix *-ya*). The process of reciting features of the landscape is, as Haley indicates, known as *ipakana yakaya* and this process is integral not only to laments, but to most other ancestral genres such as *pikono*, *selepa*, *yekia* and also *mali* (Kenny Kendoli, Personal communication, 7 March 2007).[12]

---

10 To use the word as a command by adding the suffix *-pa*—that is to say, '*ipakanapa*'—results in a command to dig a drain for water (Richard Alo, Personal communication, 27 June 2006), though it is said that *ipakana* refers to a naturally formed waterway and not one made by humans, which would instead be known as *mbekakana* (Kenny Kendoli, Personal communication, 7 March 2007). The second word in this compound, *kana*, can be translated as 'stone', as Haley identifies, but also as 'drain' (as Lomas suggests below in regard to the etymology of the Huli *iba gana*). These two words differ in tone, but because of the positioning of *kana* as the second within this compound, it is difficult to tell the difference between them. San Roque (Personal communication, 23 February 2007) explains: 'There are two Duna words "stone" and "ditch" which are distinct in tone ("stone" is convex…"ditch" is rising) and (in at least the Kelabo dialect) in aspiration (stone is aspirated, *khana*…and ditch is not, *kana*). However, if we are positing that *ipakana* is a compound in which the first word is *ipa* "water", this is not conclusive, as aspiration contrast is lost between vowels, and we would also expect some tonal changes of the two lexical elements when they are combined as a single word. A more advanced phonological analysis of the Duna tone system could perhaps resolve this.' Discussions with Duna speakers have not yielded a definitive answer to the origins of the word *ipakana*, but that is not surprising; as San Roque adds, 'it is fairly clear that a lot of the time "folk etymology" of words bears little relation to their historical origin (although folk etymologies are no less interesting for that)'.

11 I choose to spell this term without the 'i' in accordance with the orthography used by San Roque (2008).

12 Haley has written that the *ipakana yakaya* process—which she first introduces as being associated with lament performance—also precedes 'the actual performance' of *pikono*: 'A central and significant feature of *pikono* is that, although the stories themselves are held to [be] imaginary, they take place in the "real" landscape, that is at specific and named and known locations. These, I must stress, are not always named in the

Although laments play a prominent role in the musical soundscape of the Duna (see Chapter 4), the term *ipakana*, in its current usage, is not confined to this particular genre of singing.[13] Songs of foreign origin are also known as *ipakana*. We can examine what has been said of the origin of the Huli word *iba gana* (understood to have the same meaning—'song[s]'—as Duna *ipakana*) to understand how this category could have come about.[14]

In the Huli language, the term *iba gana* is described as the meeting of two words: *iba* (water) and *gana* (ditch). Gabe Lomas, a linguist who spent many years working with the Huli and the Duna between the 1960s and 1980s—a period of great change—describes how this term emerged:

> Transliterating *iba gana* from Huli yields 'water ditch/drain'. I've always understood this to refer to a ditch made to drain off water and, by association, to the sound that comes from it as the water runs along—anything from a tinkling and gurgling noise to the full rush of heavy rain water. This same label was used for humming, musical burbling, snatches of songs, and so forth. In fine, it seemed to be used as a label for music or songs outside the more easily categorised genres.
>
> Its application to songs used in church services was logical enough, since these didn't fit any traditional genres. What happened at Hoiebia, and later in the Catholic Church, was that the traditional *u* (courting song) structure and formulae also became used in church services, and these church service *u*-type songs, together with introduced melodies and formulae, became grouped under the catch-all phrase *iba gana*.
>
> I think that among the Koroba-Kelabo Duna the phrase *iba gana* is probably a Huli loan term…If this is the case, there's probably a good chance that in Duna the label *ipakana* has undergone the same process of applicaton as *iba gana* has in Huli. (Gabe Lomas, Email communication, 18 July 2006)

In essence, then, according to Lomas, *ipakana* was a term used for sounds outside any identifiable ancestral genre. This came to include new musical styles

---

actual performance. Instead *pikono* performers prefer to situate their narratives by mapping out the landscape in which the story takes place, before commencing the actual performance. This process, called *ipakana yakaiya* ("counting/naming mountains and rivers"), generally lasts for up to one or two hours, during which the narrator will name the place at which the story begins, and from there will identify all the places that feature in the story' (Haley 2002a:132). I have not experienced such a listing of places before a performance of *pikono*, however, it could be said that the process of *ipakana yakaya* is a process with a number of different contexts for its articulation, both within and without the 'actual performance' of genres.

13   Pamela J. Stewart and Andrew Strathern (2000a:90) recognise *ipakana* as the general term for 'songs' in Duna.

14   Although the languages of Huli and Duna are not closely related (Huli is classified as a member of the Engan language family; Duna as a member of the Duna-Bogaia language family), they do share a significant amount of vocabulary.

introduced by the missions. Once ancestral genres such as *u* were performed in church, they too came under the grouping *ipakana*. It is fair to surmise that this grouping was eventually extended to other ancestral genres, resulting in a broad category of 'song' that encompasses both introduced and ancestral vocalisations.

Pugh-Kitingan supports the idea that *ipakana* is a neologism, writing:

> The Huli say that the term iba gana is a recent invention created in the last twenty-five years or so to cover newer genres, such as Christian songs and European songs, which they consider to be singing. Before this, the only genre which the Huli regarded as singing was the dawanda u ['courting song']. (Pugh-Kitingan 1981:285)

She goes on to say: 'Although it originates from one person, iba gana is group music' (Pugh-Kitingan 1981:302).

For the Duna whom I questioned, however, there was no acknowledgment of *ipakana* as an introduced concept or category. Younger generations of Duna, at least, denied the term as exogenous. Ancestral forms of music, such as *yekia* (the Duna equivalent of the u courting song, and also sung by a group) were classified to me as *ipakana*.[15] There was also no discussion of *ipakana* being only for forms of music sung in groups; *pikono*, a solo tradition (which also incorporates regular audience interjections) was also classified as *ipakana*. Regardless of its origins, the term *ipakana* has now become a category for songs in contemporary Duna language use.

The following is an overview of each of the ancestral genres that can be classified as *ipakana* and that will be discussed to varying degrees over the course of this book, where further description will be provided that includes song texts, translations, explanations and corresponding sound files. The genres are presented now in alphabetical order, each with an indication of the chapter in which it will be more fully discussed.[16] A basic description of the typical melodic contour of each genre is given in notation inspired somewhat by music theorist Heinrich Schenker—stripping the melodic content back to reveal its basic core intervals. The aim in doing this is to show the distinctive melodic (specifically, intervallic) patterns that characterise each genre.

The notations have been made with C as the tonal centre for reading clarity. It should be noted that some variability does occur between performers and

---

15 Note that the verb used in combination with the word *yekia* is *undua*, or *ukundua*, meaning 'to go into' and this could also be related to the word u.

16 It is important to note the different spellings, and sometimes different terms, used by scholars in the past when discussing Duna genres. I have compiled all the various terms known to me in the discussion of each genre, to save the reader any confusion.

between song texts and this notation is meant to provide a rough indication of what is common to all of them. I have divided distinct sections of phrasing or patterning with a bar line and repeated sections are indicated accordingly. Double bar lines indicate the completion of the song, or song section in the case of *pikono*.

Heya ('*crying*'), khene ipakana ('*death songs*'), kenewa ipakana ('*sorry songs*')

The term *heya* is used to refer to the sound of crying, both stylised and not.[17] In referring to the stylised crying, the term *heya*—or *ipakana heiya* (Stewart and Strathern 2000a:92)—is interchangeable with *khene ipakana* and also with *kenewa ipakana* (though this term can be generally extended to cover all songs that elicit sympathy, which, as we shall see in Chapter 6, is a very common trait in Duna courting songs). *Khene ipakana* is a song category that includes stylised *heya* and also songs of an introduced style (for example, guitar-based songs) that mourn for the deceased. Chapter 4, which discusses the death of one particular young woman, examines the elements of *heya* and *khene ipakana* in detail. Stylised *heya* and ancestral *khene ipakana* are essentially the same genre, characterised by a limited melodic range of three pitches, two based either side of an emphasised tonal centre (see the section of Example 2.1 marked as repeated). Repetition of textual lines, based on the recitation of *kēiyaka* ('praise names', discussed further at the end of this chapter), is another feature, though this is shared by many other Duna song genres, so is not by itself a distinguishing element. Stylised *heya*, and all kinds of *khene ipakana*, is considered a women's genre, though close male relatives of the deceased are also known to sing in this way. It is the ancestral performance genre most available to women.

Example 2.1 Basic pitch structure of stylised *heya* or ancestral *khene ipakana.*

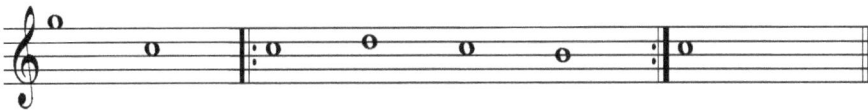

Khene ipakana typically begin with a short descent from about three and a half tones (a fifth) above the tonal centre, but the body of the melody is a clear illustration of Chenoweth's two 'poles gravitating toward centre': the tonal centre with steps above and below it, always returning back to the tonal centre between these movements and to conclude the singing.

---

17 Another Duna term for crying—*nuya*—can apparently also be used to describe sung laments (Kenny Kendoli, Personal communication, 7 March 2007); however, this term was not used to label or describe lamentations in my discussions in the field.

Mindimindi kão[18]

Mindimindi kão—also known as *mini mindi kão* (Stewart and Strathern 2000a:96) and *gao* (Haley 2002a:xxix; Modjeska 1977:161)—are songs that function as spells. Their performance context is within the *haroli palena* (bachelor cult), a social practice belonging to the pre-contact period in which boys lived and learnt from older men in the isolation of the bush, away from the women of the community. Boys might live within this cult for several years, with little to no contact with the females of their clan, until they had fully developed in body and in skills and were considered ready for marriage. As such, *mindimindi kão* are a male genre, in which the singing was led by the older men of the bachelor cult and sung by the boys generally as a group, in unison. Due to the cessation of the cult, the spells are not practised in this context anymore, but rather as examples of a practice from times past.[19] The consequences of the cessation of this cult from a social and a musical point of view will be examined in the penultiomate chapter of this book.

Haroli palena initiate Sane Noma describes *mindimindi kão* as follows:

> It was cooking sweet potatoes in the ashes and eating them, it was going to fetch cold water from the pandanus leaf water-tubes and drinking it, and on the body the hair would grow like bird feathers, like animal fur, and over the shoulders and all parts of the body the hair would flow down. At this time, people would tell the boys secret things to make them grow. These secret things belonged to the *haroli palena*... they count and speak and they sing these particular things. (Sane Noma, translated by Petros Kilapa and Lila San Roque, 22 February 2005)

Mindimindi kão hold a great amount of information for boys concerning their engagement with their natural environment. Songs tell the boys what feathers to decorate themselves with, where to hunt the bird that has these feathers, which plant leaves to clean their faces with, where and how to obtain good water for washing themselves, all in order to encourage them to stay within the *haroli palena* and make themselves into handsome men.

Mindimindi kão (Example 2.2) are characterised by the repetition of sound and text and a restricted melodic range of three tones, which is a feature of other

---

18 Note that the use of the tilde indicates nasalisation. According to San Roque, 'there is a "phonosthemic" element in Duna...words that reference activities that have a strong auditory component (e.g. whine, bark, snore) often have a nasalised vowel, and commonly begin with *k* or *kh*' (Lila San Roque, Personal communication, 23 February 2007; see also San Roque 2008:41). This is relevant to the terms *mindimindi kão* and *kẽiyaka*.

19 The only time I heard *mindimindi kão* performed was for my benefit as a researcher. I am not aware of any other contexts in which it is sung in contemporary times.

Duna song genres. And again, a vital element of the structure of the *mindimindi kão* is the use of *kẽiyaka*. When the act of performing these songs is referred to, the verb *ruwa* (speak) is utilised, which aligns this song genre with speech.

Example 2.2 Basic pitch structure of *mindimindi kão*.

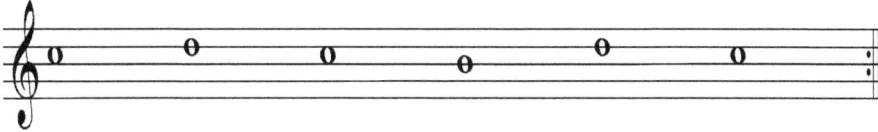

Similar to the *khene ipakana* shown above, *mindimindi kão* focus on the tonal centre and step up and down from it; however, they often (but not always) include a step up of two pitches as shown here, bypassing the tonal centre, which is uncommon in *khene ipakana*. Also, *mindimindi kão* are typically metric (perhaps due to their didactic purpose). An example of *mindimindi kão* is contained in Chapter 7.

Pikono

This form of epic storytelling is the only male ancestral genre that is performed solo, though the audience is crucial to a performance and contributes to the soundscape by giving verbal affirmations and comments on the storyline and the telling of it, and occasionally providing additional information for the singer to incorporate into their performance. Performances are given at night, typically in men's houses, and can range in length, though usually they are between three and six hours (with breaks). Although the general *pikono* melodic contour does include repetitive sections based on the typical three-pitch motif and the recitation of *kẽiyaka* (the process of which is called *ipakana yakaya*), the overall melodic range is much wider, encompassing sometimes a range of six tones (an octave) or more (Example 2.3). Much of the storytelling is improvised at the moment of performance (in accordance with the genre characteristics) and, as such, there is some stylistic variation between performers.

Example 2.3 Basic pitch structure of a *pikono* 'verse'.

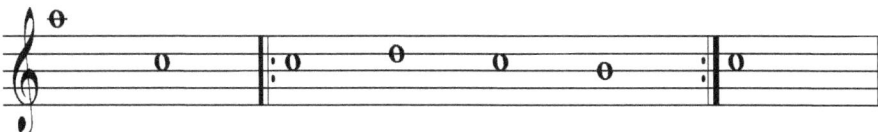

From this sketch it can be seen that the entry point of the phrase is often about four and a half tones above the tonal centre, though certainly not always; one of the defining elements of this genre is its relatively flexible and spontaneous melodic structure, particularly in the initial section of the verse, which is characterised by an extensive melodic descent (or descents). Like the repetitive sequencing within *khene ipakana*, *pikono* verses close with repeated lines based on the tonal centre, with steps above and below it, before finally alighting on a prolonged tonal centre to mark the verse's end.

Pikono is typically sung (and by 'sung' I mean intoned to a sequence of deliberate pitches); however, it can also be told as a spoken narrative. This is particularly the case when women present the genre, which happens in a private setting, mostly for the entertainment and/or moral education of children. These performances can include sung sections, particularly when a praise name sequence is to be recited or when a particular musical or sonic episode is described (see Gillespie and San Roque forthcoming).

Pikono is considered to be an extremely important source of social and other information and the knowledge evident in the texts has been used in contemporary land disputes. It has been a topic of research for other anthropologists (see, for example, Stewart and Strathern 2005). This book presents an example of male *pikono* only: an excerpt of one performance, in Chapter 5 on land and song.[20]

Selepa

The *selepa* courting songs are a male group genre, though women can participate to a limited degree. A solo male initiates the singing and then the remainder of participants join in once the text for that song has been established. Verses are usually of three or four lines in length, so the first line is sung solo and the remaining two or three lines, which are repetitions of the first line but using different praise names for each repetition, are sung in unison.[21]

The *selepa* melodic contour features just three pitches: the tonal centre, a pitch two whole tones above the tonal centre and a tone and a half below the tonal centre (Example 2.4). It also has a distinctive vocable sequence that finishes each *selepa* 'verse': *ee ai ai*.

Example 2.4 Basic pitch structure of *selepa*.

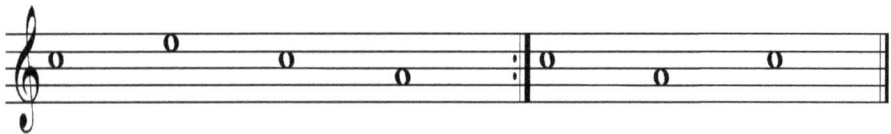

---

20 Koskoff (1998:198) notes, in the context of the study of gender and music in Europe, that 'the most important men's genre within agrarian and village contexts is the epic, or historical narrative song'. *Pikono* too appears to be the most highly prized Duna male song genre.

21 It should be noted that ancestral Duna song does not feature harmony (though, in group performances of individual *khene ipakana*, the effect of harmony can be created—see Chapter 4, Example 4.5).

The distinctive intervals of *selepa* are larger than most other purely song genres in the Duna repertoire (the genre of *mali*, discussed later in this chapter, features the largest regular intervallic steps). It should be noted that *selepa* songs can begin at any pitch in the repeated sequence.

Selepa can also be defined by its accompanying movements. In the typical performance context, men in lines of about three or four, with their arms over each other's shoulders, walk around in a circle as they sing (see Figure 2.1). A physical gap is left between each line of men and in this gap a woman may elect to walk behind the man of her choice. She may also join in the unison singing, but her vocals are very much in the background. Performances utilising these movements are no longer common, due in part to restrictions on courting events that were applied to the Duna from the period of missionisation. More commonly now, *selepa* is sung at night around a fire by a group of men as a form of night-time entertainment for them. The performance in the photograph (Figure 2.1) was more or less a 'mock-up', performed for my benefit as a researcher but also as a display for my friend Tim Scott who was visiting me at Hirane parish for the first time. The participants took the performance with varying levels of seriousness, which is reflected in part by their dress.

In her book, Stürzenhofecker (1998:24) writes of a dance that is labelled *tsole tse*, which she describes as 'a circular dance performed by men and women together'. From this description, *tsole tse* appears to be the same genre as *selepa*. Furthermore, *tsole tse* is said to be interchangeable with the term *yake* (Stewart and Strathern 2002a:84). *Yake* is the verb used in conjunction with *selepa*, so this further strengthens the hypothesis that *tsole tse* and *selepa* are one and the same (the variation in terminology is likely to be attributed to the different dialects/areas where Duna is spoken). Examples of *selepa* are presented in Chapter 5 on land and song.

Yekia

Yekia is another courting song genre. Like *pikono*, it has been a subject for examination by some anthropologists of Duna culture, largely because of the important and complex nature of the ritual of which *yekia* song is a part. More than simply 'courting parties', which is how missionaries perceived them, the rituals surrounding *yekia* 'carried deeper resonances of religious action towards spirits and life force' (Stürzenhofecker 1998:29). In contemporary times, however, 'the religious aspects have been elided and the sexual aspects exaggerated' (Stürzenhofecker 1998:29). It is said that during a performance of *yekia* in the *yekianda* (*yekia* house)[22] of times past, men would sit in the laps of the

---

22 Stürzenhofecker (1998:218) has described *yekianda* (she spells it *yekeanda*) as a ceremony. I, however, understand *yekia* to represent the song genre, and more generally the ceremony, and *yekianda* to represent the location for the ceremony (*anda* meaning 'house').

seated women as they sang, thus showing their interest in the woman on whom they sat (a similar, if more intimate and in a sense inverted, function to that of the women walking behind their man of choice in a performance of *selepa*). Stürzenhofecker (1993:403) explains that this imbalance in the representation of the various facets of *yekia* was generated by the Duna people themselves in order to protect the religious elements of *yekia* from 'unsympathetic outsiders, such as mission personnel'; however, the exaggeration of the sexual in fact defeated this purpose of protection as it was used as 'justification for prohibiting it'.[23] The song genre that remains, now that the ancestral performance context for it does not, is associated almost exclusively with courting.

Figure 2.1 *Selepa* performance.

Photo by *Tim Scott*

Like *selepa*, each *yekia* consists of three or sometimes four lines of text, with the first line introduced by one man and the remaining repetitive lines sung in unison by the whole group. Once again, as with *selepa*, here women can join in the unison singing but should never instigate a 'verse' (for women it is said to be 'hat long stat'—that is, hard to start it off [Kenny Kendoli, Personal communication, 24 June 2006]). Also, like *selepa*, *yekia*'s melodic contour is distinctive and somewhat fixed (Example 2.5).

---

23 The prohibition of Duna ancestral musical practices by various missions will be discussed shortly.

Example 2.5 Basic pitch structure of *yekia*.

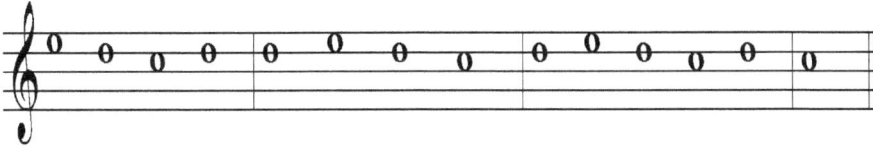

Essentially, then, *yekia* comprises three or four lines (three in Example 2.5) that begin fluctuating between the pitches of one and two whole tones above the tonal centre before arriving at it. The penultimate line closes on this tonal centre, while the ultimate line raises itself to the tone above before the whole *yekia* closes with a vocable marker on the tonal centre. When there are four lines of text, the first closes on the tonal centre and the second line closes on the tone above; however, here, in a three-line example, the first line closes on the tone above, the second line closes on the tonal centre, the third and final on the tone above again, followed by the tonal centre vocables. *Yekia* lines always alternate in this way between closing on the tone above and closing on the tonal centre.

When considering the textual structure of *yekia* (and *selepa*), one can see similarities with some features of other Papua New Guinean courting songs such as those of the Ipili-Paiela, a neighbouring but generally culturally distinct group (or groups) of people whose songs have been described by Ingemann (1968). In particular, the similarities that can be drawn are the use of just a few repetitive text lines based on alternating praise names and a vocable ending (Ingemann 1968). Ingemann represents the Ipili-Paiela (spelt 'Ipili-Paiyala') courting song vocable ending as *'ao ae'*, which appears remarkably close to the vocable ending of *yekia*, which I spell as *aiyo ai*.

Yekia is often spelt *yekea* by other scholars (for example, Stewart and Strathern 2002a:77). Sometimes *yekea* and *yekeanda* (the location for *yekia*) are used interchangeably (see Stürzenhofecker 1993:355). It is also known as *yekia auu* (Niles and Webb 1987:76), due to its verb association (see the later section of this chapter detailing genres and their verbs). *Yekia* has been likened to *dawe*, a Huli courting song genre (Stewart and Strathern 2002a:77).[24]

Laingwa is another term for *yekia*, referring specifically to the song form rather than also to the whole ritual (Kenny Kendoli, Personal communication, 7 March 2007). Stewart and Strathern (2000a:94, 2002a:80–4) discuss the song form as *laingwa*. In my discussions with Duna people, however, the term *yekia* was always used, so I reproduce their labelling here.

---

24 Other terms sometimes used for *dawe* are *dawenda*, *tauwenda* and *rawenda*, which represent different spellings/pronunciations and incorporate the term for the building (*anda*/'house') that is the location for the ritual.

Alima ('instrument[s]')

Although instrumental music is not the central focus of this book, instruments are referred to in some of the following chapters and, considering this, plus the paucity of information available on Duna music, it is important to describe here the nature of the instruments used. The Duna use several musical instruments. Instruments of ancestral origin include the *alima*, *kuluparapu*, *luna* and *uruwaya* (the drum known in Tok Pisin as 'kundu'). Instruments introduced by European contact and now used regularly by Duna people include the *luna khao* (metal jew's harp), *ngita* (guitar) and *ngulele* (ukulele), which are discussed further in the next chapter.

From the descriptions of Duna song genres in the previous section, it is clear that gender features as an important organising principle in Duna musical practice. This is typical of Papua New Guinea, particularly of instrumental music, as Lutkehaus writes:

> As distinctions of gender and the division of labour by sex are fundamental principles of culture and social organization in New Guinea, so the performance of music is structured by principles of gender... In many New Guinea societies, men and women sing, but instrumental music has long been predominantly the purview of men, and it remains so. (Lutkehaus 1998:245–6)

Musical instruments are understood in many cultures across the world to be inherently sexual and for this reason women are said to be discouraged from playing them (cf. Petrovic 1990:73). This may or may not be the case for the Duna. It is, however, true to say that Duna musical instruments sit firmly in the domain of men and this has largely to do with the performance context for instruments in the past (being associated with the *haroli palena* bachelor cult). I will now briefly describe the Duna instruments *alima*, *kuluparapu*, *pilipe*, *luna* and *uruwaya*.

Alima (*mouth bow*)

In the Duna language, the term *alima* covers the general category of instruments (including both old and introduced), but also refers to a specific instrument. The *alima* proper is made from a branch bent into an arc, with two strings between the two ends of the branch holding the branch in position and thus making a musical bow. These strings are traditionally made from tree vine, but can be made of synthetic materials in the present day. The two strings of the *alima* are played with a pick held in the right hand of the player. This pick is traditionally a small section of tree vine but can also be substituted with other materials. The two strings are struck together in the same stroke. The outer string is always left open, but the inner string is regularly stopped with the thumb of the left hand, which is holding the instrument at the bottom (the top of the instrument is held in the mouth). The thumb stops only the inner string at one place on the string, thus there are only three pitches available to the *alima*: the lower pitch of the outer open string (which is slightly longer than the inner string); the middle pitch of the inner open string; and the higher pitch of the stopped inner string (see Example 2.6 and Figure 2.2).

Example 2.6 (▶ Audio 1) *Alima*.

This is one of the few instruments that women are said to play (see also Stewart and Strathern 2002b:81). Pugh-Kitingan (1981:175) documents the Huli equivalent of the *alima*, the *gawa*, as a popular instrument for women.

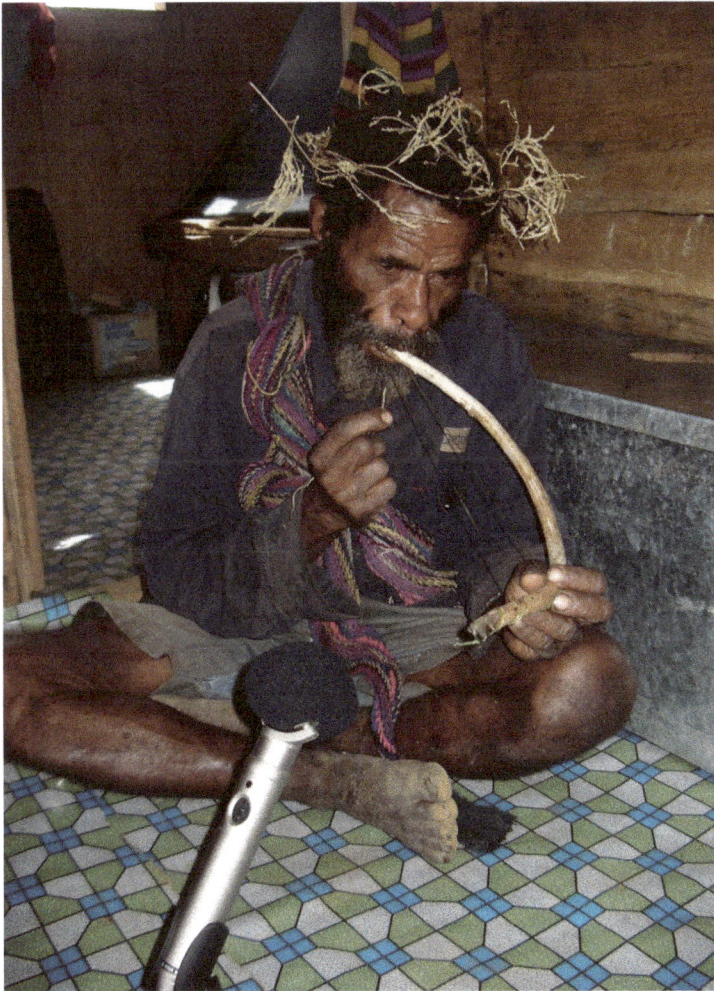

Figure 2.2 *Alima* being played by Sane Noma.

Kuluparapu (*bamboo panpipes*)

The *kuluparapu* is made of seven bamboo pipes of varying length. They are arranged with the longest pipe in the centre and the six other pipes in a circle around it. The pipes are bound together in two places: close to the mouthpiece of the instrument and again further down its body (holding only three or so pipes together at this second point). Binding is traditionally with bush materials, however, more recently other types of binding can be seen, such as strips of rubber from a car tyre. The instrument is blown lightly, with the lips never touching the pipes. There are two sizes of instrument: the *kuluparapu puka* (big *kuluparapu*) and the *kuluparapu kete* (little *kuluparapu*). Of the two models I examined, made by Sane Noma, the bigger was approximately 70 cm in length; the smaller approximately 55 cm (see Example 2.7 and Figure 2.3).

Example 2.7 (▶ Audio 2) *Kuluparapu.*

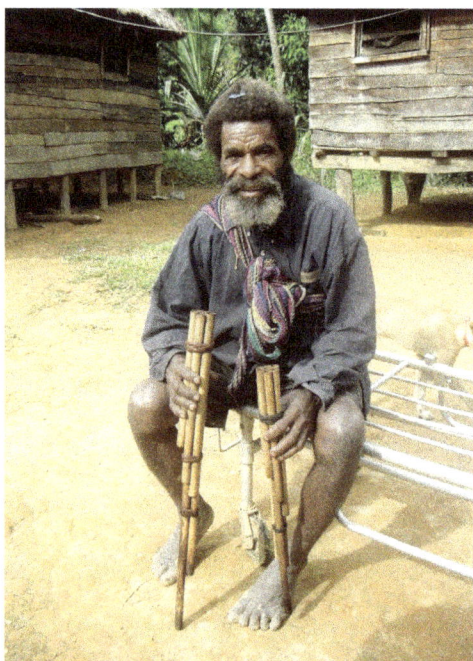

Figure 2.3 Two *kuluparapu,* held by Sane Noma.

Pilipe (*end-blown notched flute with finger holes*)

I first came across the *pilipe* in a textual reference within a *pikono* performance. Although I once saw this instrument being carried around Kopiago, I never heard it played. San Roque recorded a sound sample for my benefit on a later trip to the field (see Example 2.8 and Figure 2.4).

Example 2.8 (▶ Audio 3) *Pilipe*.

Recorded by *Lila San Roque*

Figure 2.4 *Pilipe*.

Photo by *Nicole Haley*

The *pilipe* is typically an open bamboo tube with two finger holes towards the base of the tube. It is blown through the open top. There has been mention of a second variety of *pilipe*, made from a closed bamboo tube—that is, one cut at either end at the bamboo nodes. This variety is said to be side-blown, with two finger holes at its base. Pugh-Kitingan (1981:284) reports a side-blown *pilipe* played by the Huli (known as the *honabi pilipe* or 'white person's flute') as something modelled on the European flute, which can be found in trade stores. The existence of only two holes in either version restricts the range of the instrument to primarily three pitches, plus an extended overtone series.

Luna (*bamboo jew's harp*)

Like the *kuluparapu* and the *pilipe*, the *luna* is made out of bamboo. A single piece of bamboo is cut and fashioned to create a thin inner strip that vibrates when the weighted end of it is tapped against the base of the closed hand. The mouth, placed over the cutaway section of the bamboo, provides a cavity for this vibration to resonate. There is essentially only one pitch created by the *luna*; however, in the positioning of the mouth there is a variation in timbre. The performer shapes words with his mouth against the instrument and in this way stories are told (see Example 2.9 and Figure 2.5).[25]

Example 2.9 (▶ Audio 4) *Luna.*

Figure 2.5 *Luna* being played by Sane Noma.

---

25   The people of Bosavi, also of the Southern Highlands Province, have a similar term for the bamboo jew's harp: *uluna* (Feld 1984:391). The similarity of the terms could be more than coincidental and could function as a clue to understanding the dissemination of the instrument across the province (the languages of Duna and Bosavi are not closely related).

Uruwaya

Uruwaya (see Figure 2.6) is the Duna name for the Tok Pisin 'kundu', a drum that is widespread throughout Papua New Guinea and is open at one end, enclosed with skin at the other and beaten with one hand (see also Niles 2006). *Uruwaya* is also the name of the tree from which the drum is made in the Kopiago region. It is used by the Duna to accompany dances such as *mali mapu* (see Figure 2.7).

Figure 2.6 *Uruwaya.*

Photo by *Tim Scott*

Similarities with Huli instruments

It is important to note (remembering the story of Mburulu Pango) that Duna musical instruments, in more or less their exact form, are also used by the Huli, albeit known by different names. The Huli *alima* is called *gawa* (Pugh-Kitingan 1981:183); the larger *kuluparapu* is called *gulungulu* (Pugh-Kitingan 1981:227); and the smaller *kuluparapu* is called *gulupobe* (Pugh-Kitingan 1981:220). The Huli have the *pilipe*, too, known by the same name, and they also have two models: an end-blown flute—though, unlike the Duna version, apparently without finger holes (Pugh-Kitingan 1981:272)—and an identical side-blown closed bamboo tube with finger holes (Pugh-Kitingan 1981:283–4). The Huli version of the *luna* (which Pugh-Kitingan refers to as a 'jaw's harp') is the *hiriyula*, which is similar to the *luna* but incorporates a piece of string (the Duna also used this instrument in addition to their *luna*) (Pugh-Kitingan 1981:199–217). The Huli 'kundu' drum is known in that language as *tàbage* (Pugh-Kitingan 1998:541).

Table 2.1 Duna instrument and corresponding Huli instrument names.

DUNA INSTRUMENTS	HULI INSTRUMENTS
alima (mouth bow)	*gawa*
kuluparapu puka (large bamboo panpipes)	*gulungulu*
kuluparapu kete (small bamboo panpipes)	*gulupobe*
luna (bamboo jew's harp)	*hiriyula*
uruwaya (drum)	*tàbage*

Other instruments

The Duna do not often use rattles (nor do the Huli for that matter), unlike groups in other areas of the Southern Highlands Province (Weiner 1991:167; Feld 1982:171–4). Only the Duna genre of *rawe*, which features dance movements, is said to involve the use of rattles, called *irasole*, made of dried seed pods (Richard Alo, Personal communication, 18 June 2006).[26] A brief description and an image of Duna men performing this genre with these rattles have been published by Stewart and Strathern (2000b:54, 85).

Mouth instruments as 'speech surrogates'

The *kulupurapu*, *alima* and *luna* are instruments played with the mouth. As such, when they are played, it is said that they communicate stories or direct verbal communication. Niles has made the following general observations of the *susap* (the Tok Pisin term for jew's harps):

> In Papua New Guinea, as elsewhere, the mouth harp often acts as a 'speech surrogate'. Performers use it to imitate speech patterns and phonemes in order to create the illusion of speech in a musical context. The sounds of the mouth harp are often considered to be speech that is 'disguised', in order that it not be understood by eavesdroppers… the *susap* is considered to possess love-controlling magic that men can use to attract a woman's affections. By using the instrument as a speech surrogate, the man is able to 'say' things to the woman that might otherwise be considered inappropriate. The instrument also provides impunity from rejection. (Niles 2005:83)

These qualities can be extended to the Duna *alima* and *luna*. These instruments are traditionally used as courting devices. The word *alima* also means 'friend' or 'friendship' in Duna—as in the Tok Pisin 'pren', denoting a romantic relationship—for precisely this reason. Within the *haroli palena* bachelor cult,

---

26 Stürzenhofecker (1993:378) labels the same dance as *tawe*—as do Stewart and Strathern (2002a:79)—and refers to the rattles used as *puru sole*.

boys were taught to play the *alima* and the *luna* in order to form a 'bridge' (*soko*) between themselves and their intended on their graduation from the cult (in addition to courting women at the *yekia* ritual).

The *kuluparapu*, *alima* and *luna* had particular roles within the *haroli palena*, related to this ability of the instruments to 'speak'. The *kuluparapu* is said to have had the function of waking up the bachelor cult boys in the morning. This seems paradoxical, considering the very soft and airy timbre of the instrument. It is also the *kuluparapu* that is said to 'open the door' to the *haroli palena*. The two different sizes of *kuluparapu* each had different functions in this respect. Sane Noma explained that the bigger instrument opens the door to allow a grown man to leave the cult, while the smaller instrument calls back the boys who are not yet ready to leave the cult (Sane Noma, Personal communication, translated by Petros Kilapa and Lila San Roque, 22 February 2005).

All three instruments were able to convey 'stories' to the bachelor cult members, most commonly in the form of morality tales. Interestingly, former bachelor cult leaders have played some of these morality tales on metal jew's harps to me for recording; however, they maintained that such an introduced musical instrument would not be able to be used in the context of the bachelor cult (in effect, the ancestral could come out into the modern arena, but the modern could not enter the ancestral in this case).

'Dance'

As with the term 'music', there was no collective Duna term for 'dance' in the time before Tok Pisin; dances, like songs, were referred to individually by the term for the particular genre. The Tok Pisin term 'danis' ('to dance') has, however, been adopted and is often pronounced *ndaniti* by Duna speakers. Usually though, 'danis' refers to Western styles of dancing, such as those introduced through the modern 'disco'. The more typical Tok Pisin term for traditional dances is 'singsing', which includes the entire performance, not just body movement.

Genres performed by the Duna that include body movement that I have recorded are *mali* and *selepa* (*yekia* in its traditional context also included body movement). *Selepa* can be, and is often, performed without movement and, as such, it has been classified as *ipakana*. *Mali* on the other hand is rarely performed without movement (I have heard it performed only once without movement, by a group of seated children, which was greeted with much amusement from surprised adults nearby).

This is partly because the vocal text for this genre (if utilised, and it often is not) is minimal and includes vocables that complement the body movements. I have therefore chosen to describe *mali* separately below. Stewart and Strathern (2002a:79) have briefly described other Duna dances—namely, *tawe* (or *rawe*), *komea*, *heka kiliapa* and *pilaku*, which were reported to be performed as part of the *yekia* ritual.

Mali

There are two types of *mali* that the Duna perform. *Mali mapu* is a circular dance (*mapu* meaning 'encircle, go around') performed by men, who jump up and down in the circle, facing inwards and gradually moving in an anticlockwise direction (see Figure 2.7). The *uruwaya* is used as accompaniment and the number of drums varies from just one being played to all performers playing one, according to availability. The short song text is sung by one man and a chorus of men, in two parts, follows this line of verse with unison vocables—one group calling out the first vocable, the second responding with a falsetto vocable six tones (an octave) higher. This jump makes this form radically different to other Duna genres whose melodies move predominantly in steps (Example 2.10).

Chenoweth (2000:178–9) provides a transcription of a 'singsing' genre that she calls *pe* and translates as meaning 'finish'.[27] From this transcription, and the description of its performance context as being 'sung in the big annual *sing-sing*', it appears to be a representation of *mali mapu*.

Example 2.10 Basic pitch structure of *mali mapu* based on Chenoweth's notation.[28]

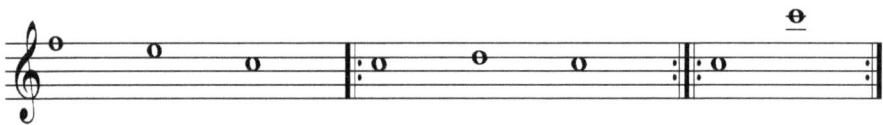

---

27   The Duna word *pe* is in fact a question marker and features prominently in lament texts, which will be seen in Chapter 4. It is unclear to me how Chenoweth came to this understanding of the word *pe* and how she came to label *mali mapu* as such.

28   In the absence of my own recording of a *mali mapu*, I have re-presented Chenoweth's data here.

Figure 2.7 *Mali mapu* performance in early 1960s.

Photo by *David Hook*

Mali mbawa is the other kind of *mali* that is performed by the Duna; however, it is generally acknowledged to be a genre indigenous to the neighbouring Huli. In this genre, men stand in two even lines facing each other rather than a circle. Once again, the *uruwaya* is used for accompaniment, but the vocals are vocables only and are sung in unison. This could be a relatively recent addition to the Duna repertoire, as David Hook, one of the first colonial administrators at Kopiago and resident there in the early 1960s, reports that he did not witness a performance of *mali mbawa* during his time there, though *mali mapu* was common (David Hook, Personal communication, 22 November 2007).

Since missionisation, the word *mali* has been used by the Duna to also mean 'year' (it is used in this context in song Example 6.11). It appears that the term was given this additional meaning by missionaries who were keen to mark the end of the year—that is, Christmas—with celebrations showcasing performances of genres including *mali* (Lila San Roque, Personal communication, 10 July 2006). Modjeska (1977:xv, plate following 296) presents a photograph of *mali mapu* being performed to celebrate Christmas in 1973.

Vocabulary: genres and their verbs

San Roque (Personal communication, 4 December 2007) explains that the terms given for Duna performance genres are not simple nouns, but 'in a sentence each term must be used in construction with a particular verb (or set of verbs) in order to be fully meaningful' (see also San Roque 2008:245–50). Therefore, in any discussion of musical genres it is important to consider these accompanying verbs, how the verbs used distinguish different genres and how they can show a relatedness between those genres that share the same verb.

A difference in verb association can represent another way of classifying performance genres besides that made by the noun or verbal-adjunct-like words. Here, however, one can see that the verb-based classification somewhat mirrors those categories of *ipakana* and *alima* as previously presented (and by default, suggests a category of 'dance' outside these first two groupings). That is, songs and instrumental music are classified into two according to the different verbs used. The exception is the genre of *yekia*, which, as previously mentioned, is associated with a verb particular to it.

Ruwa (*'to sing'*, *'to speak/articulate'*, *'to voice'*)

Ruwa is the verb associated with song genres.[29] For example, when one is instructed to sing, they would be told *'ipakana ruwa'* ('sing a song') or *'ko ruwa'* ('you sing'). The latter command, however, is also the instruction for one person to speak to another ('you speak'). The particular meaning, then, is determined largely by the context in which the word is used. To be inclusive of these two meanings, *ruwa* might be best translated as 'to voice', meaning something that is communicated verbally by a human being.

Examples

- *ipakana ruwa* ('sing *ipakana*')
- *kão ruwa*[30] ('sing *kão*')
- *pikono ruwa* ('sing *pikono*')
- *mali ipakana ruwa* ('sing *mali*')
- *selepa ruwa* ('sing *selepa*')

---

29   San Roque notes that '*ruwa* can also be used to express thoughts and desires' (Personal communication, 23 February 2007).

30   An example has been given of the construction *kão haka*; however, in this combination *haka* is not a verb; rather, a noun. To have a verbal construction one must say *kão haka ruwa* (essentially 'sing the *kão* language'), where *ruwa* is the verb (Richard Alo, Personal communication, 27 June 2006).

Haka (*'to talk', also 'language', 'word'*)

Like *ruwa*, the verb *haka* is used to indicate speech. It has some similarities to the English word 'talk' as it can be used as either a noun or a verb (see San Roque 2008:79). This speech appears, however, to be reserved mainly for non-human subjects, such as musical instruments or birds. As the word for 'language', though, *haka* relates to human beings—for example, '*Yuna haka*' ('Duna language').

Examples

- *luna haka* ('*luna* talk')
- *alima haka* ('*alima* talk')
- *kuluparapu haka* ('*kuluparapu* talk')
- *pilipe haka* ('*pilipe* talk')
- *heka haka* ('bird talk')

Sa (*'to hit/affect'*)

Instruments that are held in the hand and struck rather than associated with the mouth—for example, the *uruwaya* and the guitar—are referred to by the verb *sa*, meaning 'to hit/affect'.[31]

Yake (*'move around'*)

When referring to a *selepa* performance that incorporates the traditional circular movement of men and women, the verb *yake* is utilised. Thus, one could command one to '*selepa yakepa*' ('move around to the *selepa*'). As most *selepa* performances now incorporate only the vocal element of the genre, it is fair to classify it as *ipakana/ruwa*.

Kuru (*'jump up and down'*)

This verb has been translated generally as 'dance'; however, it is used specifically with the genre of *mali* when dance movements are incorporated (which they usually are, for reasons given above). As a command to perform *mali*, one would say '*mali kurupa*' ('jump up and down with the *mali*').

U (*'to do'*), uku (*'to go into'*)

The term *u* is, as mentioned above in describing the origins of *ipakana* as a category, associated only with the genre of *yekia* and describes the act of

---

31 This term can be heard as a command in the recorded performance of Example 5.15.

performing this genre.[32] One can announce their imminent performance of *yekia* by saying '*yekia unda*' (adding the intentive future suffix -*nda* to *u*) meaning '(I am) going to do a *yekia*'. To mark past tense, the suffix -*u* would be added—an example is the construction '*anoaka yekia uu*', which would translate to mean 'the men have finished doing the *yekia*'.

Uku is an idiomatic construction also peculiar to *yekia* and it is best described as 'to go into' or 'to go inside' *yekia*. For example, to command someone to perform a *yekia* using this verb, one would say '*yekia ukupa*'. One could also announce one's performance of the genre by saying '*yekia ukunda*', using the same future suffix as above. Also, as above, past tense can be represented with this verb, such as the construction '*yekia anoaka ukuu*' (Richard Alo and Lila San Roque, Personal communication, 27 June 2006).

From the above exploration, it should be evident that the vocabulary surrounding genres and the verbs that are utilised when discussing them are very important in the understanding of, and the classification of, performance genres. Now the language within Duna *ipakana* will be discussed.

Language features of Duna song

Kẽiyaka and repetition

All Duna ancestral performance genres that incorporate song texts use *kẽiyaka* as an integral part of their textual structure. *Kẽiyaka*, or 'praise names' as they are here translated (following Haley 2002a:123–4),[33] are additional, alternative names for the regular names for places, features of the physical landscape, flora, fauna, material objects, people and parts of a person, such as their hair. They are used not only in songs but also in other kinds of stylised speech.[34] They are not used in everyday communication; as Richard Alo once explained in Tok Pisin, 'Taim nating, ol i no save toktok [when nothing is happening, people don't say them]' (Richard Alo, Workshop presentation, Goroka, 22 June 2006)—though

---

32 The Huli term u̱, as discussed in comments by Gabe Lomas and Jacqueline Pugh-Kitingan cited earlier in this chapter, is likely to be related to the Duna term.

33 Haley does not use a tilde over the e to indicate nasalisation when she discusses this language feature; however, it is consistent with the work of San Roque. Though pronounced (and thus spelt) a little differently, *kẽiyaka* is likely to be a compound of the words *kẽi* and *haka* (considering other speech genres also use this root; see below), though *yaka*—'to name'—is also equally plausible, and is favoured by Haley (see 2008:215). It is not clear what *kẽi* signifies on its own.

34 Compound words for other speech genres include *rambaka* ('compensation talk'), a compound of *ramba* and *haka*.

they are often used as greetings (Haley 2002a:123–4). Song is, however, a very important way to consolidate—and even create[35]—*kẽiyaka* in Duna culture through repetition.

Kẽiyaka are an important feature of many Duna song texts, both ancestral and introduced, but the actual listing of *kẽiyaka* (the process known as *ipakana yakaya*, which was introduced earlier in this chapter) is vital to the structure of most ancestral song genres. Inevitably, such *kẽiyaka* listing, or 'counting', involves textual repetition, which, because of the consistent musical settings of this textual repetition, extends to musical repetition. This is evident in the musical examples that appear in this book. *Kẽiyaka* usually appear at the beginning of textual lines in the *ipakana yakaya* process and are sometimes preceded by a line of text with the regular name for a given feature/object/person in the first line of the song in order to provide a reference for the *kẽiyaka* to come (Example 2.11).

Example 2.11 *Kẽiyaka* sequence (with *kẽiyaka* terms underlined).

singayaroko	arriving there
anoa ingini <u>malu</u> liliwale peli po horaka ndu rarua rita-o	she saw a son of a man sitting there straightening his tangled *malu* hair it's said
<u>matialu</u> liliwale peli po horaka ndu rarua rita-o	saw him sitting there straightening his tangled *matialu* hair it's said
<u>nepero</u> liliwale peli po horaka ndu rarua rita-o	saw him sitting there straightening his tangled *nepero* hair it's said
<u>saiyawa</u> liliwale peli po horaka ndu rarua rita-o	saw him sitting there straightening his tangled *saiyawa* hair it's said

Taken from a *pikono* text sung by older woman Pokole Pora, and translated by Petros Kilapa and Lila San Roque.

Kẽiyaka are multiple and a fixed order of *kẽiyaka* appears to exist, so performers know in which order they will be recited. This is particularly important for those genres that are performed as a group, such as *kão*, *selepa* and *yekia*, in which one leader introduces a line of text and the rest follow his lead (these genres, as with most the Duna practise, are generally not rehearsed before a performance). The hierarchy of *kẽiyaka* appears to take into account the syllabic length of each term when they vary; it is my observation that *kẽiyaka* with two syllables will precede those with three. I have not established any other determinants of the order in which they are recited other than convention.

If this repetition, both musical and textual, is so prominent in Duna ancestral song genres, one is tempted to ask what the *function* of this repetition really is. Repetition is redundant in terms of meaning (as the audience has already heard

---

35   New *kẽiyaka* for new things, such as aeroplanes, are said to be able to be created by performers of *pikono*. Once they have introduced a term to listeners, that term can be adopted by other performers of *pikono*, and eventually it is introduced into other contexts.

and taken in the literal meaning), so it must offer more. Repetition provides, for one thing, space and time for reflection, both for the performer and for the audience. Certainly, the repetitive sequences within the *ipakana yakaya* process provoke the most emotional responses from the audience who listens—for example, the *khene ipakana* that 'really breaks the heart of a man' (Richard Alo, Personal communication, 30 June 2004) or the *pikono* that provokes an excited audience interjection such as the declarations *'home kone!'* or *'hame kone!'* ('exactly so!').

In this book, I present *kẽiyaka* in the song text translations alongside the regular word for the place/object/person. For example, when the parish of Hirane is given the *kẽiyaka* of *pakura*, I have written *pakura* Hirane. In the song texts, praise names are distinguished from other words by an underline. This is also consistent with the translations of my colleague working with Duna language, Lila San Roque.

Metaphor

Although the successful use of *kẽiyaka* in song can determine great performers and great performances, another poetic feature is just as important, and this is the use of metaphor.[36] 'Metaphor', as Love (1998:336) writes, 'abounds in Oceanic lyrics'. More specific to this context, one could say that metaphor abounds in Papua New Guinean lyrics, as several studies have testified (Feld 1982:142–3; Weiner 1991; Doherty 1995). Richness in metaphor certainly extends to Duna ancestral songs (and also to introduced song styles, as will become apparent). The texts of these songs are not often straightforward and literal. More commonly, they are clothed in metaphor in order to encode knowledge and to be valued as more artistic.

Metaphor occurs often in the Duna courting genres of *selepa* and *yekia*. This is not surprising. Love (1998:336) writes that metaphors 'safely convey… references to illicit behaviour because their meaning is inferential and therefore unprovable, protecting composers and performers from retaliation'. In this way the function of metaphor in song is similar to the function of Duna *alima* as speech surrogates: one is protected from an unfavourable response to the musical communication by hiding behind the indirect nature of it. Metaphor is also used in other Duna song genres—in particular, *khene ipakana* and *pikono*. Examples of metaphor are illustrated in the discussion of particular songs in later chapters of this book.

---

36 Of course, metaphor can be understood as a feature not only of poetry, but of all language (Friedrich 1986:23).

Language is arguably the most important aesthetic element in Duna performance. This is one of the reasons why song forms are the focus here, as distinct from instrumental and dance forms of expression. It is also why I have paid close attention to the meaning and expression of text in song in the research that follows.

Conclusion

The aim of this chapter has been to provide a comprehensive, introductory outline of Duna ancestral performance practice. This is a necessary framework for the orientation of this publication. As no previous ethnomusicology sources exist that detail Duna music in its entirety, it has been necessary to be inclusive in this outline. I began with some reflections on the origins of Duna music, touched on the 'musician' in Duna society and commented on the nature of Duna melodic structures and the Duna language as tonal. Examining the vocabulary surrounding Duna musical practice is a focus of my research, so I introduced the concept of the Duna musical categories of songs (*ipakana*) and instruments (*alima*) and described the Duna approach to what might be called 'dance'. I described the genres that I will be examining under the categories that they best fit, providing some information about the ancestral Duna practice of *haroli palena* ('bachelor cult') that is vital to the understanding of the performance context for musical instruments in particular. The importance of considering Duna verbs in relation to genres was established and verb groupings were proposed as another (parallel) way of classifying genres. Finally, language features *within* Duna ancestral song texts were explored—in particular, the use of *kēiyaka* ('praise names') and metaphor. A focus on language is also evident in the introduced musical styles that are performed by the Duna, the history and essence of which we will now consider.

3. Music and encounter

nane laip *senis nganda waya keina*	boy's life change keeps coming
imane laip senis *nganda waya keina*	girl's life change keeps coming
Ngote haka ipa mo waya keina	God's talk is like water it keeps coming

I open with a Christian song that is popular in the Duna community at Kopiago.[1] This song declares that 'laip senis', meaning 'life change' in Tok Pisin, keeps coming for boys and girls as a result of God's word that comes down like rain, never drying up. 'Laip senis' exists alongside such Tok Pisin terms as 'tanim bel' ('turn the belly', meaning to convert), used throughout the country by missions in their efforts to convert Papua New Guineans to a Christian way of life. Here, however, the term—and the song—takes on an even deeper resonance when one considers the dramatic life change experienced by the Duna people since the 1930s. So, what has changed for the Duna? How are they expressing this life change musically?

In this chapter, I endeavour to answer these questions first by examining the history of both the colonial and the missionary encounter in Duna country in and around Lake Kopiago, focusing on the kinds of musical influences of these encounters. Toner and Wild (2004:107) recently pointed out: 'Ethnomusicologists and popular music scholars have tended to neglect the processes of transmission of both local musical styles and global popular styles, and instead have focused on the meanings of the final products whether indigenous or fused.' This section concentrates particularly on the transmission of new musical influences. The second section will examine how the Duna have merged these introduced musical influences in order to sing contemporary songs about their current life experience. I will conclude with some brief notes locating this kind of musical syncretism, appropriation and indigenisation in the discourse of ethnomusicology.

The colonial encounter

In Chapter 1, I provided background to the period of first contact of the Duna with Europeans, which occurred in the mid-1930s. Although the arrival of

---

1   A shorter and earlier version of this chapter has been published under the title '"Laip senis": music and encounter in a Papua New Guinean community' (Gillespie 2007a).

the Fox and Taylor patrols on their land is generally understood to have been extremely traumatic for the Duna, photographic footage from the second patrol illustrates mostly positive exchanges between the Highlanders and Taylor's men. These photographs also hold valuable information about musical exchange during this period. In particular, one photograph shows a policeman's wife playing the mouth organ to an eager group of women in Wabag, the provincial capital of Enga Province in the Highlands region (reproduced in a plate in Gammage 1998:172–3). According to Gammage (Personal communication, 23 November 2005), Jim Taylor carried several mouth organs with him on patrol and these, along with metal jew's harps, were used for trade.[2] The popularity of the mouth organ could have resulted in part from the apparent similarity between it and traditional Duna musical instruments whose sound is also produced through the mouth, such as the *kuluparapu* and the *luna*, which are widespread across the Highlands. Gammage also writes that the Siane (from the Eastern Highlands Province) and the Purari (from the Gulf Province), who were on this patrol, played flutes at night, which no doubt would have been heard by the people of the country through which they travelled (though it is unlikely they would have been traded, as it appears they might have been associated with religion and sorcery by some of the members of the patrol) (Gammage 1998:115, 138). These appear to be the first examples of the Duna's exposure to music of cultures outside their own region of the Highlands. It was not, however, the first exposure to music other than their own; the Duna were never a closed musical community by any means, as was described in the previous chapter.

Despite the eagerness of the second patrol to establish inroads into the Highlands, it was not until the late 1950s that the Australian government, then administering the area as part of the Territory of Papua and New Guinea, began to build a government station at Lake Kopiago (see Figure 3.1). This station was to become a centre of activity for both the Duna and the government, with an airstrip and trade stores, council buildings and eventually a club for expatriates where the government officers played their chosen music on the radio for entertainment (Bill Gammage, Personal communication, 23 November 2005).

The key musical influence in Papua New Guinea at this time was guitar and ukulele music, which was first introduced to the country on a large scale during the 1940s by servicemen from Hawai'i and the Philippines (Webb and Niles 1987:54). These instruments, when played together and combined with a vocal line (and sometimes also a separate bass line), form the basic elements of stringband music.[3] By the 1960s, stringband music had become popular

---

2   Michael Webb and Don Niles (1987:52) report that the mouth organ, or harmonica, was already circulating in Papua New Guinea by the late 1800s/early 1900s, having been introduced by Australian goldminers.

3   The stringband can also incorporate a bass instrument made of large resonating tubes of bamboo or PVC, which are struck at one end with a rubber sole, producing a loud thumping bass note resembling the sound of a hand-muted electric bass guitar. When this instrument is included in the stringband ensemble, the group

in villages throughout the country (Crowdy 2001:135). It eventually reached Kopiago by radio and perhaps also through musicians in the administration. Several stringbands were later established in the community, in particular to provide the club with live entertainment. It is also possible that films were shown at Kopiago during these heady colonial days; cowboy film music has been noted as a major influence on Papua New Guinean guitar styles (Webb and Niles 1987:53) and Kenny Kendoli (Forthcoming) refers to such films in an interview.

Figure 3.1 Aerial view of Kopiago station, 1964. Note the circular parade ground and the tennis courts, now no longer in existence.

Photo by *David Hook*

Under the Australian administration, Duna men became particularly mobile (rivalry between indigenous groups in the past is one reason given for limited travel; Okole 2005:187). Men travelled as far as Port Moresby in pursuit of paid work with the administration and on plantations. In these locations far from home exposure to other musical styles and instruments was inevitable. The metal jew's harp, in addition to the mouth organ, had been an instrument of trade in Papua New Guinea since the early 1900s (Webb and Niles 1987:52) and eventually found its way to the Duna community on the men's return. The metal jew's harp proved to be a very popular instrument and its volume, tone and

---

becomes known as a 'bamboo band'—an ensemble associated with Bougainville and Madang provinces in Papua New Guinea but with origins in the Solomon Islands (see Kemoi 1996:31). In its absence, bass notes are played on the lower strings of an acoustic guitar.

robustness continue to make it favoured by many men over the *luna*. The metal jew's harp can also double as a fashion accessory/hair clip—one can be seen in the hair of Sane Noma in Chapter 2, Figure 2.3.

Despite all this musical activity around the Kopiago station, Chenoweth (1969:218), the one ethnomusicologist of the time who was working with Duna songs (as collected by others), claimed that the Duna 'have not been known to adopt any western songs'. The scene had, however, been set. In 1964, the administration officially derestricted the Lake Kopiago area (until that year it had not been possible for anyone outside the administration to visit the area) and the eager missionaries were finally allowed to enter (Haley 2002a:26).[4]

The mission encounter

The first missions to enter the Lake Kopiago area were the Lutheran Church and the Christian Missions in Many Lands (CMML), but by 1967 there were six different denominations in the area (cf. Stürzenhofecker 1998:21), with representation by the Catholic, Apostolic, Baptist and Seventh-Day Adventist (SDA) churches. Competition for land on which to establish missions in this period was so fierce that it was described as 'a gold rush for souls' (David Hook, Personal communication, 22 November 2007). Haley writes that as a consequence of increased colonial activity the ritual activities of the Duna had gradually ceased during the previous decade, thus clearing the way for the activities of the missions. This meant that in a very short time 'virtual wholesale conversion had been achieved' by the missions (Haley 2002a:26).

Scholars have compared and contrasted the impact of the colonial encounter with that of the missions, albeit from different angles. Regarding the preservation of culture in reference to the Highlands of Papua New Guinea generally, Andrew Strathern observes that

> missions always deliberately set out to alter and replace the people's own culture, in both material and spiritual terms. By contrast, the Australian Administration officers maintained a more complex attitude towards local practices. In respect of social structure, they tended to be 'conservationists': this structure must not be broken down, they reasoned, because if so, they would lose the reliable intermediaries

---

4 The administration established the Restricted Areas Ordinance in 1934 chiefly to protect missionaries and other visitors to certain regions of Papua New Guinea from the possibility of violent encounter with indigenous peoples (Bill Gammage, Personal communication, 22 December 2005).

between themselves and the mass of the people…If the Administration agreed with missions on any issue it was quite likely to be on different grounds from those used by the missionaries. (Strathern 1984:32)[5]

In his comparison of the colonial impact with that of the missions, Firth writes that

[m]ost colonial governments were skimpy, under-financed affairs… people in much of Melanesia experienced colonial rule as intermittent and sometimes mysterious demands made on occasional visits by *kiaps* (patrol officers), native police and recruiters…the outside world was embodied not in government but in the mission station with its plantations, workshops, schools and gardens, and with missionaries who came to stay, and learned the language of their congregations. (Firth 1997:255; cf. Denoon 2005:14)

Denoon also contrasts the contact Papua New Guineans had with 'kiaps' with this holistic approach as embodied by the missionaries, emphasising the role of language in encounter. 'Kiaps,' he writes, 'exercised control mainly by foot patrols. Their village visits were brief and they had to rely on Tok Pisin to communicate so they had limited insight into village affairs' (Denoon 2005:16). These arguments on the whole suggest that the most influential life change came about through mission contact.

At Lake Kopiago, early mission activity quashed what ritual activity remained after the establishment of the government station. Haley (1996:285) reports that 'the early missionaries smashed, burnt and poured holy water over ancestral *auwi* [stone relics]'. Ancestral forms of singing and ritual, such as *yekia*, were banned. Pastor Hagini (see Figure 3.2), a Duna elder and leader of the Apostolic Church in the Duna parish of Hirane, describes the reason for the banning of these ancestral practices as being that within them was believed to be the presence of Satan:

Em i pasin bilong stil, pasin bilong pamuk, pasin bilong kilim man— pasin bilong ol dispela samting i kam insait long dispela ol samting… *yekia* na *selepa*, dispela em nem bilong…samting tumbuna stori bilong ol bipo, Satan i save kam insait long dispela.

[It is the ways of stealing, ways of promiscuity, ways of fighting—the ways of all these things come inside these things (ancestral song forms)…

---

5   It is important to note, though, that there is and has always been great variation between denominations in their approach to indigenous culture (this degree of variation also applies when considering Firth's general comment on missionaries' role in communities).

yekia and *selepa*, these are the name of…these kinds of ancestral stories from long ago, Satan comes inside these.] (Pastor Hagini, Interview, 20 April 2005)

During this interview, I sang to Pastor Hagini a *yekia* I had learnt from my friend and translator Petros Kilapa, a song that his 'great uncle' Koaria (whom he referred to as his *mamane*) is said to have composed in the 1960s. Petros' mother, Pokole, had heard Koaria singing it and repeated it to Petros; he had not learnt it directly from his great uncle. The text of the *yekia* praises God—thus the biblical and the satanical are here united, or so it first seemed (see Example 3.1).

Figure 3.2 Pastor Hagini, reading at the funeral of Wakili Akuri, 17 February 2005.

Example 3.1 (▶ Audio 5) 'Lotu' *yekia.*

Ngote ngini Yesu wanda ruwata lungi kulukuluya mapu(ra)nania	when Jesus, son of God, says that he will come, the *lungi* clouds will thunder all around
alungi kulukuluya mapunania	the *alungi* clouds will thunder all around
pakala kulukuluya mapunania	the *pakala* clouds will thunder all around
ukai kulukuluya mapunania, aiyo ai	the *ukai* clouds will thunder all around, aiyo ai

This '"lotu" *yekia*' was met with consternation by Pastor Hagini. 'Ol i stilim nem bilong God [They are stealing God's name]', he declared. The name of God and the musical form declared by the missionaries as satanic could not exist together:

> Baibel i tok, Satan na God no inap bung wantaim. Satan wantaim Jisas no inap bung wantaim. Na Satan wantaim tupela i no save kaikai wantaim, i no ken sindaun wantaim, i no ken wokabaut wantaim. Tupela i narapela narapela. Na God i rausim em na i kam daun long dispela graun. Na em i yusim ol manmeri, na God tu i yusim ol manmeri. Na ol i Satan yusim long en ol i narapela samting, song bilong ol tu, na wok bilong ol tu, na sindaun bilong ol tu, kaikai bilong ol tu, em i narapela kaikai olgeta. Narapela samting. Na mipela ol mission em i narapela samting olgeta.

> [The Bible says, Satan and God cannot come together. Satan and Jesus cannot come together. And with Satan the two (Satan and God) do not eat together, cannot sit together, cannot walk around together. The two are completely different. And God ousted him and he came down to this ground. And he (Satan) used people, and God too used people. And the people Satan used are something different, their songs too, their work too, their way of life too, their food too, it's another food altogether. Something else. And we of the mission are something else altogether.]

I explained to Hagini the good intentions Koaria was said to have had in composing this *yekia*, which were, Petros said, to 'praise God's name'. Hagini acknowledged that he too had composed such songs of praise using ancestral forms when he first came to Christianity, but soon gave it up. Eventually, he conceded of Koaria's efforts: 'i gutpela, tasol i no gutpela tumas [it's good, but it's not very good].'

An adverse attitude of foreigners to the people and cultures of pre-contact Papua New Guinea was not unusual at this point in history. Schieffelin et al. (1991:265) observe: 'Traditional Papua New Guinean cultures with their body nakedness, exotic, "primitive" customs, and frequent violence were the evangelist's very image of Satan's country.' This negative attitude to pre-contact culture had a significant impact on traditional forms of Duna music—in particular, the function of the music and the context for performance. Most of these early forms of music can still be heard today, but in altered form—for example, *yekia* are generally not now performed in the presence of women and performances have been moved from courting houses to the men's house; however, this change of context has allowed for men to create *yekia* verses of politics and other issues of social dissatisfaction (examples of such *yekia* verses are discussed in Chapter

6). I once asked a young Duna man, Jeremiah Piero, why the physical aspects of *yekia* performance had ceased, why the men no longer sat in the laps of women while the men sang. He burst out in response: 'Sem [shame]!' (Jeremiah Piero, Recorded conversation, 2 March 2005). As shame is 'an emotion anthropologists have frequently analyzed as a mechanism of social control' (Myers 1986:120), it can be surmised that the missionaries fostered this sentiment within the Duna in order to control the new society they found themselves in.[6]

Missionaries on the whole preferred to introduce songs from their own churches, rather than facilitate the incorporation of ancestral song styles into Christian worship. In particular, they favoured songs with simple melodies written for children, such as *Jesus Loves the Little Children*, which was taught to the Duna of Kelabo by members of the CMML (Ian Armitage, Interview, 9 February 2005).[7] There was also sharing of resource materials between missions—in particular, the fundamentalist groups—and this served to facilitate the movement of particular songs across the region.

Despite its apparent cumbersomeness, the gramophone made inroads into the Highlands of Papua New Guinea fairly quickly. Patrol officers and also gold prospectors used it, as a published photograph by Michael J. Leahy (1967:26) reveals, but perhaps its greatest potential was as an instrument for the dissemination of Christian teachings. Representatives of both the SDA Church and the CMML have published accounts of their use of the gramophone with Duna people in particular. Not only do they describe the Duna's startled response to the sound production of the instrument, they describe the importance of teaching the Duna to operate the gramophone themselves, and describe leaving the instrument and its records for people in the community to play over and again in order to learn the teachings within, which had been recorded in their language (Were 1968:41, 54; Armitage 1969). It is very likely that Christian music accompanied these recordings of the gospel, and thus new music would have been disseminated as well.

The use of indigenous languages was a key element in the conversion of the Duna to Christianity, as was the case with indigenous groups in other parts of Papua New Guinea, the Pacific and indeed across the world. At Kelabo in the 1970s, linguist Glenda Giles of the Summer Institute of Linguistics translated the Bible into Duna and created the first and still the only guide to the Duna language (Giles n.d.). Through Giles' extensive work, missionaries became aware of the subtleties of the Duna language and were able to use this information to serve

---

6   It is also very likely that Jeremiah would have been embarrassed to discuss the topic with me—a woman of a similar age to him.

7   According to Webb (1993:106), this particular song was made popular in Papua New Guinea in the 1970s by Ray Steven's song *Everything is Beautiful*.

their purpose of converting the people to Christianity. San Roque explains that 'missionary translators use[d] the verb-endings of Duna to reinforce messages that the Christian god is "true" and a certainty'. She writes that

> the verb endings in Duna can make reference to either a) the way the information expressed in the sentence has been received (e.g., through sound, sight, personal experience, hearsay—this is the grammatical category of 'evidentiality') and/or b) whether or not the speaker is certain about the information. Christian materials (unsurprisingly) tend to favour the 'certain' and 'personal experience' verb-endings. (Lila San Roque, Email communication, 8 November 2005)

Many Christian songs were, and still are, sung in English, Tok Pisin and Duna (usually at least two of these languages in the one performance). The Duna also sing some songs in the neighbouring languages of Hewa and Bogaya, as particular Christian songs were translated as they circulated the district and were acquired by Duna attending regional bible meetings. For the comprehension of the Christian message, it was important for the introduced Christian songs (as opposed to those later composed by the locals) to be translated for the congregation into 'tok ples' (meaning the indigenous language of the place) (cf. Jones 2004:219). In the case of the Duna, the Duna people themselves carried this out through Tok Pisin. The difficulty of singing in a new musical system was not considered as challenging as singing in other languages; once the translation into Duna had occurred the songs were apparently quite easily performed (Pastor Hagini, Interview, 20 April 2005), though the missionaries themselves might report otherwise (cf. McLean 1986:36; Jones 2004:36, 61). One missionary writes of the work of one of the first Christian teachers at Kopiago (incidentally a Papua New Guinean): 'He taught the people to sing songs so different from their village chants that at first their voices could not find the notes and their tongues stumbled over the words. The children learned more quickly and sang with enthusiasm' (Were 1968:36).

Many of the schools in the Kopiago area, and throughout the Highlands of Papua New Guinea, were established and run by the missions. Christian songs therefore formed the core of music education in the schools and all school music education was essentially Western due to the identities of the teachers (cf. Niles 2001:129). In addition to the education given by the teachers at Kopiago, ABC Radio National produced school broadcasts for each grade that were listened to within the classroom, and these included songs such as *Twinkle Twinkle Little Star* and a somewhat indigenised *Here We Go 'Round the Mango Tree* (Richard Alo, Personal communication, 30 July 2006).

It is widely recognised that '[s]chooling helps to perpetuate existing ideologies, assimilate ideological challenges, and produce new ideologies in line with changing economic and social conditions' (Green 2003:264). Pertinent to the topic under discussion here is the observation that '[m]usic education participates in the construction and perpetuation of ideologies about musical value' (Green 2003:265). Songs such as *Ten Little Indians* (introduced, presumably, to teach the Duna how to count in English) appear to have been quite influential musically for the Duna. In particular, *Ten Little Indians* (Example 3.2) shares melodic and harmonic similarities with Duna Christian songs and newly composed secular songs such as those presented later in this chapter.

With the mission interest in teaching in 'tok ples', supported by a national trend in teaching literacy in local languages across Papua New Guinea, which had developed significantly by the 1990s (Litteral 1999), songs such as *Ten Little Indians* were translated into Duna and sung in the classroom. 'Indians' were replaced with 'Kopiagos' (Richard Alo, Personal communication, 30 July 2006). This song was to be further localised in at least one instance by the Rewapi Elementary School of Hirane parish—a school recently established by the local Duna people to address the need for a school closer to their homes. Their 'Indians' became 'Rewapi', referring to the children of the school, which is located in a subsection of Hirane parish known as Rewapi (the importance of land references in Duna song is discussed in Chapter 5) (Figure 3.3). I here provide a musical transcription of this song in order for it to be compared with the later transcriptions in this chapter (Example 3.2).

Example 3.2 (▶ Audio 6) *Ten Little Indians.*

ndu ketele yapa ketele itupa ketele rewapi	One little two little three little Rewapi
sondopa ketele repu ketele raka ketele rewapi	Four little five little six little Rewapi
kona ketele phou ketele ki ketele rewapi	Seven little eight little nine little Rewapi
rapaki ketele rewapi nanetia	Ten little Rewapi boys

From the very beginning of missionisation, select local people were trained to lead the churches in their own communities. These people were agnatic members of the local parish group (people who belong to it through a line of male ancestors, holding ritual and land rights to the area), such as Pastor Hagini, and thus already in a position of power and respect within their community in a traditional sense (Stürzenhofecker 1998:40; see also Stewart and Strathern 2002b:130; Strathern and Stewart 2004:62, 159, 2009:320). In the Kopiago area at the time of this writing, the churches were led entirely by Duna people (with the exception of the recent arrival of a Korean Catholic priest). This is mostly because they have the ability and do not appear to need the guidance of foreigners. Another reason behind the absence of foreign missionaries is, however, the debilitated state of Kopiago station, illustrated in the content of the songs that are analysed below. The increasing violence associated with such a lack of services also dissuades foreigners' long-term stay.

Figure 3.3 Rewapi Hirane Elementary School students dress up for visitors, April 2005.

Photo by *Georgina San Roque*

The collision of the colonial and the Christian in song

The revivalist movement of the mid-1970s was another historical factor in the spread of Christian music across Papua New Guinea. Its origins have been traced to Christian movements in the Solomon Islands from where the revival spread across Papua New Guinea westwards to the very edge of the country (cf. Robbins 2004:1–2). Pugh-Kitingan writes that the Huli language group—neighbours to the Duna—adopted non-indigenous melodic structures during the revival, which swept into Huli country from the neighbouring Foe people, and that they used these structures to compose 'thousands' of Christian songs in their indigenous languages. It is likely that these songs, and the inspiration for such composition, also passed through Duna country. Huli revivalist songs, known as Ngodenaga Iba Gana (Pugh-Kitingan 1981),[8] share strong similarities with the popular music of the time and 'may have been unconsciously derived from pan-Pacific string band music heard on radios purchased from trade stores' (Pugh-Kitingan 1984:109, cf. 1981:291). The cross-fertilisation between Christian and stringband/secular musical forms is generally accepted to be the case in Papua New Guinea and has been recognised elsewhere in the literature on Papua New Guinean music (for example, Webb 1993).[9]

Pugh-Kitingan (1981:291) identifies a melody that is 'characteristic of many of the revival songs' and she transcribes and translates this melody (pp. 585–6).[10] I reproduce the first section of Pugh-Kitingan's transcription as Example 3.3.

Pugh-Kitingan (1981:291) identifies the melody as pentatonic and describes it thus:

> The melody falls into two phrases. After opening with a rising fifth, the first phrase has a generally descending direction from the pitch a sixth above the lowest pitch. The second phrase also falls from this highest pitch and has a similar length to that of the descending portion of the first phrase.

> Each verse line falls into two parts, corresponding to the two melodic phrases in the tune.

Pugh-Kitingan (1981:292) also provides the following observation of the melody's distinct rhythm: 'A recurring [two quaver plus one crotchet] rhythm pervades the melody in this example. This is reminiscent of the regular beat in string band music and provides a further clue to the source of the tune.' All these

---

8   Pugh-Kitingan (1981:290–1) writes: 'While the term Ngodenaga Iba Gana can be applied to all types of Christian songs including European hymns, it refers specifically to songs created spontaneously by the indigenous church during the 1973 to 1976 Christian revival. Some of these have subsequently become a regular feature of Huli worship and their verses have been collected to form a songbook.' It should be noted that Pugh-Kitingan utilises diacritics in her representation of this Huli phrase, as shown in Example 3.3; these diacritics could not be reproduced here.

9   Papua New Guinea is not the only country in which Christian songs have influenced the secular. Aaron Corn (with Gumbula 2002), for example, writes of the Australian Indigenous band Soft Sands: 'Its founding members innovatively adapted earlier models of gospel composition—introduced through the influence of Methodist missionaries—to the setting of new popular songs with lyrics in Yolngu-Matha [the indigenous local language].'

10   A 'second section' of the performance of this melody, showing part-singing, has been published in Pugh-Kitingan (1984:109).

melodic and rhythmic features are evident in the Duna Christian song '*nane* laip senis *nganda waya keina*', which will soon be analysed—thus we can consider the origins of this song to be found within this same religious movement.[11]

Example 3.3 Excerpt of Pugh-Kitingan's Transcription 74.

Source: Pugh-Kitingan (1981:585).

---

11 There are some melodic similarities also with the song *Ten Little Indians* reproduced as Example 3.2, particularly in the rising and falling phrases over the interval of three and a half tones (a fifth). The similarity between this school song and the new religious songs of the time could have contributed to the song's popularity (and longevity).

A very similar melodic template as that which Pugh-Kitingan transcribed appears as a song entitled *Ega Emene*, published in a 1980 songbook, with lyrics in Huli, and described as 'a string band song, written about 1976' (Fearon 1980). The lyrics are not religious but are of unrequited love and involve self-mutilation (a topic covered in Chapter 6), as the relevant page of the songbook shows (Example 3.3b).

Example 3.3b *Ega Emene*.

Source: Fearon (1980:47).

There is therefore a historical relationship between the Christian song forms introduced by the missions and contemporary secular songs as introduced by the administration. This is evident not only in the use of similar melodic and harmonic structures, but in instrumentation: both Christian and secular music incorporate the use of the guitar. At Kopiago, boys who learn the guitar—and it is mostly young males—do so first of all in the church setting, accompanying the congregation. In church, boys can gain the easiest access to the instrument, as church members are significantly mobile members of the community with the most financial support, so are able to travel and buy the instruments and the strings needed for them. The boys then take these skills in guitar playing out of the church and into the secular music arena. This trend has resulted in whole bands forming within the Christian music scene and then crossing over to popular music (such as the band now known as Ramula Bitz—see Chapter 5).

The relationship between a particular Christian song style and contemporary secular music will now be considered through the examination and comparison of two Duna songs. First, the Christian song 'nane laip senis nganda waya keina', which opens this chapter, will be analysed. I will consider its harmonic, melodic and textual structure and then compare it with a particular contemporary song that is currently popular around Kopiago and that I have given the title of 'Memba pi nakaya' (loosely translated as 'We don't have a Member [of government]').[12]

The song 'nane laip senis nganda waya keina' is typical of Christian songs currently sung by the Duna around the Lake Kopiago area. Example 3.4 is a transcription of the common structure of this song (the corresponding recording features the second verse only).[13]

Ngote haka Ngote haka	God's talk God's talk
Ngote haka Ngote haka	God's talk God's talk
Ngote haka ipa mo waya keina	God's talk is like water it keeps coming
nane laip senis *nganda waya keina*	boy's life change keeps coming
imane laip senis *nganda waya keina*	girl's life change keeps coming
Ngote haka ipa mo waya keina	God's talk is like water it keeps coming

---

12 Many popular songs around Kopiago are not known by one particular title, so when discussing songs I usually refer to them by the first line of text or the first line of the most identifiable verse, if there is more than one. Christian-style songs in Duna usually have one verse of single short statements repeated and one verse with more variation in text, which I regard as more identifiable, as the nature of variation makes it more distinguishable from other Christian songs.

13 The melody of this song has been transcribed into the key of G to allow for clearer presentation, as this key places the melody in the centre of the staff (cf. Feld 1982:21). Also, as it happens, G is the only key in which Christian songs of the Apostolic Church at Hirane are played, and it is with members of this church that I have conducted much of my research. Transcriptions of following songs in this chapter are also in G for comparative purposes (the leading note F# does not appear at any point in the melody, thus I have not included it in the key signature; it does, however, appear in the D chord of the accompaniment).

Example 3.4 (▶ Audio 7) '*Nane* laip senis *nganda waya keina'*.

This song is here presented in two verses, each of seven bars length. Performers may, however, take as much or as little rest between verses (and between the repetition of verses) as they like (sometimes at least half a bar), so the overall length of seven bars is not a fixed measure, as will be seen in subsequent versions of this song.[14]

The chords provided in the transcription represent the chords as played by guitars in accompaniment. Each verse contains the same simple harmonic structure: the first line of every verse is tonic (I), the second line moves to the subdominant (or IV), the third line moves from tonic (I) to dominant (V), and then back to the tonic (I) again.[15] Not incidentally, these three primary chords also form the backbone to stringband music. Some stringbands play in one key only (Webb 1998:138) and such an emphasis on the tonic chord is also evident in this song, whose melody focuses on the tonic triad and the steps in between.

Melodically, each verse has the same general contour: the first phrase of four bars features an ascent from the tonal centre to three and a half tones above it (a fifth) over the first two bars and a descent of the same range over the next two bars, and the second phrase of three bars features an ascent followed by

---

14   When more than one performer sings the song, it is the strongest singer who takes a leading role, determining the length of a break and the number of repetitions.

15   Here I denote a line of text based primarily on the repetition and parallelism of words; however, I also take into account the interaction between the harmonic, melodic and textual features. The harmonic structure of this song is marked by the use of primary chords on the guitar, and it is on these grounds that I use this system in the analysis here.

a descent, which centres on two tones above the tonal centre (a third) before firmly landing back on the tonal centre repeated. It is important to note that the melodies across songs of this kind are loose in that they do not require an exact reproduction of pitches; no two performances articulate the exact same pitches and there is variation between singers when these songs are sung in unison; however, all versions follow the same basic melodic contour as described above. If the transcriptions of the melodies provided in this chapter are compared, they reveal the kind of melodic variation that occurs (comparison also shows the kind of variation in phrase length). Following both the choral church tradition and secular traditions such as stringband music, an attempt at singing in harmony is usually made when these songs are sung as a group, although as it is quite erratic and threatens to cloud the analysis, that aspect of Duna singing will not be examined in this publication.

The textual structure of Christian songs has an unwavering repetitiveness tied in with the repetitiveness of form in harmony and melody. The first phrase consists of the same statement repeated ('*Ngote haka*') or two statements of a similar meaning ('*nane* laip senis *nganda waya keina*/*imane* laip senis *nganda waya keina*'), which mirror each other. The final line of text introduces material that varies from these first two lines. Between verses, however, this final line is often the same, as in this example. Many Christian songs, including this one, use a combination of Duna and Tok Pisin languages to present their message, in order to employ those Tok Pisin terms seen by the missions as so important to conversion, such as 'laip senis' and 'tanim bel'.

These harmonic, melodic and textual features are also evident in the secular song '*Memba pi nakaya*' (Example 3.5). '*Memba pi nakaya*' was reportedly composed for the government elections of 1997 (Richard Alo, Personal communication, 19 June 2004). It promotes one of the Duna candidates for the Koroba-Lake Kopiago open electorate, Benias (Ben) Peri, and encourages people to vote for him.

Some particular characteristics of this song are worth noting at the outset. Sometimes the phrase '*Memba pi nakaya*' ('we do not have a Member either') is sung as *Memba pi naraya* ('there is not a Member either'), usually when sung by children—as this example is; however, this is grammatically incorrect. In these cases, I have given these versions the grammatically correct title (to be consistent with other versions of this song) but stayed faithful to the text as it is sung. Another feature worth noting in the performance of both Christian and popular songs is that the first and second lines, when similar to each other, are often swapped around during a performance, more as a result of uncertainty by the performers of which should come first than a conscious decision to alternate lines. This interchangeability will become apparent in the comparison of the examples presented in this chapter.

Example 3.5 (▶ Audio 8) 'Memb*a pi nakaya*' (campaign song).

yaka yaka ruwano	name, say the name
yaka ruwano nane Ben Peri yaka ruwano	say the name of boy Ben Peri say the name
haiwe pi naraya	there is not a highway either
memba pi naraya	there is not a Member either
yaka ruwano nane Ben Peri yaka ruwano	say the name of boy Ben Peri say the name

It is significant that this song complains of a lack of services (in particular a highway) in the Duna community. The Papua New Guinean local government member is, across the country, thought of as the provider of all sorts of things to the people, such as roads, schools, business opportunities and capital. In this way, the relationship between the voter and the member is reciprocal: they vote and the member provides the desired goods. This system has been labelled by one Papua New Guinean scholar as a 'cargo-cult delivery system', in which the MP is 'merely a conduit to pass on to the people what they desired', and has evolved from a history of dependence established during colonial times (Okole 2005:193). The highway, then, is not simply one of many desired services, but represents both literally and figuratively this conduit, as the road is necessary for the flow of goods and services.

This song is made up of two verses, which conform to the melodic patterns of ascent and descent as described in the analysis of '*nane* laip senis *nganda waya keina*' above. Textually, too, there are the same features of repetition present. One particular variation to note is in the beginning of the first verse. Here, the first phrase has been condensed into two bars instead of the usual four. The result is that this first verse becomes a kind of introduction to the second verse, speeding the song along to where the body of the message is contained.

A crucial aspect of the composition of 'Memba *pi nakaya*', modelled on the Christian song form as utilised in '*nane* laip senis *nganda waya keina*', is that its form is very open to textual change. So far the campaign version of 'Memba *pi nakaya*' has been used as a launching pad for at least three different versions. In this way, the song is being used as a creative site, with its text changed and manipulated to suit the topics that its performers—Duna men, women and/or children—wish to portray. This aspect of Duna creativity is also typical of ancestral song genres and this continuity in creativity will be examined more closely in Chapter 7. The next section of this chapter explores these different versions of 'Memba *pi nakaya*' and shows how this song is being used to express (and ultimately to affect the change of) the Duna's current experience of political and social instability.

Creativity and contemporary social issues

We will have to give them a lot if they are not to be disillusioned.
— Jack Hides, 1935 (in Allen and Frankel 1991:111)

The Southern Highlands Province is marked by political unrest and parts of the province, including Kopiago, remain very poor, despite oil and gas operations in the province (Hanson et al. 2001:91, 93). Elections in and around Kopiago have become increasingly violent and at the time these songs were recorded the people of the Koroba-Lake Kopiago electorate still did not have a Member of Parliament to represent them and to help work towards a change of circumstance. The results of the 2002 elections were, after some months, declared void due to voting irregularities and, as a result, the winner was required to step down. A new member was re-elected only in July 2006. The line of the song 'Memba *pi nakaya*' ('we do not have a Member either') at this time, then, was a literal description of the political situation for the Duna people. So was the paired statement 'haiwe *pi naraya*' ('there is not a highway either'). Although on most current maps the Highlands Highway is shown as ending at Kopiago (some of the more accurate maps at least show the road as unsealed), the reality has been far from that. The road has been left in poor repair for more than a decade[16] and during my fieldwork in 2005 it was rare to see a vehicle make the journey to Kopiago station. Roads are sought after throughout Papua New Guinea (cf.

---

16 Although the main cause of the poor state of the roads to Kopiago is understood to be neglect of maintenance, Robinson (2002:148) has described how the frustration experienced by the Duna people at the outcome of the 1997 election caused them to contribute to the destruction and abandonment of development in their community by damaging bridges and buildings.

Hughes 2000), but in a place with as few services as Kopiago, the lack of a road becomes symbolic of an abandoned community, a 'last Kopiago', which is truly at the edge of civilisation, as the following versions of this song reveal.[17]

The declaration of Kopiago as a remote location is, however, a declaration with two sides. Feld explains the complexity of attitudes towards development for the Kaluli people of the Southern Highlands Province and this comment can be extended to the Duna and other isolated groups in Papua New Guinea:

> Many people express a desire for a road that would connect them with the outside: they say they want development, want cash, want to participate in the economy and enjoy what they imagine to be its benefits. But the same people, the most outspoken ones about development, will be quick to tell you that they don't want *raskols* [Tok Pisin for criminals—usually young men], don't want fighting, don't want trouble with alcohol, don't want weapons, don't want population pressure on their resources. So at the same time that they desire to be modern members of the nation, they also take a certain comfort in being remote, off the grid, without oil, gas, gold, logging, or other big development projects…It is in the context of such concerns about the future that people see the resourcefulness of the past. (Feld, in Feld and Crowdy 2002:81–2)

Being the 'last place', then, can also be a point of praise. Richard Alo (Personal communication, 3 August 2006) suggests that the phrase *eke konera* ('last place') can be likened to such phrases as *mei konenia* ('steep slope'), which praises and promotes steep ground (this phrase is commonly used in songs describing certain Duna places, as will be seen in Chapter 5). Although there might be undesirable elements attached to a place that is considered 'last', or 'steep', these are still dramatic and identifying features.

One could suggest that a sense of isolation in this region of the world is a result of colonial influence; Hau'ofa (1993:7) has pointed out that it was 'continental men, namely Europeans' who introduced the view (to their fellow men and also to Pacific Islanders themselves) that the Pacific Islands are 'tiny, isolated dots in a vast ocean'. On a local level, too, it could be said that Duna people became aware of themselves as isolated only after contact with Europeans and colonialism. Certainly, it was only then that they became aware of what they possessed and how they lived in relation to the 'developed world'.

---

17 Expressing that one's place is 'last'—that is, being geographically as far from desired services as is possible—is common in Papua New Guinea. Paul Wolffram (2006:110–11) reports that the Lak of New Ireland, at the other end of the country, describe their remote district as being the 'las kona' (last corner)—a common phrase in Tok Pisin.

Disgruntled voters soon turned the election song 'Memba *pi nakaya*' as presented above into a song criticising Ben Peri, who ultimately lost the election (cf. Haley 2002b:126). Thus, a song composed for his campaign was ultimately turned against him. In the song, Peri is accused of not providing the desired services and not spending time with his own people, but rather, travelling between the town centres of Mendi and Tari in the Southern Highlands, living the good life (Example 3.6).

Once again, the melodic structure follows the conventions of the Christian song style as revealed in the analysis of '*nane* laip senis *nganda waya keina*'. This version of the original 'Memba *pi nakaya*' has been taken up as a campaign song against Ben Peri and here the notion of Kopiago as 'truly the edge' ('*eke konera*') and the 'last' place is introduced (cf. Haley 2008:222–3).

Example 3.6 (▶ Audio 9) 'Memba *pi nakaya*' (Ben Peri).

memba *pi naraya*	there is not a Member either
haiwe *pi naraya*	there is not a highway either
eke konera las *Kopiago eke konera*	truly the edge last Kopiago truly the edge
memba *pi naraya*	there is not a Member either
haiwe *pi naraya*	there is not a highway either
nane Ben Peri Mendi Tari pasinda *heka yakombe*	the boy Ben Peri passes Mendi and Tari like the yakombe bird*

* Haley (2008) identifies the *yakombe* bird as a 'swiftlet'.

Another, even more recent version of this song praises a Duna man named Peter Pex, who until the middle of 2004 held the coveted position of Kopiago Community Relations Officer for the Porgera Joint Venture (PJV), the community administrative section of the Porgera mine, which is located in another province and language area. Interestingly, it was said that this version was heard for the first time in October 2004, which was several months after Pex had been sacked from his position for a 'conflict of interest'. This version of 'Memba *pi nakaya*' seems to have been written to clear Pex's name and reputation (Example 3.7). He might have composed the lyrics himself.

Example 3.7 (▶ Audio 10) 'Memba *pi nakaya*' (Pita Pex).

haiwe *pi naraya*	there is not a highway either
memba *pi naraya*	there is not a Member either
eke konera las *Kopiago eke konera*	truly the edge last Kopiago truly the edge
home ni puka	like that
nane Pita Pex ya, Pita pi kampani *ne* *hakanarua*	the boy Peter Pex goes and talks to the company
hakayata	talk is done
hakayata pare hunia ayu peyana	talk is done now we can play

In other words, Kopiago does not have a highway or a government member—it is really the last place that receives any kind of development. Then, however, Peter Pex goes and talks to the company and now that is done the people of Kopiago can enjoy themselves, as he has obtained good things from the company for them. These good things are many and varied: the PJV provides not only compensation in monetary terms for the use of the Strickland River to deposit tailings from the mine, it provides medical supplies and assistance among other services. This song reveals the importance of the 'kampani' ('company') to the Duna and to Papua New Guinea at large—a phenomenon that Stürzenhofecker

(1998:32) points out is 'the epitome of desired change, development, and modernity'. The 'kampani' is particularly important in a society experiencing failed government representation. Like the politician whom Okole describes, however, 'the vision of the company operates in Kopiago as a cargoistic idea' (Strathern 1991:614), and for much the same reasons.

Figure 3.4 Road being created at Kopiago, 1964.

Photo by *David Hook*

It is debateable, however, whether the voicing of community desires in the 'Memba *pi nakaya*' songs is entirely an expression of 'cargo cultism'. These desires are not a product of hyper imaginings by people unaware of the functioning of the Western institutions of politics and companies. Rather, these desires are largely for real items and services that the Duna at Kopiago have already experienced in the past, mainly during the time of the colonial administration, when money from elsewhere was channelled into the community. There was once a highway (see Figure 3.4), there was a political representative and there were schools and hospitals. The Duna had all these things and then slowly lost them. These particular songs themselves are therefore songs of protest based in reality, not fantasy.

Musically, we have again the same melodic and textual structures as discussed in the preceding songs. The second and third verses feature the same kind of condensing of lines as the original campaigning version of 'Memba *pi nakaya*' presented in this chapter, in its line of *'yaka yaka ruwano'*—four bars have become two—and the effect of speeding the text to its more crucial line is also the same.

The final version of this song that I will discuss here was adapted to have a Christian message so that it could be performed in church (Example 3.8). Although the accents of the guitar accompaniment of the corresponding recording suggest different bar divisions (as does the accompaniment for Example 3.4, led by the same guitarist), I have presented the melody here as I have the previous melodies for ease of comparison.

Example 3.8 (▶ Audio 11) 'Memba *pi nakaya*' (Apa Ngote).

haiwe *pi naraya*	there is not a highway either
memba *pi nakaya*	we do not have a Member either
eke konera las *Kopiago eke konera*	truly the edge last Kopiago truly the edge
home pokua	like that
Apa Ngote khonga inu peli aru keina	Papa God He looks after us well and is here

Rather than looking to the politician or the company for support in a community with no highway and no government member, this version of 'Memba *pi nakaya*' looks to God to take care of the Duna. Musically it maintains all the hallmarks of previous versions regarding melodic shape, harmonic sequences and textual structure. In addition, as a song of God, it seems that this secular song, inspired by the Christian song style, has come full circle.

Vocabulary for introduced music

If we continue to consider the indigenous vocabulary used to discuss song forms in order to understand the indigenous conception of musical forms, we find that introduced song styles too are categorised. Two categories are used: *lotu ipakana* ('Christian songs') and *danis ipakana* ('dance songs'). The classifications of 'lotu' and 'danis' both come from Tok Pisin; however, this is not surprising as the musical forms that these terms label are also exogenous. The classification can also be described as religious versus secular content of songs (as we now know that musically these songs can be very similar). The performance context for *lotu ipakana* is primarily the church (and church-based situations such as mission school or home worship), while *danis ipakana* takes its name from the most popular performance context for secular music: the 'disco'. This is understood in the broadest sense to mean the public location for the performance of music (live or recorded) of secular content where the anticipated audience participation involves dance and includes the genre of stringband. In terms of instruments, the category of *alima*, which as we have seen applies to ancestral musical instruments, also extends to include introduced musical instruments such as the guitar (*ngita*) and ukulele (*ngulele*). The metal jew's harp, which so closely resembles the Duna *luna*, is differentiated from it by the name *luna khao* ('white *luna*'). These instruments are, however, referred to as *alima* only when they are used without vocals; a genre such as stringband that incorporates vocals will always be described as a kind of *ipakana*. Thus it can be seen that vocal musical expression dominates that of instruments (when the instruments themselves are not considered to be vocalising).

More broadly but also more hazily, the Duna make a distinction between introduced music and indigenous music in their vocabulary. This distinction is expressed as *khao ipakana* ('white songs') and *mindi ipakana* ('black songs'), respectively. I have already pointed out that ancestral Duna songs are described as *awenene ipakana*, in contrast with the *khao ipakana* that is 'white' song. *Mindi ipakana* is a term that can also be used to describe *awenene ipakana*; however, unlike *awenene ipakana*, the term *mindi ipakana* can be applied to introduced songs that are considered to be indigenised. This indigenisation is particularly apparent where the texts of songs are concerned. Songs of an introduced style and in the 'white' languages of English or Tok Pisin are described naturally as *khao ipakana*; songs of an introduced style but in the Duna language are described as *mindi ipakana* (Kipu Piero, Personal communication, 30 March 2005).[18] All the song examples given in this chapter, then, would be called *mindi*

---

18   It would be interesting, if it were possible, to complete this paradigm with a comprehension of how Duna ancestral songs sung exclusively in English and/or Tok Pisin would be classified; however, as no such songs have so far been recorded or studied, the question must remain unanswered.

ipakana; an English-language version of *Ten Little Indians*, on the other hand, would be a classic example of *khao ipakana*. Such a determining element based on text alone shows supremacy of text over musical sound. It also highlights the importance of indigenous language in the process of indigenisation.

Syncretism, appropriation and indigenisation

The essential argument of this chapter concerns how a form of Christian song—introduced initially by missionary contact but taking as a major influence the popular music of the 1970s in the shape of stringband music—has become a musical framework for the Duna to create their own songs of social protest. This Christian/popular song form is an example of syncretism at work. The definition of syncretism as the 'attempted union or reconciliation of diverse or opposite tenets or practices' (The Oxford English Dictionary 1989) is very useful when considering this song. Its form fuses the Christian song format and popular music forms—both seemingly opposing tenets representing different social values—to the point where the two influences are indistinguishable from each other in the resulting musical style.

Considering the situation surrounding the Duna's initial encounters with introduced music—in particular, the seemingly forced adoption of Christian songs—the term 'appropriation' is not accurate to describe the process by which the Duna first began to sing songs from elsewhere. Appropriation is an exercise of power on the part of the appropriators—'[t]o examine musical borrowing and appropriation is necessarily to consider the relations between culture, power, ethnicity, and class' (Born and Hesmondhalgh 2000:3)—and there seems to have been little power held by the Duna in the initial acquisition of Christian musical traditions. That position changed, however, and the popularity of the Christian revival movement that swept through the Highlands in the 1970s and the songs composed in response to this movement, assisted in popularity by the musical influences of stringband music, showed a community with the power to appropriate and eventually manipulate these introduced styles.

Alongside discussions of the appropriation of Western styles of music is the complementary discussion of the 'indigenisation' of this introduced music. The song 'Memba *pi nakaya*' and its various forms as presented in this chapter are examples of indigenisation at work in text and content. Writing on the *kaneka* music of New Caledonia, Goldsworthy (1998:45) defines indigenisation as a 'conscious process of infusing a tradition with indigenous elements in order to make it more regionally specific and representative'. In this Duna example, indigenisation has occurred primarily through the use of Duna as the language of the song text and the singing of themes specific to the experience of the

Duna. This use of text and social content is a common way of indigenising music around the world (cf. Bilby 1999:278–9). Another example of indigenisation at work is the actual constant reworking of the 'Memba *pi nakaya*' text; creativity with song texts on a set melody is a central element of traditional indigenous Duna musical invention and this is exactly what is creative in the Duna's engagement with the set melodies of the introduced material presented here. This continuity in compositional style is explored further in Chapter 7.

Music is increasingly understood to be not simply a reflection of the status quo but an active form of expression that can directly impact on experience, identity and political processes (cf. Goldsworthy 1998:58). Stringband music in Papua New Guinea in particular is recognised as an important musical form for understanding the country's concerns:

> Papua New Guinea stringband music, as an example of complex local style development, offers more than an exotic journey in syncretism. It can provide another perspective with which to view notions of global and local as they relate not only to guitars and musical style, but wider social concerns as well. (Crowdy 2001:153)

The 'Memba *pi nakaya*' songs are a case in point. As I have shown, these songs have been adapted several times to express the varied experiences of the Duna and each version is an attempt to bring about changes in their lives through the articulation of their concerns among themselves and to visitors in their community.

Conclusion

This chapter has briefly sketched the history of the Duna's initial encounters with the West through the perspective of musical practice. While the colonial encounter was the people's first experience of Western culture, it was the missions that provided systematic exposure and education in the playing of guitars, the singing of Western melodies (including singing in harmony, which is not a feature of ancestral song performance) and the translation of these melodies into 'tok ples'.

The Christian revivalist movement of the 1970s encouraged prolific song composition across the country, and one melody in particular was characteristic of such compositions. Pugh-Kitingan documented this melody as sung by the Huli people, and 30 years later the same melody continues to be popular in neighbouring Kopiago, as the analysis of just one of the many Christian songs based on this melody, '*nane* laip senis *nganda waya keina*', shows. Not only is this melody continually used to compose songs of worship ('lotu *ipakana*'), it is also used in the composition of secular songs ('danis *ipakana*').

The vibrant and continually transforming Duna song 'Memba *pi nakaya*', and other Duna songs of its kind, represents the legacy of the colonial and the mission encounters united in sound. It is a creative site that is open to change and manipulation to suit the intent of its performers. This case study shows the powerful and innovative way in which Duna people, as a non-Western (and particularly post-colonial) society, manage their present and their future through music. The creativity and innovation in Duna song across a perceived divide between ancestral and exogenous song styles will be the focus of the remainder of this book.

4. Mourning and song

aiyo Waki Waki Mbeta	oh Waki Waki Mbeta
na kota konoya angu koyana	I worry about you only, here
na aki waipe?	what will I do?
Epeni angu kenda	in Heaven only will I see you

In the early hours of Tuesday 15 February 2005, I awoke to darkness and the sounds of hysterical wailing. I said to Lila, my fieldwork companion, 'I think Wakili has died'. Hastily I dressed and ran out onto the veranda and put the outside light on. Jeremiah loomed in the darkness, and I could just make out the glint of the empty steel hospital bed he was holding. He confirmed my fears with one sentence, 'Yangpela meri i dai pinis', and I let out a howl and covered my face with my hands. Together the three of us went down to the elementary school, less than 100m away from our house, and where Wakili had been taken in order to be closer to the local health officer who was to see her the following day. That moment never came.

When Lila and I first arrived at Kopiago the previous Thursday I had asked why Wakili was not to be seen. Almost everyone we knew had turned out to greet us at the airstrip or later at the house. I had made good friends with Wakili, then nineteen years of age, on my first visit to Kopiago in June 2004. Wakili had lived with our host family Kenny Kendoli and Kipu Piero then, helping to care for their four young children—in particular the young girl Monika—and work in the garden, Kipu having no sisters who would otherwise have helped her with these duties (see Figure 4.1).

It was mostly because of her close proximity to our host family that I came to know Wakili. This trip I carried wool for her to make a 'bilum' (string bag) for herself, as she had generously given me one as a gift on my departure then, and I was keen to give something back to her. When I enquired after her I was told she was ill—simultaneously I heard the rumour that pregnancy was the cause of her illness, and that she stayed at her parents' home not only because of her illness but also for the shame of being pregnant to a man to whom she was not betrothed.

Figure 4.1: Kipu Piero and Wakili Akuri, June 2004.

A few days after our arrival Lila and I had clambered up the steep gully that was the path to Wakili's parents' home. We carried with us the wool for Wakili and a copy of *Where There is No Doctor* (a basic medical care book for those working in remote rural communities), hoping to diagnose her illness. Wakili lay under a tree with an umbrella to shade her, and when she saw I had come she said my name and held out her hand for me to hold. She was yellow and swollen and complained of aches and pains, and could not eat because of vomiting. We suspected Hepatitis but neither of us was sure—with no medical training we were at a loss to do anything. I left the wool by her side in a vain attempt to make her feel better. Little did I know that in less than twelve hours she would be dead.

As we approached the classroom on the night of Wakili's death, it felt like the walls of bamboo and grass were alive with the heat and the heaving of the bodies inside. Light was dim, the light of torches and kerosene, but it was not for this reason that her body, in the far corner of the room, could not be seen, even after it was lifted onto the hospital bed Jeremiah had brought down. Rather it was because of the many men and women throwing themselves over Wakili's body, calling out her name, and wailing both independently and together to express their grief. They stood over her, and leaned over her body in turns, flailing their arms above their heads from the moment of entering the room. In stark contrast, Lila and I stood against the back wall, speechless and with silent tears.

More and more men and women arrived over the course of the next few hours. People screamed and cried, paced with their hands latched behind their heads and called out, sometimes hitting themselves, the walls or the doors. After some time the parents and siblings of Wakili gradually collapsed to the side of the room, most likely exhausted from their grieving, compounded by their midnight vigil guarding Wakili in her last hours.

Over the next days and weeks I would have ample opportunity to study the sounds of mourning. It is important to note that the degree of mourning does vary according to the age of the deceased and the circumstances of the death. A newborn baby who died around the same time as Wakili was buried within twenty-four hours of his death, and as a consequence the mourning period was relatively short. The baby was not grieved for by the larger community in the very emotional manner, and for such an extended, continuous period of time after the burial that Wakili was. The tragic nature of the death of such a young strong woman certainly figured in the many varied outpourings of grief.

Laments and creativity

McLeod observes that music is often created at times of social stress. She writes: 'Like accusations of witchcraft then, music tends to occur at points of conflict, uncertainty, or stress within the social fabric' (McLeod 1974:113). This view may explain the outpouring of songs—and accusations—on Wakili's death. A death is usually a period of immense social upheaval for individuals, and often a whole community, and as such it becomes a fulcrum for cultural creativity, where the living have a forum for the expression of their feelings of tension and desire, and where they can make connections between the living and the dead, and the past, present and future.

Laments have been recognised as a crucial genre in the music of Papua New Guineans, and several scholars have explored laments in detail, including Feld (1982), Weiner (1991) and Suwa (2001a). Writing of the Foi of Papua New Guinea, Weiner declares that 'women's poetry is a sung message of love, loss, and grief, proclaiming the temporal ascendency of human relationship' (Weiner 1991:119). Suwa writes that 'the lament genre has been an indispensable means of poetic, often musical, expression among small-scale village communities in Papua New Guinea' and he declares that the women's crying is the only 'traditional' element left in Madang funerals (Suwa 2001a:53).

In this chapter I will explore the musical expressions surrounding Wakili's death, using as my examples recordings made within a few hours of her death through to several weeks later. I will discuss these song genres mostly in the chronological order in which the songs were sung. These death songs—*khene ipakana*, or *heya* ('crying')—focus on individual experience—initially mine, as these opening pages attest, but mainly the individual experience of the singers, in particular Kipu Piero, several of whose songs feature in this chapter. A close examination and comparison of the songs reveals common elements between them, of text and of pitch, despite the different styles from which they derive.

Inside the *khene anda*

With permission I recorded the sound of the wailing from outside Wakili's 'hauskrai'/*khene anda* ('mourning house') just after Wakili's death. A *khene anda* can be virtually any place where the deceased is located. Often, as in the case of Wakili, it is where the deceased actually died—in Wakili's case, the school classroom—as the grieving begins directly upon death. In other cases, the deceased can be moved to another location for grieving, and in these cases the sounds of grieving accompany the body as it is moved, maintaining uninterrupted crying.

As hinted in the introduction above, the initial sound in the *khene anda* appears cacophonous and without structure, but there are many layers to this emotional soundscape. At one level the sounds are spontaneous, with people bursting into the *khene anda* and crying out. On another level the grief is formulaic and repetitious, and it is this semblance of structure that allows the sounds of grieving to be sustained continuously by many in turns, throughout the days and nights at the *khene anda* before the body is finally buried some days later.

Realising the significance of Wakili's death immediately, I documented the events and sounds surrounding her death through recordings, note taking and photographs. The following is an excerpt from my field journal. It describes the sounds of the *khene anda* on the night of Wakili's death, and illustrates the spontaneous and the structured nature of the sounds:

> It was Alo [a young man, and Wakili's cousin (see Figure 4.2)] who kept a fairly steady 5 note descent...It almost acted as a bassline, in that the bottom note was like an anchor where the wailing women met his voice...it functions as a tonic note of sorts. Other women murmured on this note.

That is to say, whilst the women grieved spontaneously, the young man Alo repeatedly sang a wordless descending line over an interval of three and a half tones (a fifth). He lingered on his final note, where other voices would meet his. Alo's descent is musically depicted in Example 4.1.[1]

Example 4.1 (▶ Audio 12): Alo's descent.

The interval of three and a half tones and the role of the tonal centre in this vocal music will be seen in other musical examples in this chapter, in particular the duet between Kepo and Kipu some weeks after Wakili's death.

Another important issue, which is briefly exposed in the above journal excerpt, is the gender difference in mourning. While men who are closely related or associated with the deceased can articulate their grief in song—and an example of this will be given later in this chapter—such lamentation (and public grieving in general) is chiefly the women's domain. This can be seen in the number of examples of women's song in this chapter. It is partly this gender imbalance in singing grieving songs that drew my attention to Alo's contribution to the soundscape of the *khene anda*.

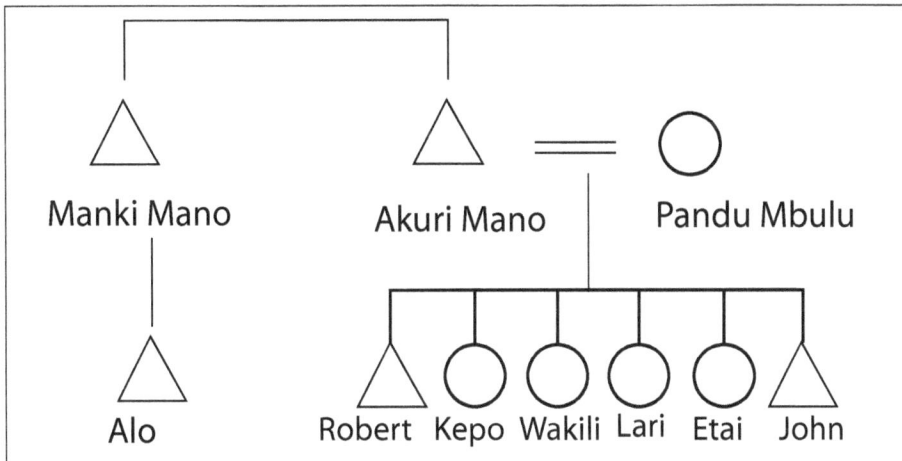

Figure 4.2: members of Wakili's family.

---

1   The shape of the descent sketched here was the most frequent, however it employs only four notes. The descent from D to B sometimes utilised a passing C (instead of the quaver D repeated), hence my journal entry describing five notes.

Women and *khene ipakana yakaya*

After the initial grieving in the *khene anda*, the dominant musical expression around the deceased is the *khene ipakana yakaya* (or 'death song counting'), so named as the song form lists or counts aspects of the life of the deceased (this will be illustrated below). *Khene ipakana yakaya* is predominantly composed and performed by women, and usually the most notable composer/performers are older women, who because of their age hold a certain power and a substantial amount of knowledge.

This relationship between gender, age and power is not an uncommon characteristic of laments around the world. Laments are performed by older, often post-menopausal, women in many cultures. Indigenous Australian laments are one example (cf. Magowan 1994a, 2001). Koskoff relates female sexuality to female musical practices and reveals an inverse relationship between female sexuality and power (Koskoff 1989:7). Applying Koskoff's view to the study of Finnish-Karelian laments, Tolbert suggests that 'women often gain power and prestige only when they are past childbearing age, which is mirrored in and/or offers access to privileged musical and ritual roles' (Tolbert 1990:44). This view is also supported by Petrovic, who writes of women's music in the Dinaric cultural zone of Yugoslavia that '[i]n post-menopausal years, village women in the Dinaric region undergo an upgrading of social status....It is then that they achieve near equality with men and there is a relaxation of the restrictions upon their freedom to communicate with men, since they are considered no longer sexually active.' (Petrovic 1990:81) It is interesting to note the apparent similarity between the laments of these regions of the world and Duna laments in this regard.

Gabriele Stürzenhofecker writes that in the funeral context Duna women have a transitional role as 'midwives at the "birth" of the spirit' (Sturzenhofecker 1998:132). There is, therefore, fertility in death (this connection is further elaborated on in my description of *yekia* courting practices located on sites associated with death—see Chapter 6).

Stürzenhofecker also writes that

> [n]arratives link the Female Spirit [Payeme Ima] to the endless oscillation of life and death from the settlement areas to the forest caves, where the dead are still thought to journey, and from which they return as pieces of life force for their individual rebirth. This cyclical process is still energized by Duna women's ritual actions and their sung laments at the time of the death of kinsfolk. (Sturzenhofecker 1998:203).

These sung laments Stürzenhofecker refers to are the *khene ipakana yakaya*.

Pokole Pora is an older woman, and the mother of Petros Kilapa, a man in his late twenties at the time of writing, and an important translator and contributor to this research (see Figure 4.3). Known to me as a skilled singer of ancestral genres such as *khene ipakana yakaya*, Pokole was present at Wakili's *khene anda* and I asked her to sing to me later in the day for recording.[2] She agreed, and produced a number of *khene ipakana yakaya* devoted to Wakili. These songs, or at least very similar ones, especially in melody, were being sung beside Wakili's in-state corpse in the *khene anda*, and were becoming increasingly audible as the sounds of hysterical grieving subsided. *Khene ipakana yakaya* are, as briefly mentioned above, characterised by the process of *yakaya* ('counting') where aspects of the lives of the deceased, in particular the names of places where the deceased has lived, are listed or counted (cf. Haley 2002a:6-7). They are often constructed of rhetorical questions directed to the deceased, asking them why they have left their earthly life. These attributes are evident in Example 4.2 sung by Pokole to the deceased (note that the range is actually six tones (an octave) lower than depicted here).

Example 4.2 (▶ Audio 13): Pokole's *khene ipakana yakaya*.

---

2   I had asked permission to record Pokole in the hope to record her singing *in situ*, however, my request was slightly misunderstood, and so she came to our hut that evening to sing instead.

antiali-o wara londo kota reyana weipe	dear mother oh, young woman torn down, will you stay or come back?
<u>*itara*</u> *londo kota reyana weipe*	young woman of *itara* Hirane torn down, will you stay or come back?
<u>*ataka*</u> *londo kota reyana weipe*	young woman of *ataka* Hirane torn down, will you stay or come back?
<u>*rapaka*</u> *londo kota reyana weipe*	young woman of *rapaka* Hirane torn down, will you stay or come back?
antiali-o <u>*yokolo*</u> *londo kota reyana weipe*	dear mother oh, young woman of *yokolo* Hirane torn down, will you stay or come back?
<u>*yalima*</u> *londo kota reyana weipe*	young woman of *yalima* Hirane torn down, will you stay or come back?

Figure 4.3: Pokole Pora and Petros Kilapa.

In this verse, Pokole asks the deceased young woman if she will come back to the community, or stay in the land of the dead. She lists the praise names (*kēiyaka*, underlined in this and other examples) for the young woman's place of Hirane (the place where she lived and which belongs to her father and his clan—further verses listing the names for Suwaka as the place of Wakili's mother and her clan were later sung). As Pokole does not use the name of Wakili, it is these references to place that identify her as the deceased. The word *kota* was translated into Tok Pisin as 'brukim' ('break'), and likened to the tearing off of a flower at its stalk, hence the English equivalent here given as 'torn down'. The exclamation *antia[li]-o* ('[dear] mother oh', where the suffix *–li* is not always used[3]) is a common one not only in Duna *khene ipakana yakaya* but in spoken expressions of grief or sorrow, and is not directed at the deceased (that is, Wakili is not here being referred to as a mother). The exclamation features especially in spontaneous outpourings of grief, as will be apparent in the following musical example.

Na panenope? ('what will I do?')

About four hours after Wakili's death, Kipu left the 'hauskrai' and returned to the house. Circling the courtyard she sang a long and grief-stricken *khene ipakana* for Wakili, within earshot of those attending the 'hauskrai', and her male relatives who, together with other men from the community, were at work constructing Wakili's coffin. Kipu's lament lasted approximately ten minutes, seven of which I was able to record through our hut wall (to later play back to, and translate with, Kipu herself). The first lines of this recording are reproduced below. The sung text is in italics, and the Tok Pisin and English translation in normal type with English in the far right column. The Tok Pisin has been included for a few reasons: it was the first translation provided to me by Kipu; it is also a helpful point of reference for analyses of the laments of contemporary popular influence that will be examined later in this chapter. Note that each line is structured as a question to the deceased, as was also the case with the *heya* sung by Pokole Pora described above.

antia wali-o antia wali-a	mama mama oh mama mama ah	mother mother oh mother mother ah
aluarena kenaka aru awanana na panenope?	mitupela save lukautim ol yelogras, nau bai mi mekim wanem?	we two care for and cradle the blonde children, now what will I do?
antia wali-o	mama mama oh	mother mother oh
antia wali-o	mama mama oh	mother mother oh
keno wara wanpis kenaka aru awanana na panenope?	mitupela save lukautim *wara* wanpis, nau bai mi mekim wanem?	we two care for and cradle the lone *wara*, now what will I do?

3   The meaning and function of the suffix *–li* is not entirely clear, as San Roque explains: 'The sequence *–li* can occur as a suffix on some kin terms and commonly occurs in *kēiyaka* vocabulary and some other specialised vocabulary items (eg. expressives). The independent or productive meaning of this form is obscure to me, but it is clear that it usually occurs in highly emotive or exclamatory contexts' (Lila San Roque, email comm., 30 November 2007).

antia wali-o	mama mama oh	mother mother oh
antia wali-o	mama mama oh	mother mother oh
keno warali wanpis kenaka aru awanana na panenope?	mitupela save lukautim *warali* wanpis, nau bai mi mekim wanem?	we two care for and cradle the lone *warali*, now what will I do?
antia wali-o	mama mama oh	mother mother oh
keno ayako wanpis kenaka aru awanana na panenope?	mitupela save lukautim *ayako* wanpis, nau bai mi mekim wanem?	we two care for and cradle the lone *ayako*, now what will I do?
antia wali-a antia wali kone antia wali	mama mama ah mama mama tru mama mama	mother mother ah mother true mother mother mother
antia wali-o	mama mama oh	mother mother oh
na wara nendeke nangayana na panenope?	mi no save go pren wantaim ol arapela *wara* meri, nau bai mi mekim wanem?	I don't go and make friends with other *wara* women, now what will I do?
no wali-a	mama bilong mi ah	my mother ah
antia wali-o	mama mama oh	mother mother oh
ko warali koanina ko kono neyape? antia wali	yu *warali* yangpela meri yet na yu no tingim na yu dai a? mama mama	You are just a young *warali* woman, weren't you thinking? mother mother
antia wali-o	mama mama oh	mother mother oh
aya koanina ko kono neyape?	yu *aya* yangpela meri yet na yu no tingim na yu dai a?	You are just a young *aya* woman, weren't you thinking?
antia wali-a	mama mama ah	mother mother ah
antia wali-a	mama mama ah	mother mother ah
na ayako wanpis na ko kono neyarape?	mi *ayako* wanpis na yu no tingim mi a?	I'm a lone *ayako*, weren't you thinking?
antia wali-a	mama mama ah	mother mother ah

In this excerpt, Kipu questions the dead Wakili. Together they used to care for Kipu's blonde children, what will Kipu do now that Wakili is dead? Both Kipu and Wakili would look after Kipu's only daughter, Monika, so what will Kipu do now? Kipu doesn't make friends easily, so what will she do now? Wakili is just a young woman, wasn't she thinking? Kipu is alone now, wasn't Wakili thinking?[4]

---

4   This kind of questioning in songs of mourning, and also the expression of a lack of family members eg. 'I have no brother/sister', is present in other groups in Papua New Guinea, such as the Kaluli and their genre of *gisaro* (Schieffelin 1976:183). Feld describes this type of linguistic construction, often expressed in song, as a key way in which the Kaluli elicit pity (Feld 1982:25-26). An orphan or an only child is seen as the epitome of personal suffering in Duna culture, and such sorry characters appear frequently in song texts such as *pikono* (sung stories). Also common is the general complaint 'you didn't tell me (before you left)'—that the singer was shocked and uninformed

The words *antia* ('mother' in Duna) and *wali* ('mother' in Huli) are used together here, intensifying the expression of woe. These words serve to punctuate each line of text, at both beginning and end. A cry out is usually attached to the end of the word *wali*, either an *-o* sound or an *−a* sound, depending on the preference of the singer at each particular line.

Duna song often incorporates Huli words, but here Huli is not the only 'imported' language. Tok Pisin makes regular appearances in this song, notably in the excerpt for the word and concept 'wanpis'. This Tok Pisin term comes from the English 'one piece', and means 'alone, without relatives, an orphan, without a mate' (Mihalic 1971:201). Its use is striking here in combination with a number of *kēiyaka* ('praise names'), which have been identified as a fundamental characteristic of Duna song language (see Chapter 2). There is '*wara* wanpis', '*warali* wanpis', and '*ayako* wanpis', all signifying Kipu's only girl child Monika. Kipu also refers to herself as an '*ayako* wanpis' now Wakili is dead. In this way, esoteric Duna language is combined with a relatively newly introduced foreign language (that is, Tok Pisin).

Another foreign element is introduced into the song text towards the end of this recording in the form of Wakili's nickname. It is quite common for Duna people to obtain shortened names or nicknames, which are given and used as a sign of affection for those they name. In this song we learn that Wakili's alternative name was Waki Mbeta (see Appendix B for the full transcription of Kipu's lament, with the use of this name for Wakili after the time of 4:59). 'Waki' is obviously a shortened version of her full name. 'Mbeta' on first glance is somewhat more mysterious. In the course of discussion after this recording it became apparent that Wakili was named after a type of tinned mackeral called 'Besta'. 'Mbeta' is the Duna pronounciation of this word, since there are no single (non pre-nasalised) 'b' or combinations of 'st' in the language. Any type of tinned food is hard for the people of Wakili's community to obtain, there being very little of it in the local trade stores (and what is there is priced far beyond the reach of most local people), so the fact that Wakili had been re-named after tinned mackeral means that she was very highly prized by those who called her 'Waki Mbeta'. It was also said that it was one of Wakili's favourite foods (see Figure 4.4).

Example 4.3 is a transcription of the first minute of the recording of Kipu's lament. The style of delivery is spontaneous, and the line between song and speech is sometimes blurred. This is typical of laments: Feld and Fox have noted that the relationship between speech and song is very close in laments, describing the mode of expression as 'verbal-vocal' (Feld and Fox 1994:39). At points Kipu's

---

of the deceased intention to die/leave them (even in cases such as Wakili's where the death is unintentional). This is evident in not only Duna song, but also Foi song (Weiner 1991:47, 140-141). The elicitation of sympathy as an important element of courting songs will be discussed further in Chapter 6.

voice creaks from emotional strain.[5] This 'creaky voice' of course is a feature of laments, one of the 'icons of crying' established by Urban and considered by Feld and Fox, the others being 'the cry break', 'the voiced inhalation', and 'falsetto vowels' (Urban 1988:389-391). These icons of crying are 'features that are linked indexically to the emotional states and affective projection of lament performance' (Feld and Fox 1994:40). Despite the spontaneity of Kipu's performance, there are particular performance conventions being observed (see Example 4.3).

Figure 4.4: advertisement for Besta Mackeral, Goroka, June 2006.

Melodically, phrases usually start (a fifth) above the tonal centre, with the exclamatory text *antia wali-o/a*. Following that initial expression is the line of text questioning the deceased, which is characterised by a rapid execution of syllables stepping between one and two tones above the tonal centre. Ending the question with the marker '-pe' the phrase is most often concluded with another exclamatory phrase, similar to the opening one, but mostly on the lowest pitch, the tonal centre. One phrase (at system 5) follows this melodic pattern, though is made up entirely of exclamations.

As this song does not have a regular beat, as is typical of *khene ipakana yakaya*, the notations here are not to be taken literally with regard to rhythm: the key rhythmic contrast to observe is between the run of syllables and the sustained notes. The run of syllables are represented here by quavers and constitute the question of the phrase and the opening of the exclamations. Sustained notes, which are often on the vocables 'o' or 'a' and which are represented here by minims, are the culmination of the exclamations, and thus appear in the initial few notes and at the very end. The end of each line is defined by a prolonged pitch (usually on the tonal centre) and a breath.

---

5   At these points I have given the pitch that I assumed she was aiming for.

Example 4.3 (▶ Audio 14, 0:00-1:00): Kipu's *khene ipakana yakaya*.

Kipu's lament is of the same genre as Pokole's given above. The range of around three and a half tones (a fifth), the stepping rapidly between pitches and the conclusion on the tonal centre are some of the features they share. Pokole's lament also opens with the exclamatory *antia* (though not *wali*) and poses a question. How they do differ is in their delivery, and this affects their textual structure. Kipu's lament is spontaneous, rapid and emotional; Pokole's is slower and more deliberate.[6] Pokole is careful to list the *kēiyaka* of Wakili's place, whereas at no point in Kipu's lament did that occur. It is possible that Kipu did not know as many *kēiyaka* for Wakili's place or was not as confident in reproducing them (she declares herself a Christian and also admits to being a 'child of the white man' due to her years of school education), however it is also just as likely that her immediate grief obstructed the careful reciting of them. Whilst Kipu used *kēiyaka* in her lament, she used them in reference to persons, not land: Wakili (and also daughter Monika) as a young girl (*wara*, *warali*, *aya*) and herself as alone, without a sister (*ayako*). The purposes of the two laments are different— Pokole's is about seeing the spirit on to a new place and tracing its past in place, whereas Kipu's, being an immediate response to the death, chastises Wakili and expresses her grief directly to her.

From the examples provided so far in this chapter, it is evident that women—and particularly older women—dominate the laments sung in the Duna community. However, the domain is not exclusive to women. Men also sing *khene ipakana*, as the next section shall reveal.

Men and *khene ipakana*

Over the next couple of days after Wakili's death, many people visited the *khene anda* of the schoolhouse (see Figures 4.5 and 4.6). The crying (*heya*) and laments (*khene ipakana*) were continuous, as different people came and went, creating an endless wall of sound. So many people arrived to grieve on the morning of Wakili's death that a side wall of the schoolhouse had to be removed and the body taken outside for the day. Wakili's family were also a continuous presence, in particular her mother and sisters, whose crying was fundamental to the soundscape.

---

6   It is possible, of course, that the different context for this performance (ie. requested, not recorded in the moment of grieving) could explain the difference in tempo and expression of Pokole's lament. However, it is the case that the highly formulaic laments such as that which Pokole sang are by nature slower and more deliberate. This is necessary for the continuation of their singing over many hours, indeed days, in the *khene anda*. Laments such as this one of Kipu's are not sustainable over such a period of time.

Figure 4.5: mourners with Wakili's body outside the schoolhouse, the *khene anda*, 15 February 2005.

On the afternoon of the third day, Wakili's body was moved in its makeshift coffin from the *khene anda* to the burial ground approximately one kilometre away. The carriers of the coffin were accompanied by a large group of men, women and children who cried as they went. Their faces, arms and legs were covered in mud to show their sorrow.[7] Once the procession arrived at the burial site, a makeshift *khene anda* was created under a tarpaulin for Wakili's coffin, and the women and children milled around this while the men finished digging the grave and building the roof structure to sit above it (see Figure 4.7).

_____

7   Applying mud to the body to indicate grief is done no matter what the weather conditions—if the days have been dry then mud will be created by adding water to the dry dirt. It can be obtained from almost any source.

Figure 4.6: Wakili's mother Pandu Mbulu (in foreground) with Kipu Piero (leaning across her) and others inside the *khene anda,* 16 February 2005. Kipu is passing a photo of her and Wakili that I took the year before and which appears in this chapter as Figure 4.1. The coffin can be seen in the corner of the photograph, wrapped in foil and sealed with adhesive tape.

There was much hubbub amongst the men whilst they worked quickly to finalise and fit the grave's roof structure. Whilst this was going on, Soti Mbulu began to sing *khene ipakana yakaya* (see Figure 4.8). He was the first man I had heard sing this genre of song clearly (I had observed a few men, namely Kipu Piero's husband Kenny Kendoli, and Wakili's father Akuri Mano murmuring what appeared to be *khene ipakana yakaya* in the *khene anda* of the schoolhouse, but the text had been inaudible). Soti Mbulu was an uncle to Wakili—her mother's younger brother. Leaning on the grave's roof structure, Soti called out first in his full voice then falsetto (another of the 'icons of crying' established by Urban), before launching into two verses of *khene ipakana yakaya*.[8]

---

8 As I did not record these verses, I have not provided a musical transcription of them here.

Figure 4.7: the *khene anda* at the burial ground on the day of burial, 17 February 2005. Note the men preparing the grave site in the background with freshly-turned earth, and the temporary *khene anda* construction in the foreground where the coffin is waiting and the women have gathered.

In the first verse that Soti sang, he articulated his sorrow at Wakili's death, using an expression common in *khene ipakana* that I have translated as 'to stomach sorrow' (*neya* here meaning 'eat'). This expression is also used in Example 4.7 later in this chapter. Soti intensifies the effect of this expression by using the *kēiyaka* for sorrow, *pape* and *yaraka* (see Example 4.4).

The second verse describes one of Wakili's activities that she performed in the garden—that is, the building up of sweet potato mounds by moving mud up onto them (see Figure 4.9). Soti asks her if she will return to do this activity again.

It is not coincidental that these verses both refer to eating, and food: food and emotion are closely linked throughout Papua New Guinea, and this important trope is further examined in the following chapter through discussions of land productivity.

As previously described, Soti is closely connected to Wakili, and this makes his singing of *khene ipakana yakaya* in the public sphere acceptable. He is also a man renowned for his renditions of traditional music such as *yekia*, therefore he is accomplished in the knowledge of the textual and musical forms of the *awenene ipakana*. It is interesting to note here that Soti's heritage is not entirely Duna: Haley records his agnatic descent showing that only his father's father comes from a Duna-speaking parish (Angora) (Haley 2002a, vol. 2:155)

Figure 4.8: Soti Mbulu sings against the coffin roof.

Example 4.4: Soti's *khene ipakana yakaya.*

ko ngaya kata papu neya kata ngoyana, antia-o	you go and make me stomach this sorrow, then you leave, mother oh
ko ngaya kata <u>pape</u> neya kata ngoyana, antia-o	you go and make me stomach this *pape* sorrow, then you leave, mother oh
ko ngaya kata <u>yaraka</u> neya kata ngoyana, antia-o	you go and make me stomach this *yaraka* sorrow, then you leave, mother oh
koya laranata ndolu weipe? antia-o	you move the mud, one time you will come back? mother oh
<u>*mopotia*</u> *laranata ndolu weipe? antia-o*	*mopotia* sweet potato mounds, move the mud, one time you will come back? mother oh
<u>*yarakatia*</u> *laranata ndolu weipe? antia-o*	*yarakatia* sweet potato mounds, move the mud, one time you will come back? mother oh

Although most Duna appear to marry other Duna, it is not at all uncommon for Duna to marry people from other language groups, particularly neighbouring ones, and this mixed heritage of Soti's (with his father's mother from the Huli-speaking area of Tari and his mother's parent's from the region of Paiela) does

not detract from his status as a performer of traditional Duna genres.

Group singing of *khene ipakana*

Kepo Akuri is the youngest woman (and, perhaps coincidentally, the only non-parent) I recorded singing *khene ipakana yakaya* at Hirane. Kepo's status as the first-born daughter to Pandu and Akuri, and thus Wakili's eldest *hakini kone* ('true sister') account for her close bond with Wakili. Kepo was a prominent person in the funeral grieving, spending most of the church service before Wakili's burial standing almost on top of the coffin or lying prostrate upon it, crying out (see Figures 4.10 and 4.11).

Kepo's grief at the loss of her sister is likely to have been further compounded by the illicit relationship her 'husband' Sakane was said to have had with Wakili.[9] It was rumoured that Wakili's illness was due to her liaisons with him, and that she had not menstruated for three months. On Monday 21 February, less than a week after Wakili's death, Sakane and his relatives from Aluni met with Wakili's relatives from Hirane, just past Kalisanda (near Wanakei) at the edge of Hirane territory. Here the Aluni people paid compensation to Wakili's family of 6 pigs and around 300 kina in cash. It seemed that Sakane was guilty as charged.

---

9   It was said that Kepo had been residing with Sakane at Aluni for some months, and though he hadn't paid a bride-price to Kepo's father, Kepo still declared him 'man blong mi' ('my man'), and the status of their relationship was public knowledge. The Duna have experienced dramatic inflation in bride-price over the last thirty-plus years (Stürzenhofecker 1998:110-118), and this, coupled with the social instability caused by colonialisation and missionisation, could see such 'de facto' relations become the norm.

Figure 4.9: potato garden, Kopiago.

The following day, exactly a week after Wakili had died, Kepo came on one of her frequent visits to Kenny and Kipu's home, the place where Wakili had spent so much time the year before she died. Pandu was also a frequent visitor, often just sitting looking out towards the lake and crying for Wakili. Both Kepo and Pandu regularly sang *khene ipakana* on the approach to Kenny and Kipu's home as well as upon their arrival. Often Kipu would be moved by their grief and join them. On this day Kepo was moved to sing for a long period of time, and her verses were particularly intricate. She stood outside our house, moving around it slightly, and was joined by Kipu for much of the singing. Kipu's physical location at the back of the house and a substantial distance from the microphone during this performance meant that her singing could not be clearly discerned. Here, therefore, I will focus on Kepo's composition, and the first two minutes of the recording where the verses are concentrated (see Example 4.5). After this analysis I will consider how the song functions as a duet.

Figure 4.10: Wakili's sister Kepo stands at the base of the coffin (which is on top of the hospital bed) supported by female relatives. Kipu paces in the foreground with hands on her head. Umbrellas are used here as shields from the sun (it was a fine day).

Figure 4.11: Kepo lies prostrate on the coffin.

Example 4.5 (▶ Audio 15, 0:00-2:01): Kepo's khene ipakana yakaya.

Wa-ki-li ha-ki-ni-o a-ntia-li wa-ne ke-no (a)wa-ya pe-le ko-la su-wa-no
ra-le ko-la su-wa-no ya-ka-le ko-la su-wa-no ya-ye-pi ko-la su-wa-no
Wa-ki-li ha-ki-ni-o Wa-ki-li ha-ki-ni-o ah a-pia ko-la su-wa-no
e-ya-pi-a ko-la su-wa-no e-ya-ne ko-la su-wa-no ku-ru-ku ko-la su-wa-no
ka-me-nda ko-la su-wa-no
Wa-ki-li ha-ki-ni-o
Wa-ki-li ha-ki-ni ah a-pua-le he-ya ma-le pu-ka-nia ko lu-ma-ka-na
a-ngi-na he-ya ma-le pu-ka-nia ko lu-ma-ka-na
ya-ka-le he-ya ma-le pu-ka-nia ko lu-ma-(ka)na a-ntia-li wa-ne
ya-ku-pi ma-le pu-ka-nia ko lu-ma (ka)na

Steep Slopes

Wakili-o antia wane antiali wane	Wakili oh mother daughter dear mother daughter
Wakili-o	Wakili oh
kanga hutia nendeke ndolu weipe?	friend of these children, when will you come back?
kangalu hutia nendeke ndolu weipe?	friend of these *kangalu* children, when will you come back?*
Wakili-o antiali antia wali-o ah antiali wane ah	Wakili oh dear mother mother mother ah dear mother daughter ah
Wakili-o	Wakili oh
rina kora suwano	from Rina mountain take water and carry it
[unintelligible]	[unintelligible]
rinako kora suwano	from *rinako* Rina mountain take water and carry it
rerepa kora suwano	from *rerepa* Rina mountain take water and carry it
antiali wane etopa kora suwano	dear mother daughter from *etopa* Rina mountain take water and carry it
kwayupa kora suwano	from *kwayupa* Rina mountain take water and carry it
[unintelligible]	[unintelligible]
Wakili hakini-o	Wakili sister oh
antiali wane keno awaya	dear mother daughter our father
pele kola suwano	break and carry the *pele* flower
rale kola suwano	break and carry the *rale pele* flower
yakale kola suwano	break and carry the *yakale pele* flower
yayepi kola suwano	break and carry the *yayepi pele* flower
Wakili hakini-o	Wakili sister oh
Wakili hakini-o ah	Wakili sister oh ah
apia kola suwano	break *apia* and carry it
eyapia kola suwano	break *eyapia apia* and carry it
eyane kola suwano	break *eyane apia* and carry it
kuruku kola suwano	break *kuruku* and carry it
kamenda kola suwano	break *kamenda kuruku* and carry it
Wakili hakini-o	Wakili sister oh
Wakili hakini ah	Wakili sister ah
apuale heya male pukania ko lumakana	*apuale* Nauwa has many *male* vines/roots that will block your way
angina heya male pukania ko lumakana	*angina* Nauwa has many *male* vines/roots that will block your way
yakale heya male pukania ko lumakana	*yakale* Nauwa has many *male* vines/roots that will block your way

109

antiali wane	dear mother daughter
<u>*yakupi*</u> *male pukania ko lumakana*	many *yakupi pele* and *male* will block your way
<u>*yakale*</u> *male pukania ko lumakana*	many *yakale pele* and *male* will block your way
antia wali	mother mother
antiali antia wane antiali antia wane	dear mother mother daughter, dear mother mother daughter
pele male pukania ko lumakana	many *pele* and *male* will block your way
<u>*rale*</u> *male ya** ko lumakana*	*rale pele* and *male* ya will block your way
<u>*yakale*</u> *ya male pukania ko lumakana*	many *yakale pele* and *male* will block your way
<u>*yakupi*</u> *ya male pukania ko lumakana*	many *yakupi pele* and *male* will block your way
Wakili hakini wane Wakili hakini-o he	Wakili sister daughter Wakili sister oh heh
Wakili hakini wane Wakili hakini-o he	Wakili sister daughter Wakili sister oh heh
<u>*antiali-o*</u>	dear mother oh
<u>*waiyeni*</u> *kupalapa*	*waiyeni* Hirane light-skin
<u>*paralu*</u> *kupalapa*	*paralu* Hirane light-skin
antiali wane <u>*awiya*</u> *kupalapa*	dear mother daughter *awiya* Hirane light-skin
antiali wane <u>*awiya*</u> *kupalapa*	dear mother daughter *awiya* Hirane light-skin
<u>*akura*</u> *kupalapa*	*akura* Hirane light-skin
<u>*akope*</u> *kupalapa*	*akope* Hirane light-skin
<u>*ipuku*</u> *kupalapa*	*ipuku* Hirane light-skin

* The term kanga in the previous line is said to be a Huli word for children; *kangalu* being the Huli *kēiyaka* for this term.

** *'ya' here is simply a vocable such as 'o' and 'ah'.*

Kepo's lament is punctuated frequently by the exclamations *antia* and *wali* and also *wane* ('daughter'), used in a similar way to the former as an expression of emotion rather than an address to the deceased. The terms *hakini* ('sister') and *keno awaya* ('our father'), however, define the personal relationship between the singer and the deceased. Initially Kepo asks of Wakili, friend of Kipu's children, when she will return. Kepo's use of *keno awaya* reinforces the *kēiyaka* that she recites that reference their father's land connections, thus identifying him.[10] Kepo, though a young woman, is confident in producing the *kēiyaka* of her parents' land. She is not a 'child of the white man' as Kipu declares herself to be—Kepo has grown up in post-colonial times, and has not had the amount of structured schooling experienced by Kipu. In this way, it can be suggested that Kepo's knowledge is more in keeping with that of Pokole's generation.

---

10   It will be recalled that any Duna person can have two or more connections to land; through the mother's side, the father's side, and through other remote cognatic ties (Stürzenhofecker 1998:90).

Mount Rina, a mountain towards Horaile (also called by its *kēiyaka* here as *rinako, rerepa, etopa* and *kwayupa*) is the first place Kepo refers to in her song, and a place to which their father is connected. Kepo instructs the deceased Wakili to get drinking water from this mountain and take it with her on her journey to the place of the dead. In the next verse Kepo tells Wakili to snap off the *pele* flower (known also by its *kēiyaka* here as *rale, yakale* and *yayepi*) and take that with her too. The juxtaposition of this verse with the Mount Rina reference informs the listener that the *pele* flower is to be found on this mountain. Likewise the following verse where Kepo tells Wakili to break *apia* (a kind of bush fibre used to make arm bands given during times of courting, also known by its *kēiyaka* as *eyapia, eyane, kuruku* and *kamenda*) and take it with her.[11]

Nauwa, the place of Akuri's mother's father, is the next of Akuri's places that Kepo refers to, through its *kēiyaka* of *apuale, angina, yakale,* and *andupi*. The many *pele* flowers and *male* vines found there will block Wakili's way, Kepo sings—and perhaps it is because of these plants that Wakili cannot easily move on to the place of the dead, and thus lingers close to home and in the minds of her family, who voice this presence in song.

Finally in this excerpt Kepo gives the *kēiyaka* for Hirane, Akuri's father's father's place (*waiyeni, paralu, awiya, akura, akope, ipuku*). She describes Wakili as being a light-skinned (*kupalapa*) Hirane person. This term is also used in the bachelor cult songs of *mindmindi kāo*, and is an ideal kind of radiant beauty associated with the ethereal. By distinguishing Wakili in this way Kepo aligns her with a non-earthly quality, suggesting her transformation into the spirit realm.

Musically, Kepo's lament is similar to Kipu's lament on the day of Wakili's death that is presented above, particularly in its use of the range of three and a half tones (a fifth). In her methodical use of *kēiyaka*, Kepo's lament is close in style to Pokole's excerpt featured earlier in this chapter. Pokole's, Kipu's and Kepo's laments are all part of the same genre—*khene ipakana*—though as Kipu does not count the *kēiyaka* of places, hers is not a *khene ipakana yakaya*.

An interesting feature of Kepo's lament is the melodic and textual parallelism that appears in the first phrase of text after the exclamations (that centres on the tone above the tonal centre, shown here as C#) and the subsequent phrases (that focus on the tonal centre). That is to say, there is a direct copying of interval structure—steps of a tone—as they map on to the corresponding syllables of text. Examples include such words as *pu-ka-nia ko lu-ma-ka-na* (compare bar 26 with 27 of Example 4.5) and *ku-pu-la-pa* (compare bar 42 with 44 of the same

---

11   The connection between courting and death here is important, and is further examined towards the end of Chapter 6.

example). These phrases of text also feature a brief drop below the tonal centre at their end-point, which is also a feature of other Duna song genres such as *pikono*. These structural features point to an expression of grief formulated and guided by established norms.

While the above discussion has focused on Kepo's musical expression alone, it should not be forgotten that this performance is actually a 'duet'. The voices of Kepo and Kipu are not completely independent in this performance, though it might seem so at first; they share many of the same pitches and their phrases conclude on the same tonic note, often simultaneously. Kipu's melodies are generally restricted to a range of two tones, in contrast to Kepo's melodies that always begin three and a half tones (a fifth) above the tonal centre. Kipu often begins just before or after Kepo's verses, and thus, there is often present the interval of one and a half tones between the singers. They also often co-ordinate the ending of their phrases, with Kipu often arriving at the tonal centre some time before Kepo (her verses generally consisting of exclamations such *antia wali-o* only, rather than Kepo's more intricate *yakaya* verses), and thus setting the place for her musical arrival.

Example 4.6 (▶ Audio 15, 0:00-0:08): Kepo's *khene ipakana yakaya* as a duet.

This kind of interlocking of voices could be described as heterophonic—that is, 'simultaneous variation, accidental or deliberate, of what is identified as the same melody' (Cooke n.d.). Therefore, '[e]ven though each voice laments distinctly, the cumulative interaction between voices draws the temporal process of the mourning event and its participants into a more dialogic arena' (Feld and Fox 1994:43).[12] Such a relationship between vocal heterophony and textual dialogism in women's laments has also been recorded for the Kaluli of Papua New Guinea (Feld 1995).

---

12 This technique somewhat resembles hocketing of medieval vocal music, which is defined by the New Grove Dictionary of Music and Musicians as '[t]he medieval term for a contrapuntal technique of manipulating silence as a precise mensural value in the 13th and 14th centuries. It occurs in a single voice or, most commonly, in two or more voices, which display the dovetailing of sounds and silences by means of the staggered arrangement of rests' (Sanders n.d.; cf. Feld 1988:81).

Although there are no examples of pre-contact musical forms with harmony, there are examples where Duna people sing together, co-ordinating their pitches and intervals. This is evident in the singing inside the *khene anda* as illustrated already with Alo's and the singing of the women. During Wakili's funeral and her uncle Soti's lament, there was also *khene ipakana* in the background matched to his. In Kepo and Kipu's lament, this kind of musical interaction is very clear—whilst the two singers are creating individual expression, they are aware of each other's performance and adapt theirs to suit the overall soundscape. It is a social process of music-making—together Kepo and Kipu support each other in grief. Also, in singing together they address Wakili's spirit and help her on her way to the place of the dead—the forest cave.

Khene ipakana of exogenous origin

Three weeks after Wakili's death, I was moving about our wooden hut at night when, over the sound of the night-time insects, I heard Kipu composing and playing another song for Wakili. This song was remarkable as it was different to all other mourning songs I had so far heard. The difference was in the musical system—this new song was clearly influenced by the Western musical forms of church and stringband music. Another difference was the existence of instrumentation. Sung six tones (an octave) lower than here depicted, Kipu accompanied herself by strumming the open strings of the guitar. I recorded her playing and singing through the wall, translating it with her the next day (Example 4.7).

This song of Kipu's had a regular pulse, and though did not seem to conform to time signatures, I have used them here for analytical purposes to reveal aspects of rhythm and duration. Phrases were irregular in beat length. Mostly the strumming of the guitar fell on the first and third beats of the bars, or the first beat of the duple time bars. During the playing (at bar 24 of this transcription), however, Kipu changed to strum on the second and fourth beats, thus giving the song a 'reggae feel'. The extra beat of rest in the previous bar seemed to prompt this change (usually Kipu only took two beats to take a breath). Bar 33 saw the strumming return to the first and third beats, as before, and she continued to strum for two more beats once she had finished singing (hence the bar of rest at the end of the transcription). The lack of correlation between the strumming and the singing, and the persistent use of the open strings (not representing any particular chord), points to an instrument used predominantly for rhythmic purposes rather than the usual melodic/harmonic function (cf. Magowan 2007:3-4), and—perhaps first and formost—an instrument that acts as a signifier of a new musical system, of a modern world.

Melodically the phrases are quite different to those represented in the examples previously shown that were sung by Pokole, Kipu, and Kepo and Kipu together. The range is much greater, however the melodic contour is very similar in that the phrases are generally descents, beginning at the top of the range and concluding on a sustained tonal centre. These descents also exist in other Duna song genres, such as *pikono*. Textually the song articulates much the same as the previous examples. Verses begin with the stock exclamation *antia wali-o*, and ask questions of the deceased. There is however no use of *kēiyaka* in Kipu's new song. The text is direct, without allusive references or metaphor.

In effect, what Kipu has done here is to set the sentiments of traditional *khene ipakana* to a modern beat and a modern instrument. The text, and even the general melodic contour, has remained the same. So too has the performance practice of this as a women's genre (during my time at Kopiago I never heard a man compose *khene ipakana* in this exogenous style). This song is evidence of a creative resourcefulness in Duna people, and in women in particular, to adapt indigenous forms of musical expression into new forms that maintain a contemporary currency in the face of colonial encounter.[13]

This was not the only exogenously inspired song about Wakili's death that Kipu composed. The following song (Example 4.8) is another example of typical indigenous *khene ipakana* song text—albeit in the non-indigenous language of Tok Pisin—set to a Western melodic style, composed in the same evening. This melodic style can be identified loosely as 'lotu' style which, as discussed in the previous chapter, is diatonic and constructed usually of four melodic and textual phrases, generally alternating between ascending and descending, with a strong triadic construction and focus on the tonal centre, and featuring textual repetition. Once again, the song does not subscribe exactly to a strict time signature, but in order to show aspects of rhythm and duration a time signature is included here (this is also the case for the transcription of the final song of this chapter, Example 4.9). Rhythm is treated loosely, especially over the ascent and descent of bars 10-11, however the focus in this analysis is on melodic content and text.

---

13 It is important to note that the social functions of indigenous *khene ipakana* and contemporary versions of this genre do not seem to be the same. *Khene ipakana* are sung from the moment of a person's death and in a manner to express and perhaps even control grief and crying, and are usually concerned with the recounting of *kēiyaka*, in particular those that refer to the land affiliations of the deceased, in order to see the spirit move on to its new place. It seems that the contemporary versions of *khene ipakana* do not arise until some time after the death (for example, several weeks as in this case), and are more reflective in their expression, more about the singer processing their own feelings rather than assisting the movement of the spirit. They could be said to lack the potency, and appropriateness, of indigenous *khene ipakana*; the lack of *kēiyaka* sequences in these contemporary versions would also play a part in this.

Example 4.7 (▶ Audio 16): Kipu's *khene ipakana* (with guitar accompaniment).

antia wali-o antia wali-o	mama mama mama mama	mother mother mother mother
na aki kone putape?	mi mekim wanem tru?	what will I truly do?
antia wali-o antia wali-a	mama mama mama mama	mother mother mother mother
na aki kone kota putape?	mi mekim wanem samting tru long yu?	what will I truly do about you?
antia wali-o antia wali-o	mama mama mama mama	mother mother mother mother
home wame nariya ko ngutiana	yu no tok wanpela samting long mi na go	you didn't tell me anything before you went
antia wali-o antia wali-a (x2)	mama mama mama mama (x2)	mother mother mother mother (x2)
na aki kone kota putape?	mi mekim wanem samting tru long yu?	what will I truly do about you?
antia wali-o antia wali-o	mama mama mama mama	mother mother mother mother
paputia norane	mi kisim sore long kaikai	I get sorrow to stomach
ko pukutiape? ka aki peya?	yu laikim a? yu mekim wanem?	you like that don't you? what are you doing?
antia wali-o antia wali-o	mama mama mama mama	mother mother mother mother
paputia norane	mi kisim sore long kaikai	I get sorrow to stomach
ko pukutiape? na aki wai(pe?)	yu laikim a? bai mi mekim wanem?	you like that don't you? what will I do?
eh antia wali-o antia wali-o	eh mama mama mama mama	eh mother mother mother mother
ye antia wali-o antia wali-o	ye mama mama mama mama	ye mother mother mother mother

In the recorded performance the second verse was repeated twice, making the length a total of four verses. Slight variation appeared between each repetition, but here I show only the melodic structure of the first singing of it (featuring the most common elements of each repetition) for clarity of representation of the overall structure. Once again, the text of each verse is introduced by an exclamation and questions the deceased, as *khene ipakana* does. The verse consisting of four short lines (not counting the repeat of the exclamation) and featuring a kind of textual parallelism in the third and fourth lines is typical of the repetitious song text structure of 'lotu' songs.

Musically, although this song belongs to the Western diatonic tradition, it shares both range and intervallic content/melodic structure with the *khene ipakana* of Alo and of Kepo. The range is generally three and a half tones (a fifth; excepting the dip below the tonal centre which only occurs once). The key interval structure is a descent over this range based on a triadic structure but also employing the pitches in-between. Thus, this seemingly modern lament hangs on pre-existing Duna musical structures and the use of language therein.

It is very likely that this Tok Pisin song arose from the process of translation of Kipu's lament (Example 4.3) from the day Wakili died. As we worked on that translation Kipu had sat with Lila and me and her husband Kenny, contributing to the translation but mostly allowing her husband to rephrase the song text into Tok Pisin for Lila and me to then turn into English. The key phrase translated from Duna to Tok Pisin in that lament is the same as the one Kipu sings here— 'bai mi mekim wanem?' The texts also have in common the reference to Wakili as 'Waki Mbeta'. It is therefore possible that in the process of translation this phrase was brought to the fore for Kipu and then used word-for-word in the subsequent Tok Pisin lament.

Perhaps the most significant element of this *khene ipakana* that merges the indigenous and the exogenous is the reference to Christianity. The combination of introduced religious beliefs with indigenous song text styles has not been found in any of the other *khene ipakana* I have recorded to date. There are versions of *khene ipakana* that incorporate references to other practices associated with white people, for example references to the activities of the deceased, such as playing ball (which will be illustrated later, in Chapter 6 Example 6.12). These tie in well with the typical *khene ipakana* text format: Soti's lament discussed above shows that the recounting of activities is often an integral part of indigenous song texts; Kipu's reference to Wakili caring for her children is another example. References to Christianity however do not appear in this pre-contact musical form. It seems that in order to sing a mourning song for Wakili using concepts of Heaven and the Last Day, a song in a non-indigenous musical system (a song in 'lotu' style, no less) needs to be created. This would be important for a woman like Kipu who participates in both indigenous and non-indigenous religious practice.

This song however is not the only version. After creating it, Kipu translates it back into Duna language, creating a new song but maintaining the key elements of tonality and text of this introduced song style (Example 4.9). She even translates the Christian themes into related Duna ones, but does not go so far as to set these themes to ancestral music. Kipu sings the Duna word for heaven, *Epeni* (which is derived from the Tok Pisin/English 'Heven'/Heaven),[14] as a substitute for the 'Heven' of the Tok Pisin song. However, rather than singing directly of the 'Las De' as she does in the Tok Pisin version, Kipu translates this Christian

---

14 Duna words always end in open syllables (vowels), and so it is common for an introduced term to be pronounced similarly but with an additional vowel at the end, eg. 'i' in *Epeni*. *Epeni* is pronounced as a 'p' rather than a 'v' because there are no 'v's in Duna, and this is the closest to one.

concept in a way that reflects indigenous concepts of ground. She sings *rindi ita rorane*, which can be translated as the time 'the ground finishes'. Entropy is an important concept for the Duna—if certain moral behaviour is not practiced, the land (and people) naturally will become infertile, and eventually life as it is known to exist will be no more (Haley 2002a:161-163; see also Stewart and Strathern 2002b:36-37; see also Stewart and Strathern 2002b:ix-xi).

Example 4.8 (▶ Audio 17): Kipu's *khene ipakana* in Tok Pisin.

aiyo Waki Waki Mbeta	oh Waki Waki Mbeta
aiyo Waki Waki Mbeta	oh Waki Waki Mbeta
mi ya wari, wari tumas long yu	I worry, I worry a lot about you
bai mi mekim wanem?	what will I do?
bai mi lukim yu long Heven tasol	I will see you in Heaven only
aiyo Waki Waki Mbeta	oh Waki Waki Mbeta
aiyo Waki Waki Mbeta	oh Waki Waki Mbeta
mi ya wari, wari tumas long yu	I worry, I worry a lot about you
bai mi mekim wanem?	what will I do?
bai mi lukim yu long las de kamap	I will see you when the Last Day* comes

* 'Last Day' refers here to the Christian 'Judgement Day'.

Example 4.9 (▶ Audio 18): Kipu's *khene ipakana* based on Example 4.8, in Duna.

aiyo Waki Waki Mbeta	oh Waki Waki Mbeta
na kota konoya angu koyana	I worry about you only, here
na aki waipe?	what will I do?
na rindi ita rorane angu kenda	when the ground finishes I will see you only then
aiyo Waki Waki Mbeta	oh Waki Waki Mbeta
na kota konoya angu koyana	I worry about you only, here
na aki waipe?	what will I do?
Epeni angu kenda	in Heaven only will I see you

Stürzenhofecker observes in the Duna area of Aluni where she worked the 'intersection of mission teaching with local ideology' and says that '[t]he Apostolic Church teaches about the impending end of the world, of the ground, and this has not only impeded attempts to put the old beliefs to rest, but inadvertently contributed to their continuation' (Stürzenhofecker 1998:74-75). Other faiths also shared this same concern about the end of the world; however, it is significant that the Apostolic Church is particularly mentioned by Stürzenhofecker, as this is the church Kipu has attended for some years.[15]

In this recorded performance Kipu repeats the first verse twice, and the second verse is sung just once, making again a total length of four verses, with the final line of the second verse again repeated. It is notable that the opening line, '*aiyo Waki Waki Mbeta*', is not repeated in this Duna version, though it was in the Tok Pisin version. Repetition of opening lines is, as I discussed above, a feature of 'lotu' song (in both Tok Pisin and 'tok ples') and as such, the lack of repetition of the opening line here may support the notion that the Duna version is one step removed from its Christian/Tok Pisin counterpart—it is moving back to

---

15   After a falling-out with her husband's relatives and fellow Apostolic church-goers, Kipu now does not attend the Apostolic Church at Hirane but an offshoot of this church, the Christian Apostolic Fellowship (CAF) church located near Kopiago station.

the original *khene ipakana* from which it was inspired. However it could just be because this is the second singing of the song, and Waki Mbeta as the subject had been well established in the first rendition in Tok Pisin, so the repetition was redundant here.

Wakili's death—the verdict

Weiner observes of the Foi that

> in traditional times...*all* deaths apart from those of the very aged were considered to be caused by sorcery....The laments for deceased relatives always had this comprehension of the ubiquity of sorcery at their core, this understanding of death as the ultimate result of the concealed jealousies and hatreds of communal life. (Weiner 1991:78)

A similar belief in *tsuwake*, or witchcraft, as the cause of unexpected deaths continues to be held by the Duna (cf. Stewart and Strathern 2002b:xvi). The cause of Wakili's illness remains unknown. Many rumours surrounded her death, touched on in this chapter's opening statements. Court took place the day after her death, charging some of the male members of Kipu's household with 'fouling' (sexually molesting) Wakili, but the results of that court cleared the men of any wrong-doing and instead fined a group of women for gossip.[16] Thus, ultimately, witchcraft was given as the cause of Wakili's death, but by whom it was not told. In late 2003 suspicion of witchcraft had resulted in the torture of several women in the community, one who died from her severe injuries, and compensation for that event was still ongoing in 2005. People at this time then were especially mindful of the consequences of accusing—and being accused—of witchcraft.

Late in January 2007, Kepo's husband Sakane (with whom she had had a baby boy the previous year), died suddenly and unexpectedly. His relatives attributed his death to poisoning by Kepo's relatives, and revenge of a violent nature was sought (Kenny Kendoli, personal communication, 7 March 2007). Sakane's and Wakili's deaths (and the deaths of most other Duna people) are not seen as discrete events but are interlinked, and thus directly affect relations within the community. Death continues to affect people's relationships through inquests, and in personal memory, and this is reflected in song texts (as shall again be seen when I return to this topic in Chapter 6).

---

16   Village courts are the most common way for local disputes to be resolved in the Highlands of Papua New Guinea. They are public events, usually held outdoors and presided over by resident older male leaders (cf. Merlan and Rumsey 1986:74-76; Goddard 2000).

Conclusion

This chapter has shown a range of typical musical responses to grief by Duna people. As I have shown, these musical responses to grief are typically female responses, as they are in many other societies in the world. These mourning songs, or *khene ipakana* ('death songs') are somewhat varied in form due to the spontaneity of their composition, but generally they incorporate a melodic descent over two or three and a half tones, with a prolonged ending on the tonal centre, and are punctuated by exclamatory phrases naming the deceased or their kin relationship (for example *hakini kone* ('true sister')) while the body of the text often delivers questions to the deceased. *Khene ipakana yakaya* are one variety of *khene ipakana*, and are distinguished by the systematic naming (*yakaya*) of places, or items within the landscape, that relate to the life experience of the deceased. These are sung at varying degrees of distance from the event of death, either sung by one not close in relationship to the deceased (for example Pokole's lament analysed in this chapter, recorded on the night of Wakili's death), or one separated in time from the death (for example Kepo and Kipu's duet analysed here, recorded a week afterwards). As such, the delivery of *khene ipakana yakaya* is notably more composed than immediate responses to death by close family/friends (for example Kipu's lament). *Khene ipakana* are an example of strong musical creativity, albeit creativity under convention.

Kipu's modern *khene ipakana* examined in this chapter feature many of the conventions of the *khene ipakana* genre, and are equally—if not more—innovative. Though her songs utilise an exogenous musical system—diatonic and under the influence of 'lotu' song—they also utilise the characteristic exclamations and questions of the deceased. As far as I know from my fieldwork these modern songs were never performed in times of intense grief but in times of reflection and sadness. They are a step removed from the grief expressed in *khene ipakana yakaya*. As such, Kipu's modern songs do not replace the role of the established *khene ipakana* but are a complement to them. These newly composed songs show an individual bridging the world of the indigenous and the exogenous for her own ends. They are valuable evidence of the creative ability and the possibility—and actuality— of musical change.

5. Land and song

mei konenia, mei konenia	steep slope, steep slope
mei konenia, mei konenia	steep slope, steep slope
mei konenia, kalipopo	steep slope, Kalipopo
mei konenia	steep slope
imane yo	girl oh
ko wanda tiani sola alimbu kone leka suwano	if you come break a real cane grass stick and hold it

Scholars working in all parts of Papua New Guinea have written of the extraordinary relationships in the country between people and their place. The Kaluli people sing of the landscape and their relationship to it, particularly in the genre of *gisaro* (Schieffelin 1976; Feld 1982, 1988, 1996). A number of publications address the effect of mining on Papua New Guinean peoples living in the Highlands region, taking into account the close relationships between people and the land in these areas (Rumsey and Weiner 2001, 2004; Stewart and Strathern 2002b, 2004; Halvaksz 2003; Jorgensen 2004). Many other works could be recalled that examine these relationships, and in this chapter I will add to these explorations through my examination of Duna land in song.

As Basso observes:

> [N]ow and again, and sometimes without apparent cause, awareness is seized—arrested—and the place on which it settles becomes an object of spontaneous reflection and resonating sentiment. It is at times such as these, when individuals step back from the flow of everyday experience and attend self-consciously to places—when, we may say, they pause to actively sense them—that their relationships to geographical space are most richly lived and surely felt....Persons thus involved may also dwell on aspects of themselves, on sides and corners of their own evolving identities. (Basso 1996:54-55)

The majority of songs I have recorded by Duna people reference land in a manner that is integral to the expression of their identity. The expression of the relationship between people and their land in art forms such as music is acknowledged as an important part of the social process of identification. Basso 1996:57) continues:

> Relationships to places may also find expression through the agencies of myth, prayer, music, dance....[people] are forever performing acts that reproduce and express their own sense of place—and also, inextricably, their own understandings of who and what they are.

Thus, people not only reproduce and express their place through creative means, they change and manipulate their identity, their place, through such forms of expression.

Haley provides a comprehensive account of the Duna people's relationship to land, revealing its complexity. She (2002a:8–9) describes the relationship as an 'intimate connection' and goes on to say: 'For the Duna, identity is inextricably bound to land and to place.' Although the concept of a strong connection to place in Duna ancestral life is understood, place is important in contemporary Duna consciousness as well (see also Stewart and Strathern 2002b; Strathern and Stewart 2004). Haley explores this in her research into the projection of Bible stories (Christianity being a modern element of Duna life) onto the landscape of old. In this chapter, I discuss both older and newer forms of Duna music in relation to land—the praising (and derogating) of it, the fertility of it and movement through it. The latter half of the chapter focuses on the music in the Duna diasporic locations of Mount Hagen and Lae, and examines what happens to Duna music when it moves away from its home. This chapter relies less on musical analysis and more on the textual content of the songs. Through this type of comparative approach, I show how particular sentiments are maintained and expressed across the musical 'platforms' of ancestral and introduced styles.

The Duna and land

'For any cultural system', Basso (1996:89) reminds us, 'what counts as a "place" is an empirical question that must be answered ethnographically'. I hope to do so over the course of this chapter, through Duna voices in song. First, though, I would like to propose that, generally considered, there are four frames of identity to which the Duna relate in terms of land and place. It is important to note that these proposed frames of identity are not to be understood as discrete in themselves but rather as permeable, or as points on a sliding scale, and are of course affected by the context in which they are employed, figuring as a tension in space-time (see Munn 1986). I have labelled these frames, in order of weakest to strongest, as national, regional, local and parish. I will now examine each of these in turn, reflecting briefly on their manifestation in music.

The concept of a national identity is barely evident in Papua New Guinea, particularly for those who live and work outside Port Moresby and other major town centres. National identity is essentially a product of independence and is under conscious attempts at construction (Foster 1995:1; Toyoda 2006:32–3). There is little sense of a national collective and this could be due in part to the decline in the quality and extent of schooling—one of the main institutions for the inculcation of nationhood but which now reaches fewer children than ever. There is a sense of individual cultures, which can be grouped together regionally but not nationally. There is, however, a view of Papua New Guinea versus the rest of the world in development rhetoric that is employed by people throughout the country, particularly in places such as Kopiago with little in the way of services and infrastructure. Such development rhetoric is sometimes used in these cases to denigrate Papua New Guinea in comparison with other, more developed nations. Musically, this division between Papua New Guinea and the rest of the world is paramount in the language of musical styles that are essentially classified in Duna as *mindi ipakana* ('black song') and *khao ipakana* ('white song') as has been elaborated on earlier.

The second identity frame I consider here is the regional, or trans-Duna identity, here being a belonging to a pan-Highlands collective (and its sub-regions). A regional identity did not exist for most people prior to colonisation, mobility being minimal. This frame of identity manifests itself most clearly in the realm of introduced musical styles. Cassettes which now circulate at Kopiago include songs by various artists in a number of Papua New Guinean languages. These songs shape people's understanding of the world outside the Duna speaking area—especially the understanding of children, who have little experience away from home, and who are inclined to replicate these songs in their original languages. An example of this kind of song which evokes regions of Papua New Guinea is one in Tok Pisin by the K-Mala Band of Enga Province. The song is popular all around the country, including Kopiago, where it circulates on cassette only (radio is not available to most there). The chorus of this song has as its text:

pasin bilong meri Wabag	the way of Wabag women
pasim garas igo daun long baksait	is to tie their hair at the back
na kamap olsem meri Aroma	and become like Aroma women

This song references not one but two regions of the world outside Kopiago: the town of Wabag, which is the centre of Enga Province and where another Highlands ethnic group—Engans—live; and an ethnic group from the Papuan region of the country, Aroma, who originate from the coast in Central Province. In this way, regional impressions and distinctions are formed through popular songs. Duna listeners appear to identify themselves in this context with Wabag people as fellow Highlanders, in contrast to coastal people. The reference to coastal people evokes a national frame of identity.

Within the regional frame of identity, but somewhat sliding towards the local frame, are a number of sub-regions of identity. The Duna place within a Hela regional identity is an example of this, and is addressed by music most explicitly by recent music releases and the dedications within their liner notes and lyrics. These recent releases are part of the agitation for the formation of a separate Hela province made up of a number of language groups from the western area of what is now the Southern Highlands Province—primarily people from the electorates of Tari-Pori, Komo-Magarima and Koroba-Kopiago (Kaiabe 2006). The idea of a Hela Province is a political goal which was first mooted in the 1960s, and which continues to gain momentum in the new millenium. An example of such a release is the Pesaps album 'Souths Ame' (Pesaps n.d.), in which the liner notes dedicate the song *Huli Medley* 'to especially all the Hela Iginis' ('Hela sons'), the majority of Hela people being Huli speakers (Kaiabe 2006).

Another example of recent Hela musical expression is the 2004 release by a band known as 'Sounds of Hela'. Although all the songs on this album are either in Huli or Tok Pisin, the liner notes declare that 'The band brought up this musical style for Hela people around the country. Also to Hela people, "Noken kisim bagarap, stap isi, stap gut" ['don't get into trouble, be calm, be good'] and co-operate with each other' (Sounds of Hela 2004).

The third identity frame that can be considered I have termed 'local'. By this I mean to suggest that local areas, such as Kopiago, are distinguished from other Duna-speaking centres, such as Kelabo (refer to Figure 1.2). Dialect differences exist between these two particular regions, which are located at opposite ends of Duna-speaking country. People identify themselves—particularly when located outside the Duna area in a place such as Mount Hagen—with the centre that most clearly represents, or services, their home parish. For example, people of Hirane would identify themselves with Kopiago station. Interestingly, people from Awi, which is close to the border of Huli-speaking country, often identify themselves as coming from the larger centre of Pori, which is within the Huli area (people from this area of the country are usually fluent in both languages).

Once again, this local frame of identity is most clearly demarcated in introduced music, rather than ancestral genres, which are mostly concerned with expressing the parish frame of identity and its subdivisions. In this local frame, areas within Duna country can be represented in the form of particular musical bands. This representation manifests itself in the musicians who form the band, and regularly the local frame of identity is also apparent in the band names. For example, the Christian band Muller Hill Gospel Singers, identified with the Kelabo area, named themselves after the Muller Range, which is a landmark feature in the area. Their second album, representing their debut into the popular music industry, was released under the name Ramula Bitz. This new name is a combination of two place names from very different regions in Papua

New Guinea: Rabaul ('Ra-') and Muller Range ('-mula') (the 'Bitz' part of the name appears to derive from the English 'beach'). Two of the band members—brothers—have mixed parentage from these two regions. It is not uncommon for Papua New Guinean bands to name themselves after a prominent feature of their home landscape. The Giluwe Rebels are another example (Webb 1993:86), Giluwe being the highest mountain in the Southern Highlands Province and the second-highest mountain in Papua New Guinea. In the case of Ramula Bitz, not only is the local identity strongly evoked in the band's title, the references to Rabaul, and the beach, again evoke a national identity.

Finally, within the most fundamental frame, and that which is clearly evident in song, the Duna describe place in terms of parishes (for example, Hirane) and the particular areas (for example, the slopes of Hirane known as Kalisanda, or 'Kalipopo') and features (for example, Hirane's Rewapi creek) within those parishes. There are at least two clans, known in Duna as *imaau'wa* (Haley 2002a: xxix), within each parish (*rindi*). For example, Hirane parish is made up of three clans: Saiya, Mberia and Haperia (Haley 2002a, vol. 2:7).

A person's parish identity, when a singular parish is declared, is often the place where they currently reside, or have resided the longest. However, Duna parish identities are multiple. The Duna social structure is one of cognatic descent, and as such, 'Duna men and women can maintain membership in more than one clan at any particular time. Accordingly many individuals and families maintain gardens and, in some cases, houses in more than one territory' (Haley 2002a:137). Duna persons very often have four parish identities: two inherited from their paternal grandparents (FF, FM) and two from their maternal grandparents (MM, MF). One's spouse usually comes from another parish, certainly from another clan,[1] but if this were not the case, then there would be less than four parishes with which they would identify. These parish identities are very important in determining a person's land rights. A Duna person might have an additional parish identity, for example if they settle in a place where neither their mother nor father has lived; however this relocation does not usually entail land rights (though some rights can be activated through working within that parish and/ or participating in its economy such as contributing to bride-price payments). A woman or man marrying and settling outside the community is a perfect example of a situation that creates an additional parish identity (Stürzenhofecker 1998: 90). Often, however, relocation occurs which draws upon affiliation to that land

---

1   In pre-contact times, marrying within one's *rindi* meant that compensation had to be paid, and if it was not, a person would be punished. It was considered 'tambu' (forbidden) at this time to marry within one's clan. Things appear to have become less rigid since European contact and there are several people who have married within their own clan (Richard Alo, Personal communication, 6 September 2006).

beyond the parents' or grandparents' generations (for further discussion on the complexity of Duna social structure, taking the Aluni Valley as its departure point, see Strathern and Stewart 2004:25-52).

Parish identities are clearly stated in numerous songs created by the Duna—those of ancestral origin and those that are influenced by introduced music. This will become more apparent as this chapter, and this publication, progresses. Groups of musicians have also named themselves after parishes: Richard Alo's stringband which was formed at Kopiago in the 1980s was named 'Auwi sola' ('Auwi cane grass') after the plant that grows at Auwi creek located within Mbara (this band will be further discussed towards the end of this chapter).[2] This is his mother's parish and is located next to his parish of residence (Aiyuguni) (Richard Alo, Personal communication, 18 June 2006). Multiple parish identities are evident most clearly in *khene ipakana*, as revealed in Chapter 4.

Through the textual analysis of a number of Duna songs, this chapter draws attention to the permeability of these proposed frames of identity. Such songs can be seen as one way in which many of the Duna at Kopiago now experience life outside of their immediate community, in the face of limited transport opportunities such as a neglected highway (as explored in Chapter 3) and the increasing price of air fares (described towards the end of this chapter in Example 5.21). I begin my analysis by examining the parish frame of identity more closely, with songs that name parishes, and their subdivisions, and that utilise the *kẽiyaka* for these places.

Land *kẽiyaka*

Invoking place names is 'a central feature of Papuan poetry' (Weiner 1991:6), including that of Duna. Haley (2002a:117–23) has written of the importance of place names to the Duna, how these names can reveal characteristics of the land, how they can reference actual events which have occurred, and the reciprocal relationship these place names often have to personal names. Haley (2002a:123–4) also describes how a place usually has several names, and that a parish is known by several *kẽiyaka* which have particular patronymic and matronymic prefixes that can be applied to it, and consequently to the people from that parish.

Place name *kẽiyaka* as they appear in Duna song are alternative names for a given place (for example a parish). They can occur singularly or consecutively in parallel lines or verses. Through these sequences of juxtaposed lines or

---

2   The Auwi Sola band is reported to have played at night at the 'hausman' near Auwi creek. In this way the old and the new would be united.

verses that list the different places where a person has lived or with which they are associated over their lifetime—such as the verses which make up *ipakana yakaya*—the singer creates an impression of movement through landscape, as will be discussed shortly. Like the place names used in the songs of the Kaluli (Feld 1996:102-03), the Duna therefore can create actual trails through song.

Place references expressed in ordinary language and as praise names are evident in *awenene ipakana* such as *ipakana yakaya*, *yekia*, *selepa*, and *pikono*. However, they are also evident in contemporary song. In a later section of this chapter entitled 'Moving through the landscape', several examples of contemporary songs that use *kēiyaka* for places will be drawn on.

Praising (and denigrating) land

Traditional Duna musical forms listing the *kēiyaka* of places have as one function the praising of the land which they are singing about, hence the translation of this term as 'praise names'. Example 5.1 is a *mali mapu*, a ceremonial dance genre with sung text, whose primary function is to praise land.[3] The text of this song was provided by Robert Kendoli, whose father is from Aiyuguni, hence the reference to Ania mountain, part of which is in that parish. Any of the men from that area can form the necessary group to sing this song and praise their land by evoking its dramatic scenery.

Example 5.1: *mali mapu* text.

waiya ralua na wanda nawayanda na riya	*waiya ralua* rain will come or it will not come, (the mountain) it tells us
noya *mina* aupa	my *mina* Ania is getting dark
amina aupa	*amina* Ania is getting dark
arange aupa	*arange* Ania is getting dark

There is also a hidden meaning in addition to the literal. A man in the performing group may look at a woman whilst singing this *mali mapu* to make his feelings, and the hidden meaning, known to her, as if he were asking her: 'Are you going to cry or not? It looks like your face is downcast/dark' (Richard Alo, Personal communication, 26 July 2006).

Yekia courting songs also have as a core function the praising of land (Example 5.2):

---

3   This *mali mapu* was not performed for recording but rather recited as an example of this genre, and then discussed. A performance would require a number of men and a clear space, and these conditions were not available at the home in Mount Hagen where this discussion took place. Hence I am unable to provide a musical transcription of it.

Example 5.2 (▶ Audio 19): *yekia.*

heka *upia* nginitia *ralu* sopara *upia* rata phakanania ripurane kena	sons of *upia* bird of paradise *ralu* place down there, bird of paradise sits and will fly, early in the morning you will see
rano *upia* rata phakanania ripurane kena-o	Rano *upia* bird of paradise sits and will fly, early in the morning you will see
erano upia rata phakanania ripurane kena-o, aiyo ai.	erano Rano *upia* bird of paradise sits and will fly, early in the morning you will see, *aiyo ai.*

The phrase *heka upia nginitia* is used to address men from the parish of Aluni. My collaborator Richard Alo is addressed with the singular form of this, *heka upia ngini*, as his father's mother (FM) comes from that parish.[4] *Upia* is the praise name for a particular bird of paradise, and *ralu* the praise name for 'place'. The river Rano, which creates the border between Aluni and the parish of Horaile, is listed, followed in the next line by its praise name, *erano*.

The song describes the birds of Aluni, which can be seen early in the morning. There is also a hidden meaning within this song. It addresses the Aluni boys, telling them that the girls of Aluni (signified by the birds) who live near Rano river, go to the garden early in the morning. It suggests if the boys want to see them, they too must go out early. Flying is a reference to the movement of their grass skirts.

In singing about the girls from Aluni in this way, using the praise names for people of the parish of Aluni and the place of Rano, the singer is praising or promoting this ground. Often, in the context of courting, such a verse would be sung by a man from this parish of Aluni, who wants to express the positive attributes of his place in order to attract a bride to his parish. However, as in this case, it can also be sung by someone from another parish, who might like to praise the girls from Aluni and encourage other men to pursue them, or who would like to reveal to an Aluni woman listening that he is interested in her.

New song styles can also have the function of praising land. Example 5.3 with its repetitive refrain *mei konenia* ('steep slope', after which this publication is entitled) serves to praise the area within Hirane known as Kalisanda, which slopes down to the shore of Lake Kopiago (see Figure 5.1). Here the area is known by its affectionate nickname 'Kalipopo', so named in the 1980s after the neighbourhood of Kalibobo in the seaside town of Madang, Papua New Guinea,

---

4   A person usually has several praise names, due to the multiple parish identities they inherit. Generally people with that same parish identity call the person by the name pertaining to that parish. For example, Richard Alo lists his praise names as *kulu ngini* (for the parish of Yalia, where his FF comes from), *heka upia nane* (for the parish of Aluni, where his FM comes from), and *kayako nane* (for the parish of Mbara, where his MF and MM comes from. Richard's friend Kenny Kendoli, who has Aluni heritage, would call Richard *heka upia nane*, whilst someone from Yalia would greet him as *kulu ngini*, and another from Mbara would acknowledge him as *kayako nane.*

which also fronts the water—albeit an altogether different kind. The place Kalibobo became particularly well known across Papua New Guinea through the popularity of the Kalibobo Bamboo Band, whose two cassettes were hugely popular in the late 1970s and early 1980s, often being played in the stores of Mendi and Tari (Steven Feld, Personal communication, 28 February 2008). In this way a kind of modern *kēiyaka* for a Hirane land feature has been created, and a national frame of identity is also gently evoked.

Example 5.3 (▶ Audio 20): *'mei konenia'*.

mei konenia, mei konenia	steep slope, steep slope
mei konenia, mei konenia	steep slope, steep slope
mei konenia, kalipopo	steep slope, Kalipopo
mei konenia	steep slope
imane yo	girl oh
ko wanda tiani sola alimbu kone leka suwano	if you come break a real cane grass stick and hold it

This version was sung unaccompanied by a group of young women; however, it is likely that the song was originally composed for a local Duna stringband. Incidentally, this song is built on the same melodic and harmonic formula as the Christian song style introduced in Chapter 3 with the song *'nane laip senis nganda waya keina'* (Example 3.4). It is yet another musical example that supports the finding that Christian and secular songs inform each other.

This song can also be compared to Example 6.7 of Chapter 6 which also uses the phrase *sola alimbu leka suwano* ('break a cane grass stick and hold it'). This phrase describes the need for a walking stick, in this case made of the local cane grass, to climb up the steep slopes of Kalipopo. The song presents the steep slopes as a distinguishing feature of the area—the praise arises as other areas nearby do not have such a dramatic and impressive land feature.

Steep slopes can also mean unproductive or fragile land, land that is difficult to traverse. The fact that the girl who is desired might struggle to walk to Kalipopo unless she takes a walking stick may well be a deterrent for her. The following song, which begins in Tok Pisin[5] and then moves to Duna, declares that once the girl in question has seen Kalipopo, she will return to where she comes from as she will be dissuaded by its steep slope. The praise name for *rindi*—*ralu*—is used which gives added emphasis to the singer's place, as it does in other song examples.

---

5   The text for the first verse of this song is an adaptation of the chorus of the song 'Kerema', released by the band Hollie Maea in 1990 and sung by Robert Oeka, whose lyrics are: 'Maunten wara bilong Kerema miks wantaim solawara/Kerema yu no save, yu yet kam na lukim' (the mountain water of Kerema mixes with the ocean/Kerema you do not know, you yourself come and see). Kerema is a coastal town and the provincial centre of Gulf Province—again, part of a national framework.

Figure 5.1: Kalisanda, or 'Kalipopo'.

Example 5.4 (▶ Audio 21): 'maunten wara bilong kalipopo'.

maunten wara bilong kalipopo	the mountain water of Kalipopo
go miks wantaim L.K.	mixes with Lake Kopiago
yu no save, yu yet kam na lukim em (x3)	you do not know, you yourself come and see it
imane apona	girl over there
kalipopo nakeyatiani	if you haven't seen Kalipopo
ipa rokania ipa apona	water aplenty, water over there
keyata ko riyanda	look and you will want to go back (home)
no ralu kalipopo mei konenia	my *ralu* place Kalipopo is a steep slope
imane apona	girl over there
kalipopo nakeyatiani	if you haven't seen Kalipopo
no ralu mei konenia	my *ralu* place is a steep slope
keyata ko riyana	look and you will go back (home)
imane apona	girl over there
kalipopo mei konenia	Kalipopo is a steep slope
keyata ko riyana	look and you will go back (home)

Such a negative song seems to effectively discourage girls from marrying into the place described. However, one Duna man, however, explained that even though a man might express such views in song, the girl to whom he directs his singing would still come to live with him, as she would have already made a promise to him that she would do so (Lepani Kendoli, Personal communication., 14 July 2006). Richard Alo supports this sentiment as he claims that when a woman hears her lover singing a song which denigrates his place, she will become even more enamoured of him and dismiss the poor qualities of his land, choosing to remain with him (Richard Alo, Personal communication, 24 July 2006). In effect these songs, and others like them, are a test of the woman's love: even though her lover's land might be poor, if she truly loves him she will marry him anyway.

It is not only new styles of song which give voice to negative sentiments about one's own place. Many *yekia* courting songs too have such content, inducing the same 'sori' (Tok Pisin for 'sympathy') effect in the women who are listening. Such negative *yekia* are likened to popular songs such as Example 5.4, the two genres having been described as 'wankain' ('one and the same') though they have 'narapela nek' ('a different melody') (Lepani Kendoli, Personal communication, 14 July 2006).

The *yekia* that is Example 5.5 describes the men of Hirane parish calling out to the women of Hagini parish to rouse themselves and move to Hirane to be with them, but the women choose to marry elsewhere.

Example 5.5 (▶ Audio 22): *yekia.*

riyata ole alandorane <u>kolo</u> wanetia <u>ralu</u> sopana pawa miniya ima mininda rutia waleso	we sang out in the afternoon to the *kolo* Hagini daughters' *ralu* place below in the yard, 'move, women come and move (to Hirane)' but they married
<u>hora</u> pawa miniya ima mininda rutia waleso	*hora* Hirane, the yard, 'move, women come and move (to Hirane)' but they married
<u>akura</u> pawa miniya ima mininda rutia waleso	*akura* Hirane, the yard, 'move, women come and move (to Hirane)' but they married

Haley (2008:225–6) argues that these *yekia* of negative sentiment, where men in particular decry their place, are becoming more frequent at Kopiago due to the displacement of Duna masculinity in the present day. However, the denigration of person and place—recognised by some as the rhetorical device of meiosis—is a common and established device used in courting songs throughout the Highlands of Papua New Guinea (cf. Strathern 1974), as shall be discussed in Chapter 6, and these songs should be considered in that light.

The food of place

There are many examples of food references in both traditional and newer forms of Duna song. One example which has already been considered is Soti Mbulu's *ipakana heya* of Chapter 4. In one of his verses he refers to the deceased Wakili as having cared for the sweet potato mounds, and asking if she will come back to tend them again. *Yekia* courting songs, too, often have food as a central theme—typically the enticing of a wife through depicting the land as rich and fertile:

Example 5.6 (▶ Audio 23): *yekia.*

<u>kolo</u> nginitia <u>ralu</u>, <u>kolo</u> nginitia <u>ralu</u> sopara kolo iri ruwanokua nakeyao mbatia reipe?	the *kolo* nut pandanus Horaile sons' *ralu* place, the *kolo* nut pandanus Horaile sons' *ralu* place down below has plenty of *kolo* nut pandanus, I could tell you but are there some here who haven't seen it?
<u>rano</u> <u>anga</u> <u>kolo</u> iri ruwanokua nakeyao mbatia reipe?	the *rano* Horaile place down below has plenty of *anga kolo* nut pandanus, I could tell you but are there some here who haven't seen it?
<u>erano</u> <u>anga</u> <u>kolo</u> iri ruwanokua nakeyao mbatia reipe? aiyo ai.	the *erano* Horaile place down below has plenty of *anga kolo* nut pandanus, I could tell you but are there some here who haven't seen it? *aiyo ai.*

This *yekia* verse (Example 5.6) was sung for recording by a man named Jim Siape, who has already married a woman from the parish of Horaile. It appears that not only is he literally praising Horaile as being a place with many nut pandanus trees, but that he is praising the many girls that can be found there (represented by the common metaphor of nut pandanus).[6] The singer may have as one of his intentions the encouragement of the other men at the *yekia* to follow his example and marry from there.

Selepa courting songs can also refer to food (Example 5.7):

Example 5.7 (▶ Audio 24): *selepa*.

hiru hama noma hutia waru pina haya akupa	this *hiru* clearing used for fighting is full of mud so get your net and catch *haya* fish
lope waru pina haya akupa	*lope* Kaguane is full of mud so get your net and catch *haya* fish
kalope waru pina haya akupa, ee ai ai.	*kalope* Kaguane is full of mud so get your net and catch *haya* fish, *ee ai ai.*

The verse describes the ground as so muddy that you could catch fish in it as if it is a lake (Kenny Kendoli, Personal communication, 25 July 2006). Thus it praises Kaguane as being a fertile land with much food to offer.

The *selepa* verse that followed this one in this recorded performance (Example 5.8) asks the woman if she has the skills to break up the materials in order to make a fishing ring to catch the *haya* fish in Lake Kopiago (see Figure 5.2).

Example 5.8 (▶ Audio 25): *selepa*.

yangoli-o aku lekanatia, ko koneipe?	woman, to break the fishing ring, do you know how?
kapia haya aku lekanatia, ko koneipe?	*kapia* Lake Kopiago *haya* fish, to break the fishing ring, do you know how?
kapiako haya aku lekanatia, ko koneipe? ee ai ai.	Lake Kopiago *haya* fish, to break the fishing ring, do you know how? *ee ai ai.*

The composer of this *selepa* verse, Kenny Kendoli, explained to me that he was employing parable talk: when asking the woman if she knows how to work with the fishing ring, he is implying that if she doesn't, he will show her—thus they would come together as a pair of lovers. Exactly the same sentiment, but with regard to catching fish in the hand rather than a net, is expressed in the stringband song beginning with the line '*ipa auwi karuya raroko*' presented later in this chapter under the discussion of diasporic song.

Kahn (1996:175) writes of the Wamira of Papua New Guinea that hunger for them is not only a physical state but an emotional one. Feld (1982:27–8) and

---

6   The figure of the nut pandanus is a common way of alluding to women in Duna song, often used to refer to their genitalia, particularly when the nut is described as ripe and exposed with the breaking open of its hard covering to reveal the soft fleshy meat within. *Yekia* is full of such sexual metaphor, as many other Duna song genres also are.

Schieffelin (1976:26–7, 72) report the same for the Kaluli. It is also the case for the Duna. Food production is tied up in social relationships with others—those who help work the garden and those who eat the produce—and to be without family is to be without food (and vice versa).

Stewart and Strathern (2002a:77) support the view of food production being central to relationships (and relationships encompassing death) when they write: 'Being with people means making gardens, producing food, and sharing in its consumption, and death is the negation of this process. The Duna people have made this fact central to their courting songs'. Of course, the importance of food for relationships extends beyond courting: consolidating relationships through eating together, or providing another with food, is often evident in the oral stories of the Duna such as *pikono*.

It appears that missionaries realised early on the importance of food in relationships and they used this connection when composing songs to entice people to Jesus. This can be seen in the following Christian song, which begins with the repetitive refrain *Yesu epo* (Example 5.10). It contains comparisons between knowing Jesus and eating the traditional Duna foods of pig and (more recently) chicken, claiming that those foods are not sweet (*epo* being similar to the Tok Pisin sense of the term 'swit', also meaning 'tasty') when compared to Jesus. The third verse, in this version sung by Duna people living in Mount Hagen, opens up to include foods of far-away regions.

Figure 5.2: Duna fishing ring, Lake Kopiago.

Example 5.9 is the opening lines of a woman's *pikono* recorded in 2005; its text clearly shows the link between the orphan girl's lack of family and lack of food.

Example 5.9 (▶ Audio 26): *pikono.*

(translation provided by Lila San Roque)

paye imane ndu kho pi hanga raonorua rita	right, there was a girl living there it's said
imane ndu kho pi kho antia hinia nariya-o	the girl she didn't know her mother
kho apa hinia nariya-o	she didn't know her father
kho hanga raonorua rita	she lived there it's said
kho hanga rao rita-a	she lived there it's said
kho raoka raoka raoka raokaya hapia rao ayu rao hapia rao	she was staying staying staying she lived before she lived then she lived before
ayu raoya hanga raoka po	then she was living there making her life
kho hina pi hinia naraya-o	she had no sweet potato
mbou pi ndu naraya-o	no garden either
hina khei pi ndu naraya home po	no sweet potato runners either and that's how it was
kho antia amene homerape sako	she didn't know about her mother and father
kho hanga raonorua rita-o	she lived there it's said

Example 5.10 (▶ Audio 27): *'Yesu epo'.*

Yesu epo Yesu epo	Jesus is sweet Jesus is sweet
Yesu epo Yesu epo	Jesus is sweet Jesus is sweet
Yesu epo kupalini konera	Jesus is sweet my true love
Yesu epo	Jesus is sweet
ita nayaroko epo neyana	when I eat pig it is not sweet
heka nayaroko epo neyana	when I eat chicken it is not sweet
Yesu epo kupalini konera	Jesus is sweet my true love
Yesu epo (x2)	Jesus is sweet (x2)
Madang taro *nayaroko epo neyana*	when I eat Madang taro it is not sweet
Sepik saksak *nayaroko epo neyana*	when I eat Sepik sago it is not sweet
Yesu epo kupalini konera	Jesus is sweet my true love
Yesu epo	Jesus is sweet

Another version of this song contains a verse which substitutes pig and chicken for the processed and extremely desirable (and, in Kopiago, unobtainable) brand-name foods Ramu Sugar and Oksapmin Honey:

Ramu suga *nayaroko epo neyana*	when I eat Ramu sugar it is not sweet
Oksi honi *nayaroko epo neyana*	when I eat Oksapmin honey it is not sweet
Yesu epo kupalini konera	Jesus is sweet my true love
Yesu epo	Jesus is sweet

So, references to food have been maintained in the Duna Christian repertoire throughout social (and dietary) change, encompassing foods grown at home, imported, or experienced in other provinces.

Introduced song styles, sung by both men and women, can also complain of a land's lack of food (Example 5.11).

Example 5.11 (▶ Audio 28): *'kalipopo nane rokania'*.

kalipopo nane rokania	Kalipopo has many boys
imane nduna kho wanda konotiani	if a woman thinks to come and marry
ko hutiani homo wamo ruwanda ko wayeni	if you come and say this and that (is not good about me), you cannot come
ko hutiani aki kone noaepe? riya ko yauna	if you come, what will you eat? they will ask, you will cry (from hunger)
ko hutiani ko hutiani	if you come, if you come
ko hutiani aki kone noaepe? riya ko yauna	if you come, what will you eat? they will ask, you will cry (from hunger)

Again, by describing one's place negatively, sympathy in the listener is elicited. Kalipopo might not have a lot of food to offer, but if the song is effective in its intent as a song of enticement, she will come anyway, with or without her walking stick of cane grass (refer here again to Example 5.3).

Moving through the landscape

As was discussed earlier in this chapter, and as has been seen in Chapter 4, *khene ipakana* is a song genre that moves through the landscape by listing various places of that person's life in juxtaposed verses. However, there are more literal ways of moving through the landscape in Duna song. The genre *pikono* usually involves a journey of some description, in which convention necessitates the recounting of a number of places and the *kēiyaka* of these places (the process of *ipakana yakaya*) through which the protagonist travels. There are also snapshots of sub-journeys within these broader frameworks: in one *pikono* the singer Kiale

Yokona describes the setting sun, reciting all the names of the places where the last rays of sun fall (see Figure 5.3). Example 5.12 represents the first segment of an almost four minute description.

The same *pikono* contains an *ipakana yakaya* sequence that refers to Rabaul, Bougainville and Port Moresby (Example 5.13). Such references would not have occurred in pre-contact times, as the knowledge of such far away places was not readily available.

Figure 5.3: sun setting over the Highlands.

Example 5.12 (▶ Audio 29): *pikono.*

(translation provided by *Lila San Roque)*

*horame rane yarita**	so it was it's heard
ake naneka imane ngana pi kono imaneka naneka ngana pi konoyaroko	what then, the boys thinking the girls would leave first, the girls thinking that the boys would leave first
ulu alu wapena kho honga neya yarita	the *ulu alu* wape sun was no longer near it's heard
etona marapia mburipi nene rao apoya kata	it went across and sat down over on the peak of *marapia mburipi* Kunai mountain
etona yarita kaka kayiamba rao etoya kata	across it's heard sitting at Kaka mountain at Kayiamba mountain

kiraya epana wuandu aporane yarita	burning across there blazing over it's heard
rina yarita epana yarita-e	it's heard over there it's heard
[audience member: peta kana wane]	*[peta kana* Aluni daughters]
kira aporane alu ali ruwata rana	burning over and then at the place of the one called *Alu Ali*
yawa yapale ndu po kuru poko etoya kata	leaping across to a *yawa yapale* Aku place of mine
pari pere ndu po kuru poko etoya kata	leaping across to a *pari pere* Aku place of mine
apona piri pere ndu po kuru poko etoya kata	leaping over and across to a *piri pere* Aku place of mine

* The word yarita is a very common one in pikono, often punctuating the end of lines. It has here been translated as 'it's heard': essentially the word identifies the singer of the pikono as a third person, someone who has heard this story from another, rather than having experienced it first-hand, the suggestion being that the pikono is a story being told now about things from the distant past that have been described before). (cf. Gillespie and San Roque forthcoming.

Example 5.13 (▶ Audio 30): *pikono.*

(translation provided by *Lila San Roque*)

ngayeni yarita	going yet it's heard
reke epa kona singata keyaroko-o-m	they reach an outcrop and look around
wana raya ipa solowarana raya etona ripu ripai ngorane keyaroko	the ocean sitting there stretching on and on and they look across the white-capped waves
anga wane opo ndu potia rao eto	the daughters opo Rabaul ones of mine sitting on the other side
kokopo ndu potia rao eto	*kokopo* Rabaul ones of mine sitting on the other side
etona lapalo ndu potia rao etotiana	across there the lapalo Rabaul ones of mine sitting on the other side
anga wane lapulu ndu potia rao etotiana-e	the daughters *lapulu* Rabaul ones of mine sitting on the other side
hoyaki keya etona ke eto keyaroko	looking back to this side and looking over to the other side
repe nepetia khunuya etona kiata ndu potia rao etotiana	the ones with white eyes white teeth across there the *kiata* Bougainville ones of mine sitting on the other side
etona kiata panguna ndu potia rao apotiana	across there *kiata panguna* Bougainville ones of mine sitting away over there
etoyaki yarita etoyaki sura kepo sapura ndu potia rao etotiana-e	the far side it's heard on the far side *sura kepo sapura* Port Moresby ones of mine sitting on the other side

So the reciting of locations in *pikono* is not restricted to local places. In its listing of these foreign places the above excerpt of this *pikono* recalls to mind a Christian song which describes travelling to Rabaul, Ok Tedi, Mount Hagen, Port Moresby in order to escape inevitable death. The relevant verses are reproduced here (Example 5.14).

Example 5.14 (▶ Audio 31): *'ipa sipi sayata'.*

ipa sipi sayata Rabaul ngutiani	if you go on a ship to Rabaul
khene ko pi wanania	death will come with you
antia kone antia Yesu sanda	mother, real mother, get Jesus
riya wano	turn back and come
(x2)	
heka mbaluta Hagen ngutiani	if you go on a plane to Hagen
khene ko pi wanania	death will come with you
antia kone antia Yesu sanda	mother, real mother, get Jesus
riya wano	turn back and come
sia hatiata Ok Tedi ngutiani	if you go by foot to Ok Tedi
khene ko pi wanania	death will come with you
khane kone khane Yesu sanda	brother, real brother, get Jesus
riya wano	turn back and come
heka mbaluta Hagen ngutiani	if you go on a plane to Hagen
khene ko pi wanania	death will come with you
khane kone khane Yesu sanda	brother, real brother, get Jesus
riya wano	turn back and come
Air Niuginita Mosbi ngutiani	if you go with Air Nuigini to Moresby
khene ko pi wanania	death will come with you
khane kone khane Yesu sanda	brother, real brother, get Jesus
riya wano	turn back and come

Contemporary songs are, however, not only about far away places or experiences. Example 5.15, composed by teenager Rodney Kenny and sung for recording by him and his peers, is a typical short song praising home by setting it at the end of a journey and showing a feeling of 'sori'—in this case understood to be 'an exclamation of gladness' (Mihalic 1971:180–1)—at arriving there.

Example 5.15 (▶ Audio 32): *'ipa ikili mbiteya'.*

ipa ikili mbiteya karia kendei rakiya	cross water Ikili, go over Mount Kendei
ipa rano mbiteya ipa tumbutu mbiteya	cross water Rano, cross water Tumbutu
karia pauwa rakiya singa romara	go over Mount Pauwa and arrive up
sori-o no <u>ralu</u> <u>pakura</u> singa romara	oh! to my *ralu* place *pakura* Hirane arrive up

Another version recorded six weeks later shows minor textual changes: it replaces 'sori-o' with *singa romara*, and *pakura* with two other praise names for Hirane, *auwi* and *yungu*. This is further evidence to support the argument (highlighted at various points throughout this text) that the song texts of the Duna, both of ancestral and introduced origins, are in a continuous state of flux.

Other songs are stories of attempts made by people to leave their home, but for various reasons, such as the journey being too difficult (or expensive), or the feeling for home too strong, are unable to. Example 5.16, recorded with some of the same young boys, combines both sentiments.

Example 5.16 (▶ Audio 33): *'akalu nene nene keno raroko'.*

akalu nene nene keno raroko	on top of (Mount) Akalu we two sit down
wia peretia hewa karia pima apima wia peretia	slope across, the Hewa mountains Pima and Apima slope across
nganda ruwata ngayaroko	we say we are going, we try to go
hatia ukarua oro daro hatia ukarua	the road is long between Oro and Mount Daro, the road is long
kono kandora	our thoughts (to go) were cut
kono kandora no rindi auwi yungu kono kandora	our thoughts (to go) were cut, our land *auwi yungu* Hirane, our thoughts (to go) were cut
sokomaro	the view
sokomaro akalu nene kata sokomaro	the view from on top of Akalu where we are, the view
si bruk a noya auwi yungu si bruk a	the waves break at my *auwi yungu* Hirane, the waves break

The feeling of nostalgia in regard to place has been addressed by a number of scholars (cf. Schieffelin 1976:179; Weiner 1991; Basso 1996:54). In particular, one scholar of Duna, Stürzenhofecker, writes of this sentiment as it pertains to women. She writes that women's nostalgia for their natal place is expressed by the composition of song about various localities of that place (Stürzenhofecker 1998:151). According to her, women are only united with their natal place after death, that is if they move away during marriage (Stürzenhofecker 1998:97). In the context of this reference Stürzenhofecker is no doubt writing of ancestral song, though in my experience the composition of newer styles of song also expresses this kind of nostalgia. This is evident in the musical examples shown in this chapter.

Songs of journeys are popular both at home in Kopiago and away, as will be reiterated in the following section. A common element of the journey song is the arrival of a letter, which instigates the journey or experience. This next song was composed by a young man Lepani Kendoli in the town of Mount Hagen to illustrate the journey undertaken by myself and Lila to reach our fieldsite of Hirane (Example 5.17). Although no letters were actually written summoning us to travel to Hirane, poetic licence was taken by Lepani to fit the story to the familiar plot motivation.

Example 5.17 (▶ Audio 34): *'Kirsty Lila ne anene'*.

Kirsty Lila ne anene Mosbi karoko	Kirsty and Lila the pair at Port Moresby
pepa *yapa pi home kata nariya singa romatia*	two letters, from where they did not know, arrived up there
Kirsty Lila ne kheno Mosbi kheno raroko	Kirsty and Lila the pair were sitting at Port Moresby
pepa *yapa pi Mosbi kata singa romatia*	two letters to Port Moresby arrived up ther
pepata *sata keyaroko*	they got the letters and looked at them
anene pi yungupakura kone wano rirarua	the two to *yungu pakur*a Hirane true must come, the letters said
(x2)	
home rirane aneneka	like this they (the letters) said, the pair
Mosbi siti *ya Mount Hagen e kone singa romatia*	(left) Port Moresby and to Mount Hagen true they came up
ane(ne) singaya M.A.Fta	the pair arriving up, to MAF
wanania yaroko L.K. kone hongo are neya rita	they came and asked, L.K. is not near they were told
home rirane	like this they (MAF) said
singa romaya Kopiago kone singa romara	arriving up there to Kopiago, arrived up there
singa romaya	arriving up there
singa romaya aku(ra) <u>*rewapi*</u> *kone singa romara*	arriving up there at night to *rewapi* Hirane true, arrived up there
home rirane	like this they said
home porane no <u>*auwi yungutia*</u> *siya reina*	like this it happened, my *auwi yungu* Hirane people hold them
home horane	like this they came
home horane <u>*auwi yungu*</u> *nginitiaka siya reina*	like this they came, the *auwi yungu* Hirane sons hold them

Thus Lepani has myself and Lila moving through the frames of identity from the national, starting at Port Moresby, to the regional as we arrive at Mount Hagen in the centre of the Highlands region, on to the local area of Kopiago by plane, and then finally arriving at our parish location of Hirane where we are welcomed by our friends. I will now consider movement in the other direction— the Duna who have travelled away from their home parishes and settled outside.

The Duna diaspora

Despite the close connection Duna people have to the place of their birth and of their family, a sizeable number of Duna now live outside their home communities. Reasons for relocating are many, and the period of time that they stay away is variable, from a few weeks up to several years, or even a lifetime. The most populous Duna diasporic communities in Papua New Guinea are known to be in the cities of Port Moresby, Lae, and Mount Hagen, and the mining communities of Tabubil, Ok Tedi, and Porgera. In 1983 Nicholas Modjeska produced a radio program using recordings made by Don Niles of stringband and *yekia* of the Duna settlement at Six Mile in Port Moresby, which showed even then a musically active diasporic community (see Modjeska 1983).[7]

In this section I will consider the general nature of such migration in Papua New Guinea, the kind of music which results from this experience, and then I will profile the Duna diasporic groups in Mount Hagen and Lae with whom I have spent time in between my travels to their home area of Kopiago. These friends have sung many songs for recording, and I will examine some of these songs here.

Of course, the Duna are not the only language group in Papua New Guinea to undertake migration in large numbers. There is ample literature in the fields of anthropology and human geography (not to mention the research of statisticians in Papua New Guinea) which addresses the phenomenon of migration (see for example May 1977; Goddard 2001; Umezaki and Ohtsuka 2003). A full discussion of it would be beyond the scope of this research. Suffice it to say that overwhelmingly it seems that the primary reason for migration, at least for the adult male population, is the search for employment ('painim wok', a phenomenon so common in Papua New Guinea that one of the nation's most

---

7   Although I acknowledge that the term 'diaspora' has particular historical and religious significance in referring to the Dispersion of Jews, I use it here more loosely, and in a manner that is increasingly more common in academic research, to describe any group of people living away from their original home. In this case I use it to describe Duna people who are living outside of the place of origin of their language group in the Southern Highlands of Papua New Guinea. In common with other recent literature I use lower case to further remove the term from its historical association. For a discussion on contemporary definitions of the term 'diaspora' and some of the controversy surrounding the use of the term, see Lewellen 2002:159-170.

popular rock bands was named such). Other reasons for relocation given by Duna people include schooling (for the child population), illness (that is, the need to visit a working hospital/clinic, since the availability of health services in Kopiago itself ranges from extremely limited to non-existent), and the need to escape difficult family situations (such as domestic violence).

There are at least four settlement areas in Mount Hagen with significant numbers of Duna. These areas are known as 'T' School, New Town, Bata Compound, and Dobel (more or less in order of size/prominence—this last area is significantly further out of town on the road to the airport). The gathering point for Duna speakers in the town centre (at least in the years 2005-2006) was on a corner outside a strip of shops on Wahgi Parade, one of the town's main roads, and from where the inter-provincial PMVs (Public Motor Vehicles) depart.

My informants and collaborators in Kopiago who had come to town and were staying with their relatives who lived in the 'T' School settlement first introduced me to these settlement areas. The 'T' School settlement area is named after the nearby school, Hagen Primary School. The name 'T' School is an abbreviation of territory school, which was a term used in the colonial period to label those schools that provided for the Territory of Papua and New Guinea (now known as national schools); this was in contrast with 'A' schools, or Australian Schools (now known as international schools) (Kevin Murphy, Personal communication, 1 July 2006). Because of these family relations, my experience of the Duna diaspora in Mount Hagen focuses on this one settlement area, and most of the recordings I have made of this diasporic group were conducted there in 2005 and 2006.

It is worth describing the nature of 'settlement' before I proceed to describe the songs created and/or performed by those living in such an environment. Generally the Duna inhabitants of 'T' School have appropriated the use of Hagen town land by a purchase in some form from the local government. The story of how one household head, Brian Iri, obtained his block of land is typical of settlement in this area (see Figure 5.4). Brian recalls that around 1989 he obtained his current block of land at 'T' School from a man from Wabag (in Enga Province) who was staying there. He offered him 600 kina for it, which the man took immediately, as he was reported to fear the end of the world with the approaching millenium and was keen to return to his home in Wabag. Brian described the Hagen settlement areas during this time as 'weslan bilong gavman' ('government wasteland'); however, he explained that once town became full of settlers, they were asked by the government to 'register' their blocks of land, which involved paying a fee. In 2002, when Brian registered his land, he paid 200 kina for it. But in order to actually obtain the title for the land, Brian would need to pay the government several thousand kina, which he currently is unable to do (Brian Iri, Personal communication, 24 July 2006). Thus, there appears to be several layers to the process of acquiring land for non-Hagen settlers.

The first striking thing about the recordings I have made at 'T' School is that many performers chose to preface their first recording of songs and stories with an unprompted statement introducing themselves and their place of origin: '*No yaka --. No rindi --.*' ('My name is --. My parish is --.') Although people often introduced themselves before recording a song or story during my fieldwork in Kopiago, rarely did they volunteer a statement aligning themselves with a particular Duna parish. Most likely this was because many of the people were already in their parish when the recording took place, and the knowledge of this was taken as a given. Those recorded at 'T' School were out of their home environment, and keen to make the connection to their own place clear, therefore defining to me their own identity in relation to land.[8]

The second striking thing about the songs recorded is the continued prominence of place names in song. I had somewhat naively expected that when one was removed from one's place, the songs sung would also be so removed, but this was not so. Not only are a number of songs set in Duna places, which serve to reinforce the singers' identity, there are also one or two songs with contained references to places in the town of Mount Hagen. Example 5.18 describes love letters coming down Wara Gerimb (see Figure 5.5), the creek in Mount Hagen which marks the outer border between the 'T' School settlement area and the land owners of Mount Hagen (it will be recalled from earlier in this chapter that the arrival of letters to instigate action/experience and often a journey is a common feature of secular Duna song). This song was sung by three women from the Kopiago parish of Suwaka who live near this creek: initially they began the song with the words *imane yapa* ('two women') but when I pointed out jokingly that they were three, they quickly changed the opening lines.

Example 5.18 (▶ Audio 35): *'imane itupa pi'.*

imane itupa pi ngerimb raroko	three girls at Gerimb were sitting
leta itupa pi ngerimb ulitiaka siya peretia (x2)	three letters down Gerimb creek floodwaters were carried
hona pi rōya sata	they swam and got them

---

8   I do not mean to suggest that the expression of land identity is more important for the dislocated than for the Duna living in their *rindi* ('parish'). Those 'at home' express their land identity regularly, and one important way is through song, as I have shown. What I suggest here is that the Duna at home do not seem to have the need to explicitly introduce their land affiliation outside of song, unlike the diasporic community.

yaka yaroko keno keno ruwTanda rirarua	reading it, (the letter) said that you and me, you and me are becoming sweethearts
ruwanda ruwata riya karoko	so it said and we were sweethearts
riya karoko lima ala rutiaka lembo kutia	we were sweethearts and the sweethearts from before were angry
lembo lembo korane	they were angry angry
ko momoya no ralu L.K. leka riyara	it just seems like I live here, my place is L.K., I have turned back
ko momoya no ralu L.K. leka riyara	it just seems like I live here, my place is L.K., I have turned back

Figure 5.4: Brian Iri and family at their block in Mount Hagen, 2006.

The women sing of sitting by Gerimb creek in Hagen when letters are carried downstream to them on the water. These letters are Hagen letters, and it is suggested that they are written by Hagen men, who would like to befriend these women. They are courted for a time by these men, but their 'sweethearts from before' (that is their Kopiago lovers) are unimpressed. So the women leave their new Hagen liaisons, declaring their home to be Lake Kopiago, and describing their presence in Hagen as something only temporary, almost an illusion (*ko momoya*).

Most of the songs sung by the Duna diaspora in Mount Hagen (except for the Christian ones) focus on expressing the feeling of being away from home, away from the land to which they are connected. Themes include the forgetting of home and family and developing madness when encountering the sea for the first time, or when becoming attached to a woman from a coastal area (the travelling protagonist in these songs is usually a man—I have not heard any Duna songs where a Highlands woman is described as falling for a coastal man). Example 5.19 was sung for recording by the same group of three women as above, and using the same melodic and harmonic schema as the previous song (another example, then, of melodic recycling). Note the reference to crossing various waters (*ipa mbiteya*) and arriving up (*singa romara*), very similar textual lines to that sung by the young boys Hirane parish presented earlier in this chapter. It is very likely that this well known song formula informed the boys' efforts.

Example 5.19 (▶ Audio 36): *'hewa* Mande *ngi'*.

hewa mande *ngi*	on Monday at daytime I left
hewa mande *ngi karia weri rakiya no hora*	on Monday at daytime I left and went over Mount Weri and came
(x2)	
ipa pori mbiteya ipa sakali mbiteya	crossing water Pori crossing water Sakali
singa romara yungura tari singa romara	arrived up at Yunguru Tari airport arrived up
singa romata karoko	arrived up and while there
Air Niugini karia Ambuaneneta panga kutia	Air Niugini over Mount Ambua the plane passed
horata poko romaya	into this I climbed up
poko romaya POM siti kone singa romara	I climbed up, to Port Moresby city true I arrived up
singa romata karoko	arrived up and while there
karoko Papua walitiaka salo kutia	while there a Papuan woman messed up my thinking
salo salo korane	messed up, messed up my thinking and so
salo korane antia apatia pi konda kora	messed up my thinking and so my mother and father also I forgot
salo korane yamali raotia pi konda kora	messed up my thinking and so my lover who is waiting also I forgot
home porane solwara si keya kono kandora (x2)	like that it happened, seeing the salt water sea my thoughts (of home) were cut

The women who sang this song for recording claimed it as their own creation, but another Duna person, Lepani Kendoli, claimed to have heard it at Kopiago station in the early 1980s by a group of male performers. It is very likely that the melody and the textual structure are in a sense recycled materials from previous sources (as we have seen in the creation of Christian songs inspired by stringband songs and vice versa). So whilst it is the song of these women who may have tailored the text to their purposes, it is unlikely to be completely their original.

It is said that when such a song as this is heard it can drive women (the lovers who have been abandoned by wandering males) to cut off their fingers, or parts of their fingers, with grief (a common way in the Highlands of Papua New Guinea for a person to show they have experienced a personal tragedy), or to commit suicide by drowning themselves (Lepani Kendoli, Personal communication, May 2005). Of course, such a response to song is not reserved for newly introduced forms of music; the courting songs of *yekia* and *selepa* can result in the same reaction. This will be further explored in the following chapter.

It is important to note that songs like these are sung both by those of the diaspora and at home in Kopiago—if they are composed away from home, the songs certainly return home with the singers and circulate amongst the people there. The popularity of these songs, particularly with the younger population, sees them potentially serving as a dissuader to travel, listing all the terrible experiences that could befall those who choose to leave home. Many songs address particular anxieties related to absence from home, such as the death of parents, the difficulty in finding the money needed to return to 'ples', and the singers' own death and return home in a coffin.

Example 5.20 (▶ Audio 37): '*antia yo* moni *ndu ngi*'.

antia yo moni *ndu ngi*	Mother oh give me some money
apa yo moni *ndu ngi*	Father oh give some money
kei nguina Lae siti	I will go and see Lae city
kei nguina	I will go and see
kei ngayata moni *ndu pi*	Having gone to see, some money
waepame kol boksi	instead of sending, a coffin box
waeweinia	I will send
kaki kano ipa auwi kokera	bury me at Auwi creek bend
kaki kano	bury me

Figure 5.5: Wara Gerimb.

In Example 5.20 the singer asks his parents for money to travel to the city of Lae, a coastal city in the Morobe Province of Papua New Guinea where many Duna people now live. The suggestion is that the singer would find employment there and have enough money to send some home to his parents (presumably to pay back this debt plus some extra for their living). However, he imagines that he might die in Lae, and the money he obtains while there will have to go towards buying his coffin. Finally, he expresses his wish to be buried at the bend in Auwi creek.

Another song example has both transport problems and death in its lyrics (Example 5.21). Although there are no parish references or praise names used, it is still a place-identifying song as it firmly declares, in the language of home, that the creators, and the performers, of the song do not belong to their diasporic location, but to the home where their mother is to be found.

Example 5.21 (▶ Audio 38): *'no* Mosbi *ngata karoko'.*

no Mosbi ngata karoko	I went to (Port) Moresby and while I was there
no antia khene rarita	my mother I heard had died
(x2)	
home rirane riyanda ruwata	when they said that I thought of going back
waki yaroko MBA ratia mani pukarua (x2)	while asking, these MBA* (tickets) the price seems too high
home rirane no wanda hatia naraya	when they said that I had no way of coming
antia ko yaka memori na siya reina (x2)	mother your name as a memory I hold it here with me

* MBA stands for Milne Bay Air, an airline that once provided a service to Kopiago. This airline service is said to have ceased operation in the region sometime in the 1990s, and so the reference to it in this song gives an indication of the age of the composition.

The composition of both Examples 5.20 and 5.21 is attributed to the Auwi Sola stringband (Richard Alo, Personal communication, 23 July and 16 September 2006). The stringbands of Kopiago have always named themselves after parish locations. The Auwi Sola stringband is no exception. The band has had a number of members since they were formed, but all members are from the same clan (Okopa clan, from the parish of Mbara), hence the name of the band identifies one of the group's places of origin. In 2006 I travelled with Richard Alo from my base in Mount Hagen to Lae in order to meet up with members of the Auwi Sola stringband living there (see Figure 5.6).

The city of Lae is perhaps the most important industrial centre in Papua New Guinea. Because of this, it attracts many Papua New Guineans from other provinces looking for work. The Duna population is no exception, and there has reportedly been a continuous presence of Kopiago people and their families in Lae for over twenty years. The main centres for Duna living in Lae are at the settlements of Four Mile and Chinatown.

In travelling to Lae, I was interested to study how people sang about place when they were not actually living in it. One of the first songs recorded there was a very joyous song referring to the Auwi creek (Example 5.22), the band's namesake and the boys' clan area (see Figure 5.7).

Example 5.22 (▶ Audio 39): *'ipa auwi'.*

ipa auwi karuya raroko	while sitting there blocking Auwi creek
ipa wenatiaka pikipakatia	fish in the water jump up and down
(x2)	
sanda ruwata ngayaroko	you think of getting (fish), while going there
sa kuteni sola siritiaka ruwa nguanania	if you become confused, the cane grass spirits will tell you
(x2)	

In this short song the singer describes the way to catch fish in Auwi creek: 'blocking' the water by sitting in it with legs open and outstretched, facing upstream (while another boy above channels the fish downwards). When the person sitting in the water attempts to grab them, they jump up out of the water and down into it again. The singer explains to his audience that if they would like to learn how to catch fish in this way, the spirits from the Auwi creek where the cane grass ('pit-pit') grows will teach them.

By referring to Auwi creek in this way, and describing it as a fertile place with many fish, this song serves to praise the ground of these clansmen/ band members. However, this song is also a courting song. It was explained to me that the spirits described actually represent the band members themselves, who would be keen to show a girl how to catch fish in order to entice her to his place.

Water spirits, or *ipa siri*, were important for courting in times past, helping men to send messages to the girl whom they desire (this will be further expanded upon in the next chapter). This song therefore is a modern kind of *yekia* or *selepa*, with a hidden message to attract a girl.

It can be seen that songs with specific reference to place, and showing an interaction with the environment and expression of beliefs from the 'taim bipo' (or 'time before white contact') are still very important to people performing in introduced musical styles, even among the Duna diaspora.

Figure 5.6: members of the Auwi Sola stringband playing in Lae.

It is perhaps unsurprising to note that in Mount Hagen and Lae, people were keen to tell ancestral stories and sing lotu and popular songs, but it was not always easy to find anyone willing to sing ancestral genres. On two occassions *yekia* were sung to me in Mount Hagen for recording, but this was the only sung ancestral genre I was able to record among the diaspora. Some of these *yekia* had contemporary political content, and will be presented in a later chapter on politics and song. Several *pikono* stories were told in Mount Hagen, but they were very short, and only in the spoken form, not sung. It is relevant to note that the telling of a *pikono* in the sung style during the day—that is, out of context—is said to incur the risk of the singer's anus closing up (Richard Alo, Personal communication, 20 June 2006). Such an experience is something known to Duna people through narratives—see for example the 'Man without an anus' story collected by Nicholas Modjeska and reproduced by Nicole Haley in the Appendix of her thesis (2002a vol. 2:187). Considering that my only visits to Hagen's 'T' School settlement were during the daytime, this would explain the performance of *pikono* in spoken form only there. It appears then that place may be important in the performance of ancestral song genres in another sense—that of the physical setting for performance.

Figure 5.7: Auwi creek, Kopiago.

Conclusion

This chapter reveals the close relationship of the Duna to the land and how this relationship is reinstated and manipulated through song. A continuity of song text content is shown across songs that originated in ancestral times, and those songs composed in an introduced style. Songs at both ends of this spectrum are concerned with singing about place, particularly about a (usually the singer's) particular parish and the sites within that parish. *Kēiyaka* for places are used across the spectrum of songs. References to food in relation to the fertility of land appear often. Many songs are concerned with moving through landscape: examples include *khene ipakana* (which can list multiple parishes), *pikono* (which often recount journeys), Christian songs and stringband/secular songs.

Themes such as these are evident also in the songs of the Duna diaspora, as shown in the songs I have discussed which were composed by Duna people living in the towns of Mount Hagen and Lae. People in these locations are keen to use both speech and song to declare their parish identity, but they can also sing of places within the diaspora itself, thus incorporating their away-from-home experience into their identity and life stories. Songs of moving through the landscape in the form of journeys are common, as they are at home (many songs of being away return home with people and circulate amongst the people there), and many of these journey songs express the challenges of being away, and the difficulties encountered in attempting to return home. Many of these songs of landscape, food and journeys are songs of love. Land is closely connected with relationships in Duna culture, especially in relationships with the opposite sex, and it is now to the process of courting that we turn.

6. Courting and song

meri *suwaka*, tingting bilong yu	woman from Suwaka, if you think to
prendim mi, no ken prendim narapela man	befriend me, you cannot befriend another man
salim pas i kam long *yungu pakura*	send a letter to *yungu pakura* Hirane

This chapter explores songs associated with obtaining or maintaining relationships with the opposite sex. As in the previous chapter, here the focus is on song texts and song function. I choose to label the songs featured in this chapter 'courting songs' rather than 'love songs'. This is because I am writing of songs that have courting as their specific function. Stewart and Strathern also choose to use the terminology of 'courting' over 'love' and for more or less the same reason. They write:

> Courting songs may also be referred to as love songs but the term 'love songs' begs the question of the sense in which the word 'love' is being used…Love is in any case a broad and diffuse category and our aim is to look for specific modalities of sensibility that appeal to a combination of values and senses. (Stewart and Strathern 2002a:29)

It has in the past been suggested that 'love' is a relatively new concept for the Duna, introduced by Christian teachings. Ex-missionary Were (1968:35–6) writes of the initial mission work at Kopiago station: 'the missionary showed pictures and talked of the Bible and of God who loves people. Kagi and his kinsmen could not understand this at first, especially the part about love.' While I personally do not agree with this view, it is not the purpose of this chapter to theorise the nature, the presence or the absence of a Western concept of 'love' in Duna society.

I have visited Duna courting songs already in this publication. Chapter 2, in its description of Duna ancestral music genres, gave information about *yekia* and *selepa*, the two song genres whose primary function was to court women. In Chapter 5, we saw how these courting songs praised the land of the singer and often that of his desired woman. In Chapter 3, we discovered that the courting practices that took place during the performance of these genres were banned from contemporary Duna life. This ban was never in fact lifted and although it is seemingly not enforced in any way by the local church leaders, these practices appear to have not resumed. Actual song forms, though actively discouraged, proved harder to remove.[1] Listening to previous recordings made by Peter White (1970s) and Don Niles with Nicholas Modjeska (early 1980s), it appears that these song forms remain largely unchanged in terms of their sonic structure.

This chapter will first consider how the banishment of *yekia* and *selepa* courting practices has given the function of these genres an unexpected turn, opening them up to express contemporary experiences. I will focus particularly on the genre of *yekia*, the ancestral courting song genre to which I have had the most exposure, illustrating its application to the political experience. I then turn to introduced styles of courting songs and practices, revealing the continuity that comes about partly as a result of the suppressed expression of past practices. I examine the elicitation of sympathy by a singer as an important aspect of courting songs across the Highlands, in both old and new genres, and the effect such an emotion can have on the listener. To conclude, I revisit the event of Wakili's death in order to explore the relationship between courting and death in Duna song.

New application of the old

The following *yekia* (Example 6.1) was sung by a group of Duna men at Six Mile, a settlement area in Port Moresby, in 1983, and was recorded by Don Niles of the Institute of Papua New Guinea Studies in collaboration with Nicholas Modjeska. The text, which I transcribed and translated with Richard Alo in 2006,[2] expresses a new context for *yekia* as entertainment among men only.

---

1   Yampolsky (2001:179) points out that it is the intangible nature of music that allows it to survive over time: 'Not only is music a powerful symbol of ethnic identity (and all other identities), it is an intangible one, one that can retain its power when other more tangible proofs—such as a society's autonomy, its land, its forests, its religious practices, its economy, its settlement patterns, its traditional modes of clothing—have been arrogated or crippled or outlawed by authorities or abandoned by the society itself. In the face of many pressures toward social integration and uniformity, intangible symbols such as music are sometimes all that people can retain of their identity.' Regarding the Duna, Stürzenhofecker (1998:160) claims that 'certain patterns of thought survived this ritual demise' of Christianity. She suggests that beliefs and practices associated with death are examples of such patterns of thought that might have survived due to being camouflaged or veiled by Christian practices—that is, they were not explicitly in contradiction with the new doctrine. This might account for why laments have survived better than other sung traditions. My own observation on the night of Wakili's death supports Stürzenhofecker's suggestion: in my field journal (2005–2007:18), I wrote '[i]t is as if grief is the only place the West can't touch here'.
2   Modjeska used some of the Six Mile recordings, including this *yekia*, for a National Broadcasting Commission (NBC) radio program. His notes for this program, provided to me by the Institute of Papua New Guinea Studies, include a similar, but not identical, translation of this *yekia* (Modjeska's translation does not make reference to giving cassowary pinions). The translation I provide here, however, is considered to be more accurate (Kenny Kendoli, Personal communication, 7 March 2007).

Example 6.1 (▶ Audio 40) *Yekia.*

ayu kone ali yekianda ipatu hondu pakuru iki yapa nane yaneta sandapa <u>wara</u> naraya pina	right now we sit down outside the *yekia* house, we were given two cassowary pinions from another boy as there are no *wara* women here
<u>ngina</u> iki yapa nane yaneta sandapa <u>wara</u> naraya pina	we were given two *ngina* Awi Logayu cassowary pinions from another boy as there are no *wara* women here
<u>angina</u> iki yapa nane yaneta sandapa <u>wara</u> naraya pina	we were given two *angina* Awi Logayu cassowary pinions from another boy as there are no *wara* women here

In this *yekia*, the men deplore the absence of women at the *yekianda* (*yekia* house). They complain that men have to give each other gifts of courtship, such as cassowary pinions, because women no longer attend *yekianda* to be courted. It is most likely that the Duna men were singing figuratively here. In Port Moresby, in 1983, the Duna population was unlikely to have been constructing *yekianda*—the ritual of *yekia* being curtailed in Duna-speaking country more than two decades prior. Furthermore, *yekianda* are usually constructed over sites of death such as the place where a person has died or their former residence or they are constructed during the time that a secondary burial is taking place (Stewart and Strathern 2002a:78), which would have been difficult in the city of Port Moresby to which these singers had relocated.[3] Therefore, the men are altogether 'outside' the *yekianda* and regret the lack of this form of courting available to them. Some Duna men, however, find their situation humorous in that they are faced with only men to sing to and therefore court; this is indicated by spoken interjections and bursts of laughter throughout the recording session.

Another *yekia* (Example 6.2), recorded more recently and in an entirely different context, reverses the gender absence. Recorded in Hirane parish at Kopiago in 2005, it is sung by a solo woman (Pokole Pora) for women (Kipu Piero and myself) and describes a group of women meeting together, but without the company of their men.

Example 6.2 (▶ Audio 41) *Yekia.*

<u>wara</u> apotia kewa hila sangao kua aya alia nawayatia	those *wara* women came as a group bound together, but the boyfriends did not come
<u>ela</u> kewa hila sangao kua aya alia nawayatia	*ela* white women came as a group bound together, but the boyfriends did not come
<u>elape</u> kewa hila sangao kua aya alia nawayatia	*elape* white women came as a group bound together, but the boyfriends did not come
<u>rukupe</u> kewa hila sangata ngo kua aya alia nawayatia, aiyo ai.	*rukupe* white women came as a group bound together, but the boyfriends did not come, *aiyo ai*.

---

3 Building houses for courting on top of burial sites inevitably links courting with death. This connection between courtship and death is explored further towards the end of this chapter.

Yekia composed in recent times are open to references to the contemporary world in which Duna people live. In Duna society, modernity came hand-in-hand with the change of performance context of the genre and thus elements of a new lifestyle and repression of ritual surrounding courting songs encourage new topics to be introduced (as we will soon see in detail when songs of politics are examined). This *yekia* describes me and my fellow female researchers from The Australian National University (namely, Lila San Roque and Nicole Haley), who often travelled together to Kopiago but without our partners. The praise-name sequence *ela, elape* and *rukupe* represents white people; the fact we are a group of women is implied by the first line, which uses one of the Duna praise names for women generally: *wara*. The praise-name sequence, however, is commonly used to refer to items associated with modernity as introduced by white people, such as aeroplanes, so equally in this *yekia* we could also be described as 'aeroplane women' (Kenny Kendoli, Personal communication, 7 September 2006).

This is the only *yekia* I have discussed here that has been composed and sung by a woman. I have established that this is a men's performance genre in the *yekianda* setting; men initiate verses with their own or with pre-existing lines of texts and other men join in at the second line. Women could join in the singing with the other men at the second line, but under no circumstances would a woman initiate a *yekia*. Outside the *yekianda* and the courting context, however, women are able to create their own *yekia* or replicate those they once heard in the *yekianda*.

It is notable that the only *yekia* I have heard by Duna women are sung/initiated/led by the older generation of women (aged about fifty-five years or more), who experienced *yekia* either in the *yekianda* themselves or through their older sisters who attended the *yekianda* (there could be *yekia* created by younger women, but any such examples are as yet unknown to me). The musically similar Duna ancestral courting genre of *selepa* is another genre I have heard sung only by the older generation of women. Among Duna men, there seemed to be no such generational distinction in performance—both *yekia* and *selepa* are popular with younger men (aged about thirty–forty years) as well as their fathers' generation, and I have recorded boys as young as eight years attempting *selepa* (though their lack of knowledge of multiple praise names makes their performances very short, and quite amusing to their parents). So the courting genres *yekia* and *selepa* remain largely male performance genres.

Men today sing *yekia* among themselves in men's houses, makeshift or otherwise. By way of an example of a makeshift men's house, most of the *yekia* presented for me to record have been sung in one particular hut belonging to Kenny Kendoli and Kipu Piero (see Figure 6.1). This hut is used primarily for cooking, but also to house male guests who are visiting temporarily (women who are visiting generally sleep with Kipu and the children in the family home). Thus, of an evening, this 'hauskuk' (cooking house) sometimes functions as a men's house, where cooking by the hearth is a key feature. Men are said to encroach on the space of the women and dominate the shared space in the contemporary setting (Stürzenhofecker 1998:142), and the monopolising of the 'hauskuk' space is a classic example of this.[4]

Figure 6.1 Kipu Piero (foreground) stokes the fire in her family's 'hauskuk', with friend Juli peeling potatoes and daughter Monika looking on, April 2005.

Despite invitation, I have chosen not to record in, or even enter, a true men's house, of which there is at least one established in every Duna parish. They are the reserve of men only and I have chosen to follow this gender distinction. Makeshift men's houses are also maintained by this unspoken rule, evident in the following fieldwork account. On 15 March 2005, my hosts at Hirane arranged for an eminent *pikono* singer who was visiting the area to sing a *pikono* for my recording in the above described 'hauskuk'. Kiale Yokona had sung a *pikono* just the previous evening in the Hirane men's house and though we were invited to enter, my fieldwork companion, Lila, and I instead experienced a

---

4   Duna men and women use space differently for socialisation. Men congregate at the markets, while women are rarely seen in groups (for fear of being accused of witchcraft) and see other women only while in their homes, at a funeral place (*khene anda*) or perhaps working in the garden (though gardens are often a place for solitude). Men are less likely to be seen alone, as it is when they are alone that they could be the targets of a witch (Stürzenhofecker 1998:148–50). This use of space seems to be reflected in music: men usually sing in groups, while women often sing alone (though this is changing with church singing).

short section of his story through the wall before returning to our hut. By the time Kiale had arrived the next night to sing in the 'hauskuk', eight or nine other men had set themselves up in the hut with cigarettes, sweet potato and a glowing fire, with coffee provided by myself on their request. Women and children were banished from the hut and I felt the significance of my admission as I set up to record. The event of his *pikono* telling (including its intervals) lasted for more than three hours. When the performance ended and I was told that it was all over, I assumed it was. Lying in bed not long afterwards, I heard the unmistakeable melodic shape of *yekia* and I then realised that there was a lot more to the evening than what I had been permitted to experience.

In the absence of women, the primary function for *yekia* as courting songs has diminished, thus opening up the genre to other functions, such as singing songs of political protest.

Courting politics

We have seen how modern elements in Duna society and experience can be introduced into *yekia* with the example above of a *yekia* describing the behaviour of white women. By and large, however, the majority of *yekia* performed by Duna people that sing of modern experience describe events and sentiments of contemporary politics. In this way it can be said that the courting function of *yekia* continues, but this time it is voters and votes that are being courted. This kind of adaptation of courting songs is similar to what has happened in another part of the Papua New Guinea Highlands—the Melpa region in the Western Highlands Province, where a traditional genre of sung tales *about* courtship has been used in an election campaign to compose and perform an allegorical tale about how a certain candidate would court the vote (Rumsey 2006b:331–2).

The next three *yekia* (Examples 6.3, 6.4 and 6.5) were sung by a Duna man, Lekari Lombaye, who was resident in Mount Hagen during the 2006 Koroba-Lake Kopiago by-election. The compositions describe elements of that important event and contain both a literal meaning and a figurative one.

Example 6.3 (▶ Audio 42) *Yekia.*

upia nginitia *ralu* sopana *(na) papa hundalu hatia karutia irina* sarere *etota kenda*	Mbara *upia* red birds of paradise sons' *ralu* place down there, (on them) at Mbara I have closed the door, next week Saturday I will see
akapa hundalu hatia karutia irina sarere *etota kenda*	(on them) at *akapa* Mbara I have closed the door, next week Saturday I will see
akuya hundalu hatia karutia irina sarere *etota kenda, aiyo ai.*	(on them) at *akuya* Mbara I have closed the door, next week Saturday I will see, *aiyo ai.*

Example 6.3 literally describes the red birds of paradise from the parish of Mbara. The birds and the lowlands area where Mbara is located share the same praise name—*upia*—Mbara being a place where these birds are found in abundance.[5] It is on these birds that the singer of the *yekia* closes the door, and on whom he will look in, next week on Saturday, the suggestion being to see whether they have escaped or not.

At the time this *yekia* was recorded (5 July 2006), 'next week Saturday' was the anticipated end of voting in the Koroba-Lake Kopiago by-election. Of course most *yekia* in any context have a hidden meaning and the true meaning of this *yekia* was something other than locking up birds and checking on them later. Here the birds represent the people of Mbara and the singer describes blocking their independent voting by instructing them all whom to vote for (in most cases clan affiliation to a candidate determines how the majority of people in the electorate will vote). When he checks on them at the end of the voting period (that is, when the votes are counted), he will know who gave their vote to another and who listened to him; those who listened to him will have voted for his desired candidate, thus achieving a win for that candidate.

Another *yekia* sung by Lekari directly after Example 6.3 was recorded uses a similar song text structure, but names two prominent men from the Hewa-speaking area of the Southern Highlands Province, which backs onto the Duna-speaking area, to identify the place in question (Example 6.4). From Wanakipa, on the other side of Mount Apima, Salo Auwale is known to be a 'fierce man' with many wives, while Wualo Tupiao was once married to a Kopiago woman and this is his Duna connection (Richard Alo, Personal communication, 26 July 2006).[6]

Example 6.4 (▶ Audio 43) *Yekia.*

apima Wualo Salo ruwata rayaneya hewa ralu sopana hundalu hatia karurua ngina sarere nduta kenda	Wualo and Salo of Apima they say, of the Hewa *ralu* place down below, now I go down and I close the door, in one week I will see
pima hundalu hatia karurua ngina sarere *nduta kenda*	*pima* Hewa people, now I go down and I close the door, in one week I will see
apima hundalu hatia karurua ngina sarere *nduta kenda*	*apima* Hewa people, now I go down and I close the door, in one week I will see
apopa hundalu hatia karurua ngina sarere *nduta kenda, aiyo ai.*	*apopa* Hewa people, now I go down and I close the door, in one week I will see, *aiyo ai.*

---

5   The praise name *upia* is usually applied to the Duna parish of Aluni; however, it also represents general lowland areas (Kenny Kendoli, Personal communication, 7 March 2007). The context of this use of *upia*—that is, immediately preceding the listing of praise names specifically belonging to Mbara parish (*papa, akapa* and *akuya*)—further clarifies its meaning here.

6   According to Richard Alo, these men are not from Mount Apima exactly; the singer made an error.

Lekari provided the above two political *yekia* verses as examples of what one would sing in support of candidate Ben Peri (who is, incidentally, the candidate Lekari supports). When I asked him what the supporters of another candidate might sing—for example, the supporters of candidate Petros Thomas—Lekari provided the following *yekia* (Example 6.5).

Example 6.5 (▶ Audio 44) *Yekia.*

ale karuka ralu roma kuru hundalu hatia karurua ngonia sarere nduta kenda	*ale karuka* Auwi Lagayu people's ralu place above, I went and closed the door, in one week I will see
ako hundalu hatia karurua ngonia sarere nduta kenda	*ako* Auwi Lagayu people, I went and closed the door, in one week I will see
andako hundalu hatia karurua ngonia sarere nduta kenda	*andako* Auwi Lagayu people, I went and closed the door, in one week I will see
paliako hundalu hatia karurua ngonia sarere nduta kenda, aiyo ai.	*paliako* Auwi Lagayu people, I went and closed the door, in one week I will see, *aiyo ai.*

This *yekia* appears almost identical to the previous one when their texts are compared. On closer examination, however, it can be seen that the difference between the songs of the supporters of the two candidates lies in the place references. It appears that those in the parish of Mbara, and those who live around Mount Apima, are mostly supporters of Ben Peri, and those living in the area of Auwi Lagayu, though they used to support Ben Peri, now mostly support Petros Thomas (Kenny Kendoli, Personal communication, 26 July 2006). Once again, as we have seen in the previous chapter on land and song, key song information is held in the references to places.

Yekia have taken on a new and important role in Duna musical life, due in part to the restrictions placed on their original courting context. They are a forum for debate and decision, and—as is evident in other examples—the inevitable expression of dissatisfaction that surrounds the introduced experience of contemporary politics. The genre continues to thrive with this new application and courting continues in a sense as its function.

Contemporary courting practices

Introduced styles of song often reveal in their texts the new ways in which women are generally courted. One of the primary forms of contemporary courtship is through the letter, as Example 6.6 indicates.

Example 6.6 (▶ Audio 45) 'Meri *suwaka*'.

meri *suwaka*, tingting bilong yu	woman from Suwaka, if you think to
prendim mi, no ken prendim narapela man	befriend me, you cannot befriend another man
salim pas i kam long *yungu pakura*	send a letter to *yungu pakura* Hirane

In this song, the singer addresses a woman from the parish of Suwaka. He tells her that if she wants to become his lover she cannot simultaneously obtain another man's affection; rather, she should send a letter to the singer to establish their relationship. Although this recording was sung by a number of Duna men, it is identified as the song of Jim Siape, who led the group. He is from the parish of Hirane (it is his father's parish) and his wife is from the parish of Suwaka. Jim's use of the *kēiyaka* for Hirane—*yungu* and *pakura*—reaffirms this identity. Once again, we can see the importance of land references in the formation of identity in song.

The movement of letters through the landscape is significant. Often the letters of courtship travel down in the water, as illustrated in the song cited in this previous chapter that describes letters travelling down Wara Gerimb (Example 5.17). Tools of literacy, such as the letter, are obviously introduced phenomena to the Duna. A message travelling down through the water, however, echoes the way of the past, when *ipa siri* (water spirits) would carry the sentiments of a man to his sweetheart and back again (Lepani Kendoli, Personal communication, 11 July 2006). The role of the *ipa siri* in courtship was referred to briefly in Example 5.21. The next song illustrates more directly this relationship between lovers and the water spirits who bring them together.

Example 6.7 (▶ Audio 46) *'Sola alimbu leka suwano'*.

ruwa nguanania rewapi siritiaka ruwa nguanania	they will talk, the Rewapi water spirits, they will talk (to you)
imane yo, sa ngutiani rewapi siritiaka ruwa nguanania	girl oh, if you lose your way the Rewapi water spirits will talk (to you)
waya kata, waya kata sola alimbu leka suwano	you come, you come break a stick of cane grass and hold it

Sung by a group of men and women in this recording, this song appeals to a certain young woman that if she would like to come up to the Hirane area of Rewapi (a subsection of Hirane parish adjoining Kalipopo), she need not worry about getting lost, as the Rewapi water spirits (*rewapi siri*) will guide her way. When she does come up, however, she should break off a piece of cane grass and use it as a walking stick (*sola alimbu leka suwano*) in order to help her climb. The implication is that Rewapi is located on a steep slope, not a flat area, as is Kalipopo (see Example 5.3),[7] which is identified and praised with the phrase *mei konenia* (steep slope). It will be recalled that the woman visiting Kalipopo is also instructed to use a walking stick.

---

7   The phrase used in Example 5.3 is *sola alimbu kone leka suwano*. The word *kone* (meaning 'true', 'really') is sometimes added to existing song texts for emphasis and to decorate otherwise sustained notes with an additional two-syllable pattern.

As is the case with the Auwi boys of Example 5.22, the *ipa siri* of this song are said to represent the Rewapi boys who are offering to show the girls the way to their home. This metaphorical representation is a continuation of the layered meanings present in *awenene ipakana* such as *yekia* and *selepa*.

Water spirits appear in many courting songs. Example 6.8, composed by a group of young women about 2002–03 and sung by them for recording in 2004, describes the locations where men (as *siri*) are sighted.

Example 6.8 (▶ Audio 47) *'Itape koke'.*

itape koke auwi ho irina	Itape river bend and Auwi creek is over there
wayapere sopa reyana	Wayapere grassland is down there
auwi karaka siritiaka khana yapa siyata ole ndoletia	the Auwi frog-like water spirits carried two stones each at dusk

At a metaphorical level of interpretation, the frog-like water spirits again refer to boys. Some reasons have been given for the existence of this metaphor: the boys of this area (near Auwi Creek in particular) are slender, not at all fat (Kenny Kendoli, Personal communication, 25 July 2006); the boys do not have a lot of pig money (that is, they are not wealthy), do not eat well, do not have good 'bilas' (body decoration) and—in the case of Example 5.21 where catching fish is described—they spend their time playing in the water rather than tending gardens, which would be a more fruitful pursuit (Richard Alo, Personal communication, 6 August 2006). In another opinion, the boys of this area appear like *ipa siri* when they put mud on their faces (Deni Kilapa, Personal communication, 7 August 2006), which is something done for decorative and/or emotionally expressive purposes (for example, to show grief at the memory of the deceased). Whatever the reason, or combination of reasons, the metaphor of young men as *ipa siri* is well established in Duna song.

The song describes the boys down at Auwi Creek carrying stones and it is implied that they are carrying gifts to give to their girlfriends. The song ends with a play on the word *ole*, a shortened version of the word *olele*, which is the name of the type of cicada insect heard at dusk and which lends its name to that time of day. This abbreviation, *ole*, is followed by a playful nonsense term, *ndole* (with the addition of the past visual/[sensory] suffix *-tia*). Kenny Kendoli (Personal communication, 25 July 2006) muses that this verbal construction, *ole ndoletia*, might represent the sound of the two stones being hit together.

Siri are important in the Duna belief system of the 'taim bipo' (time before), and reference to them, in particular their role in courtship, metaphorical or otherwise, is here seen to continue into introduced forms of music adopted by the Duna.

Guitars as courting instruments

Two of the three songs in the previous section—Examples 6.6 and 6.7, whose recording was led by men—were composed as guitar songs. This is significant as it gives an indication of the performance context for the songs. Secular guitar songs are often created for the purposes of courting, as Example 6.9 details.

Example 6.9 (▶ Audio 48) 'Manki *pakura* pilaim gita'.

manki *pakura* pilaim gita	*pakura* Hirane boy plays guitar
pilaim ngurale pairap pairap	plays ukulele 'pairap pairap'
meri *suwaka* sikirap wantaim	Suwaka girl desirous
raitim leta	writes a letter

This song describes a modern courting scene: a boy from Hirane parish plays guitar and ukulele 'pairap pairap' (meaning 'noisily'); a girl from Suwaka parish becomes desirous of him (and his playing) and writes him a love letter. Significantly, a gender divide is foregrounded: the male is playing the string instruments; the woman is listening and responding in turn. This is typical of Duna musical practice regarding the guitar (and ukulele). Women sometimes play guitar privately to accompany Christian songs, but usually it is men performing with this instrument, and women joining in by singing, and perhaps moving their bodies in time. In the home, outside a public performance realm, women are more likely to attempt to play the guitar. I have heard my female friend Kipu sing this song and accompany herself on the guitar, using 'imitation' chords and with the song lyrics changed to sing about her male and female dogs courting. Unsurprisingly, the gender roles in the lyrics did not change, even with this entirely different species (the male dog played guitar while the female dog swooned).

The lyrics of this song are as malleable as other Duna song texts—ancestral and introduced—and while this version was recorded by a group of Hirane girls, people from different parishes can tailor it to their needs. For example, in another recording, Kipu sang of the 'manki *upia*' playing guitar and the 'meri *yungu*' full of desire writing a love letter, accompanying herself again with the guitar. The names *yungu* and *upia* are praise names for the parishes of her and her husband (Hirane and Aluni respectively). In this more personal version, the gender role as expressed in the text for guitar playing as male is preserved, even though in this recording she was the one in fact doing the guitar playing. So, song texts are malleable, but not without convention. Despite such efforts as Kipu's, guitar and ukulele playing in public remains the domain of Duna males rather than females (see Figure 6.2).

Figure 6.2 Hirane men and boys playing music, February 2005.

Courting through musical instruments was important to the Duna in pre-contact times and today some men continue to win over women through their skill at playing the *kuluparapu* (bamboo panpipes), *luna* (bamboo jew's harp) and *alima* (mouth bow). The Duna use the introduced instruments guitar and ukulele for courting in much the same way (though one important and notable difference is that the guitar is not said to 'voice stories' as ancestral instruments are said to). In fact, these new instruments are so closely associated with courting that married men report having their guitars confiscated and their musical activities curtailed, even in the home, by their wives. It is in the 'disco' setting where guitars, and guitar-based songs, are brought into the public realm by Duna men—generally the young and unmarried, who are keen to find a lover.

The disco

The disco in Papua New Guinea is a continuation of the stringband *pati* ('party'), which has been present in the country since the 1950s. According to Crowdy (2001:140), '[*p*]*atis* generally consisted of dances in an enclosed area with one or more stringbands performing. Admission fees were often charged and refreshments made available.' Six-to-six parties (conducted between the hours of six in the evening and six in the morning) eventually developed into an electric arena with the use of 'power bands' (bands using amplified instruments such as electric lead and bass guitars, and keyboards) (Webb 1993:107–8). Although at Kopiago attempts were made to form power bands with the inventive use of radio equipment, and later the purchase of electric guitars, keyboard and drums by one particular aspiring politician, the lack of a reliable source of electricity was a primary hindrance to such musical activity. The acoustic stringband remains, at this stage, the principal form of group instrumental music for the Duna.

Stringband music in the less remote parts of Papua New Guinea is considered by some to be unfashionable and associated with earlier attempts at playing guitar music in the 1970s and 1980s (Feld and Crowdy 2002:80–1). For those far from town (and even village) life, such as the Duna, stringband music is, however, a connection with the wider world and the world of which they aspire to be a part. Feld (in Feld and Crowdy 2002:81) writes of the Bosavi people's relationship to *gita gisalo*, their local form of stringband music: 'It [*gita gisalo*] is the Bosavi way of connecting with PNG modernity; it is their jump from making pre-modern PNG music to modern PNG music. For Bosavi people, the fluency in this new music is really just like gaining fluency in *tok pisin* and English.' The same can be said for the Duna.

Richard Alo described to me the stringband performance scene at its height in the 1980s. At this time, he was the 'captain' of the Auwi Sola stringband. There were several stringbands in the region at that time and stringband 'resis' ('races' or competitions) were held at events such as the celebration of Independence Day. Groups would come to Kopiago from parishes such as Aluni, and even as far away as Kelabo (see Figure 1.2). At these competitions, prize money could be won (amounts of about K60–80), which would then be divided between the members of the group. This was in the period before Richard married. He then explained that after he married, he felt ashamed to play the guitar in public—for example, during the day at the market—preferring, if he played at all, to play at home at night. Even then he recalls that his wife frowned on such activity, leading him to eventually give away his playing and his instruments (Richard Alo, Personal communication, 18 June 2006). This account reinforces the belief in the guitar as an important and effective means of courting.

Stringband competitions are rarely held in Kopiago anymore. This could be due to the relative scarcity of working guitars, though in 2005 there was no shortage of guitar strings available for purchase at the local market. It could be due to the movement of young men, who would otherwise have formed such groups, out of their home environment in search of work (see the section in the previous chapter on the Duna diaspora). Not least, however, it could be due to the proliferation of the cassette culture in Papua New Guinea developing the listening side of Duna musical practice.

Instead of using live bands, discos at Kopiago now most commonly use pre-recorded music in the form of cassette tapes played on a portable stereo for entertainment. Discos are the first point of contact for many people with cassette culture (listening, responding, borrowing, copying and trading). Before the disco, trade stores were a place to convene and listen to cassettes and the radio, and this still occurs, but at a reduced level. It is the disco that is the main forum for exposure to cassette music (and, as has been discussed in the previous chapter, the forum for the formation of identities and knowledge of the outside world). It is also the disco that provides the only form of night-time public courtship, thus it can be considered an extension of one of the functions of the *yekianda*.

The following fieldwork account, taken from one of my field notebooks, describes the unfolding of regular discos in Hirane parish, which were held within earshot of our house (see Figure 6.3):

7 April 2005

First disco at Hirane. 'DJ' was Peter Kambua, whose house is close to the mission station. He brought his own ghetto blaster and tapes. The tapes he bought in Tabubil [a mining community in another province] when he went to visit his sister (he caught a plane from Kopiago). Most of them are from the ubiquitous Tumbuna Tracks Studio in Madang. 'Med Wagi', which I have, is one of these tapes.

When we arrived (8pm) they were just starting, with a bonfire but no lamp. The girls, they said, were hiding by the road and wouldn't come until there was a light (they were afraid, the boys said). A pole was across the path, channelling people into the fenced off area. Admission 50t.

The scuffling of the dancing was sometimes louder than the music! Boys just danced with boys, as no girls present [at that stage].

14 April 2005

A week later a more successful disco was held. A lot more men attended, and by 10pm approximately six girls had arrived (ourselves [me, Lila and Lila's mother who was visiting at the time] not included), though hiding themselves with headscarves and umbrellas (though no rain) and sticking very much to the side, often behind the mother figure selling handfuls of peanuts. A man was also sitting on the ground selling peanuts, and two groups of men sat nearby playing cards. Next to them was the tarpaulin area, under which the 'DJ console' was set up. This consisted of Peter's stereo and tapes, hooked up to a battery, and all resting on top of a newly-made wooden platform/bench. Later flashing fairy lights were hung overhead (courtesy of Lila). On the corner of the tarpaulin tent hung a kerosene lantern (what was much sought after on the first evening).

Men danced with men. Their movements were surprisingly angular, with rigid folding and unfolding of the body, and jagged knee-lifting. We wondered how women would ever get involved in the dancing: the only one dancing was Kipu, who danced with an old (declared 'crazy') man every time, going up to him and saying "Scuse mi', 'dancing' with him and then leaving him at the end of the song. I wondered how much this kind of interaction was successful as a courting ritual, and how much it replaced *yekia* and *selepa* movements as courting dance.

Then a man called out between the songs: 'All women must ask a man to dance now' (in Tok Pisin). Amazingly the men stood around waiting for a proposition—amazing as the girls still stood to the very side and had barely revealed their identities, let alone identified men to partner. No-one but Kipu went forward [it is significant that she is already a married woman with several children, so was not taken seriously as a courting participant—also her role as chaperone for three white women on this occasion is likely to have prevented any advances], and so the music went back on and the men continued to dance in pairs and groups of three.

We left at 10pm. I imagine that more women eventually arrived and the atmosphere loosened up, as by 6am when the final song was played, I heard the distinctively loud laughs of Juli and Sendi [two teenage girls, eligible for courting].

23 April 2005

Today I'm dubbing Peter's disco tapes. Lately (and always?) the discos have been going 'til 6am more or less exactly, adhering to that six-to-six standard. This going-to-6am attitude is expressed/reinforced in some of [the lyrics of] these disco songs eg. 'six oklok pinis na mi no save...' ('it's six o'clock already and I don't know [what to do]').

The above account illustrates the typical set-up and structure of the disco as it is held in the Kopiago region. It also describes to a point the divide between men's and women's participation in the event. What it does not describe are some of the more negative aspects of discos as perceived by the Duna community, especially in certain contexts, such as someone's death.

To hold a disco close to the time of a death, particularly the death of a significant member of the community, is considered inappropriate and could even suggest that the participants in the disco were in part responsible for the death that occurred. It is not only discos that are avoided at this time, but also ancestral dances and songs and the killing of pigs for consumption—essentially any public activity that is considered enjoyable. It is necessary that 'ol mas i stap bel sori'—that is, people should be sorrowful and express their sorrow. If happiness is expressed then suspicion is aroused (Richard Alo, Personal communication, 24 July 2006). The practice of avoiding ceremonial/celebratory activities at the time of a death is of course not limited only to the Duna. Schieffelin (1976:25) writes that the Kaluli do not hold ceremonies at funerals 'for Kaluli feel it is improper to jiggle a dead person with dancing. Besides, after a death people are grief-stricken, somber, and angry and are more in the mood for murder than ceremonial dances.'

An example of this kind of conflict occurred during my fieldwork at Kopiago in April 2005. The community leader and former local government councillor Simon Hongei was reported to have drowned when his canoe overturned in a body of water not far from Lake Kopiago (his teenage daughter who accompanied him survived as she knew how to swim). A day or two after his death, when members of the community were still grieving over his body at the *khene anda*, others were preparing to hold a disco at Hirane parish. Those grieving began to ask why this disco was being held. Richard Alo, who was at the *khene anda* at this time and who heard this talk, declared that he would go and find out and put a stop to the disco, which by this time had already begun. In the aggression that reportedly ensued, he took one of the speakers and smashed it onto a tree, effectively putting an end to the dance. He later explained to me that it was for the good of the Hirane people and the visiting Australians that he protested to the disco in this way—he did not want to see any of us implicated in Simon's death (Richard Alo, Personal communication, 24 July 2006).

Apart from the consequences of discos immediately after deaths, holding discos is generally frowned on by other community members because it almost guarantees sleeplessness, resulting in tiredness and a loss of productivity the next day. They also attract people from outside the immediate area, who might not be welcome. Strathern and Stewart describe a disco in the Duna parish of Aluni in 1991, which was held as a fundraiser for local projects. They write: 'As an experiment in fund-raising the discos were not repeated, because they caused so much trouble. For days before and after them outsiders, male and female, came into the area, playing cards, drinking alcohol, and disturbing local patterns of decorum' (Strathern and Stewart 2004:110).

Figure 6.3 Site where Hirane discos were held in 2005. Note clearing for dancing and fence constructed out of plant materials.

One of the key aspects of Duna life at stake in the disco scene is the issue of sex and discos. Controlling sexuality is considered important for the Duna as without this control the marriage system is threatened (Stürzenhofecker 1998:120), and this in turn threatens the social and economic future of the entire community. In the past, the restraint of desire was important to Duna people (Stürzenhofecker 1998:130). Stürzenhofecker (1998:121) writes that 'a perceived crisis in control over sexuality could stand for a perceived crisis in continuity itself, since such continuity is seen as dependent on the orderly sequencing of the creation and payment of debt arising from sexuality [that is, bride price] over the generations'. Considering this, then, one can see why there has been general objection, particularly by older Duna people, to the discos held at Hirane and elsewhere.

Bride price and song

Although the economics of courtship is partly what throws the discos into disrepute, young Duna people are conscious of the obligations of bride price payments expected of them by their families. Songs are often composed with the issues of money and of bride price in the foreground, and these songs, composed with guitars, would have been intended for the public party context. I now present two such popular songs (Examples 6.10 and 6.11).

Example 6.10 (▶ Audio 49) *'Imane ketele'.*

imane ketele ketele konenia	really little little girl
antia apaka ita moni *nanda rita ma ritape? (x 2)*	your mother and father say they want to eat pig money, did they tell you to go (to me)?
ma ritako	if they told you to go (to me)
ma ritako ipa wala kendo nay[i]a randa wano (x 2)	if they told you to go (to me), at water Wala drink from the leaf spout, come and sit down

Here the male singer addresses a young woman, who appears to have been sent away by her parents to find a suitor. The singer assumes that the parents are hungry for 'pig money'—that is, they are greedy for bride price, which in large part is made up of the gift of a number of pigs, some of which are consumed directly in celebration of the marriage. He invites the girl to drink from water Wala through the leaf spout there and rest by him. He is prepared to entertain the idea of marriage to her.

Stewart and Strathern present a courting song from the Duna genre of *laingwa* (accepted to be the same genre as *yekia*, as explained in Chapter 2) with a similar meaning in the final line of text. This line is *'ko tanda rakuku rapa'*, which they translate to mean 'drink water, come and sit down' (Stewart and Strathern 2002a:80–1). The authors suggest that the song that centres on this line 'reflects the actual social pressures on a newly married wife to stay at her husband's place and not visit her own kinsfolk's area, where she might become disinclined to return to her husband' (Stewart and Strathern 2002a:81). This was very much an ancestral ideal; from my experience of contemporary Duna living, it is not always the case that Duna women move to their husband's area—often men chose to live on the land with which their wife strongly identifies. There are various reasons why this might come about: the wife's land might provide better employment opportunities, more fertile land, refuge from a clan or parish dispute or an opportunity to strengthen ancestral ties the man himself might have to his wife's place. Although the Duna text that Stewart and Strathern provide differs from that which I have presented above, the meaning as taken from their translation appears to be the same. Thus it can be said that this sentiment and the ideal that it invokes, now set to a contemporary guitar-based song, have been carried over from the ancestral past.

Young women are under a considerable amount of pressure from their parents to accept a marriage proposal, as parents want to receive the bride price. It is not uncommon for relatives to assault ('paitim') the girl if she is unwilling (Richard Alo, Personal communication, 24 July 2006). Similarly, men are under pressure to find the large sum required to pay the bride price. During recording, Example 6.10 was followed directly by Example 6.11, effectively its partner song, concerning bride price and how to raise the payment.

Example 6.11 (▶ Audio 50) *'No awa'.*

no awa mali mbatia ngaya hapia kheneo (x 2)	my father some years ago he died
imane ka wanda ayia kuri patia no ita moni *paka sandape?*	girl you come asking me often, but from where will I get pig money?
ita moni *naraya pina*	I do not have pig money, it is so
naraya pina anoa yane ralirua ko ngano	I do not have, it is so, so find another man and go

Here the singer explains that because his father has died he is disadvantaged as far as raising the required bride price is concerned (paying the bride price is not the sole responsibility of the suitor but of the whole family or clan). He tells her instead to leave him and find another man to marry. Rather than his message being to dismiss his bride-to-be, however, the sentiment expressed in this song encourages sympathy ('sori') from the woman. It suggests that she might be moved to accept his proposal without a bride price payment, which is increasingly common for Duna people, who, for complex social and economic reasons, must endure rising bride price payments but without a similar rise in income for most (Stürzenhofecker 1998:110–18). 'Sori' is a sentiment integral to courting songs in many areas of Papua New Guinea (and indeed across Melanesia), in both ancestral and introduced styles of song.

'Sori'

The Tok Pisin term 'sori' (meaning essentially sympathy) is most commonly evoked in courting songs through statements of self-denigration by the singer/composer.[8] A number of researchers working in Papua New Guinea have documented this phenomenon from an anthropological perspective.

Andrew Strathern has published a collection of courting song texts (*amb kenan*) of the Melpa people of the Western Highlands Province. In these songs, *kond* (sympathy or pathos) features prominently, often literally, in the lyrics (Strathern 1974). He also discusses *kond* in relation to Melpa songs in a later, co-authored publication (Stewart and Strathern 2002a). Stewart and Strathern (2002a:119) write: 'The emotion of *kond*, which predominates in the [courting] songs, reveals a certain balance of sensibilities, the wish for an ideal outcome combined with a regret that it may not be possible.' They go on to describe

---

8   In Duna language, the term 'sori', in this sense, is *khenowa* (to be/feel sorry, 'stap sori', is *khenowa kana*) (see San Roque 2008:264–6, and also p. 94, concerning expressions of sympathy).

kond as 'a highly positive, if ambivalent, emotion, expressing how people feel bonded to one another yet recognize their separation. It accurately captures the uncertainties of the life phase of courtship and marriage; as well as the ultimate realities of life and death themselves' (Stewart and Strathern 2002a:212). Some Melpa marriages do result from the singing of courting songs (Stewart and Strathern 2002a:63) and this suggests that the sentiment of *kond*, when used to attract the opposite sex in song, is an effective one.

Of the Kaluli, Schieffelin (1976:131) writes: 'People who are disappointed or frustrated in their desires and feeling sorry for themselves sometimes express their feelings and try to strike a sympathetic image by breaking spontaneously into song.' Feld (1982) explores the poetics of sorrow in the Kaluli sound world extensively in his publication on the topic. Weiner (1991) too writes of such a sentiment in Foi song. So it can be seen that 'sori' is a concept translatable across many language groups in Papua New Guinea and is an integral part of performance genres.

Reactions to 'sori': self-mutilation

In the previous chapter on land and song, I presented an example of a song about travelling in which a Duna person leaves his home for Port Moresby, and at the end of the journey he has lost his thoughts of his family and lover (Example 5.18). I mentioned that this kind of tragic song can elicit violent reactions from the listener against their own person—for example, cutting off a part of their finger. This happens when the listener—it could be a man or a woman—is consumed by their emotions, their passion. To cut off part of the finger is acknowledged as a sure way to elicit sympathy, and in the case of a man returning home (it is rarely a woman embarking on journeys away from home), could unite the lovers again once the woman has shown the man what she has done to herself over him.

If the lovers do not, or cannot, reunite (for example, if the woman marries another in her lover's absence), the stump of the finger acts as a mnemonic to the relationship that once was so cherished. It is said that if the woman becomes unhappy in her marriage—for example, if her husband beats her or they become very poor—she will sit alone, hold the stump of her finger and cry. She might return to her former lover eventually, and listening to love songs on cassettes is reported to occasionally provoke people to run away from unhappy marriages and back to their lovers.

Of course, such dramatic reactions are not only the domain of these newer *denis ipakana* ('disco/dance songs'). The courting songs of *yekia* and *selepa* can equally break the heart of a lover. A woman can be driven to self-mutilation if another is chosen over her during this time of courting. If a man desires a woman who is being courted by another man through *yekia* performance, he would form his own group of men and sing *yekia* close to the rival group in order to win her affections, to praise his place well, showing his riches so she would choose him instead (Kenny Kendoli, Personal communication, 26 June 2006). If, however, he is 'out-sung' by a richer man, or a man better skilled at the courting genre who can describe and praise his land in a more appealing manner, he could inflict harm on himself (Richard Alo, Personal communication, 24 July 2006).

In the most extreme cases, a lover can commit suicide over a relationship. This appears to be largely a female response and is often used as an act of vengeance by the woman towards her family and/or husband in order to create economic havoc in their lives (remembering the concept of bride price).

Courting and death

Earlier in this chapter, I mentioned the connection between courting and death in Duna song[9] through the physical location of the *yekianda* of pre-contact times on top of the grave sites of ancestors. In such a physical setting, *yekia* performances fostered a sense of renewal as relationships for the future were instigated virtually on the graves of the past (Nicole Haley, Personal communication, 28 November 2005). There are, however, more ways in which this connection between courtship and death is maintained, and one of the key ways—more readily transferable into the new performance context—is through song texts. To explore this further, we shall now return to the death of Wakili to revise some of the observations made in that earlier chapter in a new light and to consider another lament composed for her by Kipu Piero.

Death is connected with courting in the lyrics of many *khene ipakana*. In Chapter 4, Example 4.4, Kepo Akuri sings of her sister Wakili breaking the *apia* plant off as she travels away from the land of the living. This plant happens to be one of those used in making armbands and armbands are one of the items given in courting (another is the cassowary pinion, which was sung about in one of the *yekia* examples earlier in this chapter). Kepo appears to be suggesting to Wakili that as she goes she should take *apia* with her in order to make armbands to give to the dead men that she is about to join. Such a sentiment is common, though usually expressed more directly, in laments sung by other Duna women (Kenny Kendoli, Personal communication, 7 March 2007).

---

9 A similar dialectic also seems to occur for the Foi. Weiner (1991:151) writes that times of sorrow are also times of courtship/enticement.

In an excerpt from another lament (Example 6.12), Kipu Piero sings for Wakili to join dead men in a game of ball and to flirt with them by just throwing them a glance (not staring but being modest).

Example 6.12 (▶ Audio 51) *Khene ipakana ('re lene keno').*

antiali wane <u>pakala</u> nane mbalo weinania re lene keno	dear mother daughter, the *pakala* cloud boys a ball game they will play, you must just glance at them
antiali wane <u>isiki</u> nane mbalo weinania re lene keno	dear mother daughter, the *isiki* Port Moresby boys a ball game they will play, you must just glance at them
antiali wane <u>wasiki</u> nane mbalo weinania re lene keno	dear mother daughter, the *wasiki* Port Moresby boys a ball game they will play, just glance at them
antiali wane <u>ela</u> nane mbalo weinania sokoma rano	dear mother daughter, the *ela* aeroplane boys a ball game they will play, you must sit down and view
antiali wane <u>pakala</u> nane mbalo weinania sokoma rano	dear mother daughter, the *pakala* cloud boys a ball game they will play, you must sit down and view
antiali wane <u>yuwei</u> nane mbalo weinania sokoma rano	dear mother daughter, the *yuwei* cloud boys a ball game they will play, you must sit down and view
antiali wane <u>eperi</u> nane mbalo weinania sokoma rano	dear mother daughter, the *eperi* Port Moresby boys a ball game they will play, you must sit down and view
antiali wane <u>pakala</u> nane mbalo weinania sokoma rano	dear mother daughter, the *pakala* cloud boys a ball game they will play, you must sit down and view
antiali wane <u>yuwei</u> nane mbalo weinania sokoma rano	dear mother daughter, the *yuwei* cloud boys a ball game they will play, you must sit down and view

This lament was recorded while Kipu was washing some clothes by hand (see Figure 6.4). The lament is reflective, formulaic but not strictly structured. Almost absent-mindedly, she repeats each line, alternating praise names as they come to mind, not in their anticipated sequential order as they would be performed in public. When I checked this translation with Richard Alo, I acknowledged with him song text differences between this lament and those I have recorded in the past by older women (such as that of Pokole Pora in Example 4.2). I suggested that although the text differed slightly, the 'nek' (melody) remained essentially the same. Richard disagreed, citing again the textual differences in further detail. He shook his head, saying that Kipu's lament did not sound good, that the singer should not jump from one clan to another and back again as Kipu had done, as that did not show enough 'sori'. The fact that Kipu began every line of this lament with the exclamation *antiali wane* was also, he claimed, not traditional. He concluded that she must have been practising (Richard Alo, Personal communication, 16 August 2006). In arguing against melodic similarities by citing textual differences, it was proven once again to me that in Duna ancestral song, the text is paramount—so much so that one does not have a vocabulary, or indeed a need, to describe melody as a separate concept, apart from labelling its genre. Further to this, it is textual inventiveness (within convention) that is prized by the Duna; melodic inventiveness is generally not prized.

This lament is non-conventional in the features expressed above; however, there is another striking difference in the text. The activity in which the dead men are engaged is a game of ball. It is unclear what type of ball game is being referred to in this lament as several are currently practised in the Lake Kopiago area. These include basketball, volleyball and rugby league. All these are introduced games from the colonial period, which is indicated in part by the English-derived term for ball, *mbalo*. It is significant that from Kipu's vantage point sitting at the table outside her house the local place for playing ball games—most commonly basketball—would have been in her line of vision. This could have inspired the reference to ball games in her lament. References to flirting with the eye (*re lene keno*) would have appeared in *awenene khene ipakana*; however, the setting for such flirting would not have been the same. In many ways, though, this lament is a continuation of the laments of times past—it addresses the deceased, is ruled by repetition and utilises a very similar melodic contour (based on a restricted three-tone refrain). Particularly, it maintains through the text a connection between courting and death in the absence of the *yekianda* and in doing so contributes to the understanding of fertility in death (as described in Chapter 4).

Conclusion

This chapter has taken a circuitous journey through the courting songs of the Duna, moving from ancestral courting songs to the introduced, and back again. It has been deliberately circuitous in order to blur the boundaries between what I continue to identify as ancestral and introduced forms of song. I began and ended with examples of ancestral song that incorporated elements of the new; *yekia*, in its new performance context out of the *yekianda* and away from women, is now often composed with politics in mind, while *khene ipakana* incorporates references to introduced social activities. Contemporary courting practices were revealed to show continuity with the past—in particular, the movement of love messages through the water and the metaphorical reference of men to water spirits. Courting through the playing of musical instruments was seen to continue in the use of the guitar (and ukulele) and parallels were drawn between the *yekianda* and the disco as night-time courting rituals.

Figure 6.4 Kipu sings while washing, with daughter, Monika, by her side.

Themes of times past were shown to continue in song texts and in particular the elicitation of sympathy ('sori') and reactions to that emotion in ancestral and introduced genres was shown to be crucial in courting songs for the Duna (and indeed across Papua New Guinea). Finally, the relationship between courting and death was explored with the revisiting of Wakili's death and the examination of an additional lament composed for her.

This chapter develops the premise that ancestral songs can look forward while introduced songs can look back, building on the experiences and understandings of the past. It is in this way that a continuum of musical practice is forged. Now we will examine continuity at the very beginning of musical practice—the creation of songs.

7. Creativity and preservation

no ken wari, no ken surik	don't be concerned, don't back away
traim na wokim tasol	just try and do it

The previous three chapters have been concerned with illuminating the continuity of theme, text and function between Duna songs of ancestral and foreign origin, or the endogenous and the exogenous. This chapter will be concerned first with the creative process itself, as it applies to Duna song creation. Both ancestral and introduced song styles display a similar approach to composition, in particular the recycling of melodic material in songs of the same genre, and this compositional process can be seen as another form of continuity. This in turn reveals continuity in what is regarded as a key element of Duna song form: textual innovation. Consequences of this creative approach for the preservation endeavour are considered, before the chapter then turns to the views of the Duna themselves on the maintenance of their own traditions and some of the ways in which they have sought to do this.[1]

Continuity in creativity: 'traim na wokim tasol'

The process of creativity is epitomised in the words of one popular song, 'traim na wokim tasol' ('just try and do it'), cited above.[2] One must acknowledge, however, that creativity does not start from nothing. Liep (2001:1) describes creativity as something that 'bursts forth when elements, which were already known but apart, are brought together by inventive people in a novel way'. He goes on to define it as the process whereby 'something new is produced through the recombination and transformation of existing cultural practices or forms' (Liep 2001:2) and declares that '[e]very creative effort must emanate from familiar forms and methods of production' (p. 6). As such, structural resources are in place in any creative endeavour and Duna song is no exception. Subscription to melodic and textual conventions can be considered the primary requirement for successful song creation for the Duna. I now address those conventions that are shared across the spectrum of Duna musical practice.

---

1   This chapter presents the views of Duna men only; the opinions of Duna women on the creativity and preservation of their musical practices appear to be far less frequently voiced.

2   Jebens (1997:43) also draws on the Tok Pisin expression 'traim tasol' ('just try it') to describe the 'traditional and continuing readiness to experiment with innovation' in regards to religion in one community of the Southern Highlands Province.

Regarding the creative process it is important to remember what was stated in Chapter 2: for the Duna, the creation of songs is an egalitarian process. Also, the roles of performer and composer are intertwined, resembling the 'singer-songwriter' figure in popular Western music. As set out in Chapter 2, distinctive melodies exist for distinct Duna ancestral genres. This is how the genres, and in turn their functions, are identified. The same can be said of introduced styles of song. Many songs are based closely on the melodic format of the Christian revivalist song style and this melodic format has been circulating among the Duna at least but most likely also beyond for several decades with little change. This can be seen when Pugh-Kitingan's notation of a performance of *Ngodegana ipa gana*, recorded in 1975 and reproduced in Chapter 3 (Example 3.3), is compared with my own notation of '*nane* laip senis *nganda waya keina*' (Example 3.4). Any melodic change in the recycling of the Christian revivalist song format is likely to have resulted from the different textual settings applied to that melody—for example, the addition of repeated notes to account for additional syllables (which is the case for the latter of the above two examples). It is clear that the recycling of distinct melodic formulas is integral to the creation of Duna ancestral songs and this practice continues in the creation of songs in introduced styles.

If melodic material in Duna song is generally formulaic then innovation must occur in another aspect of song composition. As suggested above, this occurs in the aspect of text. The creation of poetic texts is held in high esteem across Papua New Guinea (see Schieffelin 1976; Feld 1982; Weiner 1991; Rumsey 2006b). Although the quality of this poetic invention might be variable, for the Duna, textual innovation can be seen across song styles due to the fixity of melodic features of the songs. This invention is, however, guided by convention and, perhaps not surprisingly, the same conventions guide both pre-contact and post-contact song forms. These primary conventions are word substitution and the repetition and the parallelism in which this results.

In both solo and group ancestral performances, textual lines are repeated several times. This often occurs through the process of *ipakana yakaya* (explained in Chapter 2), which by definition is concerned with the listing of various landscape features using their *kēiyaka*. This occurs in a textual (and melodic) frame, whereby each *kēiyaka* (usually heading the line) is substituted by another on repetition of the frame. Thus a kind of textual parallelism occurs.

Such a feature is also apparent in newer Duna song styles, whether or not the word (or phrase) substituted is a *kēiyaka*. For example, consider the song text of the standard Christian song type showcased in Chapter 3:

> *nane* laip senis *nganda waya keina*

> *imane* laip senis *nganda waya keina*

In this example the first word of each line is different, as in the typical *ipakana yakaya* process of ancestral music, while the rest of the line (which I referred to earlier as the textual frame) remains the same. A similar textual construction showing word substitution in the first line and also resulting in parallelism is apparent in the many 'Memba *pi nakaya*' songs of Chapter 3:

> memba *pi nakaya*

> haiwe *pi naraya*

Because of the high value placed on textual innovation, songs constantly change, though textual phrases and motifs are sometimes reused (this is discussed in a later section on authorship and ownership). Melodic material, though flexible to a point in accommodating new texts, remains in contrast relatively static.

Until this point, the musical systems of ancestral and introduced music have been considered as separate entities. This is primarily because of the separate origins of these systems. We might now consider whether there is a continuity of musical sound also present.

Musical similarities between the endogenous and exogenous

The most effective way to consider a possible continuity in musical sound is to map the musical systems onto each other and observe where the elements coincide. It has already been established that Duna ancestral song (and instrumental music) is largely non-metric. What similarities there are, then, would be revealed in the area of pitch.

We have seen that the tonal centre and pitches of a tone and two tones above it are important in Duna ancestral genres—for example, *yekia* (see Example 2.5). These pitches correspond to the whole tones of the Western diatonic tradition; they could be conceived of as being the same as the first three degrees of a major scale. The employment of a semitone below the tonal centre in such genres as *khene ipakana* and *pikono* is also suggestive of the Western musical system, as it corresponds to the 'leading note' or seventh degree of a scale, which is raised from a tone to a semitone below the tonal centre. This similarity is indirectly identified by Pugh-Kitingan (1981:362) in her cipher notation, which depicts this pitch as '7' and also occasionally '7b' (to indicate a whole tone below the tonal centre or what would be known in the Western tonal tradition as a flat seventh), with a dot under both occurrences to indicate its belonging to the octave below.

In the Duna composition of Western songs, however, this seventh degree is rarely utilised—nor is the fourth degree of the major scale. This is pertinent; it is the quality of these two tones that partly defines the conventions of the Western diatonic system. In the Duna songs composed in the Western musical system, particularly those songs in the style of the Christian revival songs, the pitches most common are the tonal centre, a tone above it, two tones above it (a third), three and a half tones above it (a fifth) and four and a half tones above it (a sixth). This can be seen clearly in Example 3.3. Thus, the 'new' Duna system can be seen to correspond with the common pentatonic scale,[3] as Pugh-Kitingan (1981:291) also identifies when describing the Huli revival songs.

Although the pentatonic scale should not be seen as the foundation of Duna ancestral music, the first three pitches of it, as mentioned above, feature heavily in that system. The higher pitches (and larger intervals) can also be said to feature in some ancestral genres; often the beginning of *pikono* phrases utilises these degrees; also the tone and a half below the tonal centre of the *selepa* melodic contour (see Chapter 2, Example 2.4) correlates to the sixth degree of a major scale.

The pitches employed by the Duna in their singing of ancestral genres of music are therefore comparable with those pitches utilised by the Western diatonic system. Such observations in musical 'continuity' are not so much examples of either of these two musical systems shifting to encompass the other as an example of where the systems might meet—what they might share in terms of melodic convention. These similarities do more to explain the Duna's ultimate acceptance of a new musical system (as described by Pastor Hagini in Chapter 3) than to explain any organic adaptation of one system to another. Therefore, in my argument, the similarity of musical systems is necessary to contemplate but in reality plays little role in an overall musical continuity. What is most important to note regarding continuity on the compositional level in terms of musical elements (aside from text) is, as described above, the recycling of melodic material within all genres of Duna song.

Authorship and ownership

Earlier I argued that textual innovation was a highly valued aspect of Duna song creation across time, but that it was also common for certain phrases or motifs to be reused. This raises the question of song authorship and, by extension, song ownership.

---

3   The common pentatonic scale is understood to be the major scale of the anhemitonic pentatonic collection of scales (that is, scales without semitone intervals), most commonly represented by the tones C-D-E-G-A (Day-O'Connell n.d.).

Toynbee (2003:104) writes: 'Authorship, in all forms of culture including music, is of a profoundly social nature.' For Duna song, this is particularly and temporally so. The moment of authorship of a Duna song, for the majority of songs of ancestral and foreign origins, occurs at the moment of performance; songs in their final form are seldom rehearsed beforehand. And the moment of performance is a social event; most songs are performed not individually but as a group and in a particular social context such as grieving, courting or celebrating.

For the Duna, songs are often described with reference to particular performances or, more specifically, performers. This is essentially because of the level of textual innovation apparent. Kenny Kendoli recently described his favourite *pikono* stories in terms of the performers who told them (it is important to remember here that *pikono* is the only ancestral Duna song genre intended to be performed solo):

> I have three *pikono* favourites. One is a *pikono* man named Urungawe Pukani, in a performance of Kiliya's, another is Amina Kelo, in a performance of Luke Ranga from Yokona…

> They're favourites of mine. I really like them and these two are the ones that I really enjoy. Another one is Yeripi Pake,[4] well there are a lot of stories about Yeripi Pake but one story is that a woman took him to the cannibal areas to fight. This was a story told by Teya. (Kendoli [translated by Lila San Roque] forthcoming)

Duna songs rarely exist as static works reiterated without variation. This applies to Duna song genres across the board and ties closely with the value of textual innovation in songs. Although some genres, such as *yekia*, utilise common imagery and textual features, they also allow for the creation of new poetic features. Singers who create successful variations become known as particularly effective performers and these variations can be attributed to their name until they are eventually incorporated by others into future performances, thereby becoming standard features themselves.

The Duna understand that once a song has been performed, the format is available to others to use. Still, the changes that are made are not always viewed as favourable by the original author (when that author can be identified). In the following interview excerpt, Richard Alo expresses his dissatisfaction

---

4   Stewart and Strathern (2002b:41) describe a *pikono* plot with a character named Irimi Pake, who they identify as being the same as Yerepi Pake. There are also other *pikono* characters with names that begin with 'Yerepi-' (see Stewart and Strathern 2002b:42–4, 2005:94).

with a version of a guitar-based church song that he had composed in the local Apostolic Church at Kopiago, and which I had recorded in 2005 being sung by a group of Duna women in Mount Hagen:

> Em ol kisim nau, sampela long namel long song bilong mi, ol kirap na rausim na ol putim nupela toktok bilong ol i kam na go insait…Dispela [nupela tok] em mi no putim long en, ol putim i kam igo insait…Mi no save wanem lotu o wanem manmeri putim i kam igo insait, mi no save… Mi ino gat hamamas long dispela.

> Mi gat planti ol songs bilong mi long haus lotu bilong Apostolic. Olgeta manmeri save singim raun…Mipela [yangpela manki] save holim gita na singsing. So ol kisim long het na, taim yu pleim dispela song [recording] bilong yu, bai yu harim ol meri mix up long singsing—narapela bai kirap na arangim narapela word, na narapela bai wokim bilong en yet i go, bikos ol ino klia gut long song we mipela komposim long en. Ol ino rekordim gut na ol pleim na ol mekim olsem. So ol bilong stat bilong sing em oli singim stret where mi singim long en. Long namel ol lus tingting bilong en…stail bilong ol i kam insait…Dispela [nupela tok] mi ino putim long en…ol i faul long singsing we mi bin mekim long en… Mi no wanbel long dispela singsing.

> [They all took it, and some of the middle of my song, they got rid of that and they put their own new words in…This (new text) I didn't put there, they put it in…I don't know what church or what people put it inside, I don't know…I'm not happy with it.

> I've got plenty of songs of mine (used) in the Apostolic church. All the people sing them around the place…We (young boys) would hold the guitars and sing. So all the people would get them (the songs) in their heads and, when you play this song (recording) of yours, you will hear all the women mix up the song—another will get up and arrange another word, and another will do it her way, because they all aren't clear of how we composed the song. They don't remember it well and they all play it and do that. So at the start they all sing it the way I sang it. In the middle they forget it…their own style comes inside…This (new text) I didn't put in it, they all got it wrong the song that I composed…I'm not in agreement with this song.] (Richard Alo, Interview, 2 July 2006)

Richard's words show a number of aspects of song transmission and composition. Richard suggests indirectly that the song that he composed should be sung the way he originally composed it; however, he can only express his dissatisfaction with the new product; he is unable to control the use of his song in any way (it is unclear though whether he is unhappy with that fact it has changed at all or whether it is the new text that he specifically dislikes). Richard outlines how songs (specifically in the church performance context) are committed to memory by the congregation and sung outside the original performance context by many (at one point in the interview he commented that the textual changes in the women's performance of his song were lacking in religious praise). Importantly, he comments (and extensively throughout the interview, singing the two versions more than once) only on the textual change of the song; he does not comment in any way on the melodic material or vocal style of presentation. The focus, then, is on textual innovation. Finally, the real composer of this song fluctuates in Richard's account from being himself ('mi') to the group of boys with which he first performed the song ('mipela') and then back to himself again. Thus, again it can be seen that authorship of a song cannot be removed from the first performance of it; authorship essentially establishes itself in the performance of the song, rather than in a prepared product.

From the above we see that some sense of authorship can be claimed for Duna songs; however, ownership of these creative moments as such is not asserted. This lack of ownership rules is in marked contrast with other parts of Melanesia. For example, Ammann (2004) reveals that a very high level of importance is placed on song ownership for the Tanna people of Vanuatu. In other areas of Papua New Guinea, such as Kanjimei (located geographically and culturally between the Sepik region and the Highlands), there are strict rules of song ownership, in which songs can be purchased from the composer and compensation must be paid for the misappropriation of songs (Darja Hoenigman, Personal communication, 11 September 2006).

Suwa, in his study of the music of communities in the Madang district of Papua New Guinea, suggests that ownership of songs can come about as a result of efforts in song preservation. He (2001b:92) writes that after the colonisation of the Madang area 'the significance of *singsing tumbuna* was transformed' and '[a]n old dance, which might previously have been exchanged throughout the region, subsequently became a cultural property for one community'. Suwa (2001b:93) identifies that the concept of cultural conservation and ownership, as it is known in the West, is an ideal adopted by these communities. If this preservation ideal is indeed an exogenous one, let us consider, then, the extent to which the Duna might engage this ideal.

Preservation

As we have seen, the Duna value textual innovation in songs across the spectrum of musical influence. Therefore, songs themselves are constantly changing, though one could say that the melodic material—through melodic recycling due to the importance of melodic markers for genres—is generally preserved. This constant changing in practice appears to overshadow the Duna's desire for song preservation. Such an attitude is not unusual in Papua New Guinea; Suwa implies as much for the coastal song tradition he studies. Closer to home, Niles suggests of the Ku Waru people of the Western Highlands region that for their genre of *tom yaya kange* at least, creativity in the text is important in a performance. For this genre, performers present their narratives in 'a metrically and melodically highly regular and predictable framework'—one that 'enables listeners to focus on the constantly-changing poetry of the text' (Niles 2007:119). Similar to the Duna, then, for the Ku Waru, song preservation comes about through fixed melodic structures, but the focus (and value) is on textual innovation.

One could argue that an apparent strong sense of individual agency could diminish any inclination towards the idea of 'preservation'.[5] An example from my fieldwork at Kopiago highlights this possibility. In an interview at Hirane parish with the renowned *pikono* singer Kiale Yokona (see Figure 7.1), the topic of the many young Duna men's interest in guitar music arose. This activity was aligned with European ways and was contrasted with Duna ancestral interests such as the performance of *pikono*. Commenting on this, Kiale (Interview, 16 March 2005) said that he personally chose to continue in the ways of his father. There was no concern expressed for the actions of others in his generation or the next (though he did express, when asked, that he expected that his young son would in time learn to perform *pikono*). This 'every man for himself' or 'it's his affair' attitude (Strathern 1979) could affect the maintenance of these traditions.

Another example of individualism and its effect on preservation can be seen in the following comments of a Duna cultural leader and spokesperson. During a series of performances staged for Tim Scott and myself in 2005 (one of which is captured visually in Chapter 2, Figure 2.1), an older man was present, overseeing the dress, decoration and performance by the Duna men (see Figure 7.2). Afterwards I asked of his background. He said that his name was Pati Kweria and he was a man of mixed Huli and Duna descent (see Figure 7.3). Pati was recognised by some as a kind of cultural ambassador for the region, having travelled to Singapore in the mid to late 1970s with a Huli group to promote Papua New Guinea with the funding of an unspecified Australian company and with the support of the Koroba-Lake Kopiago MP of the time, Andrew Wabiria (Pati Kweria, Interview, 21 April 2005).

---

5   Early anthropological literature argued that Highlands societies were highly individualistic; however, the new Melanesian ethnography—in particular, the writings of Marilyn Strathern (1988)—argued against this claim, suggesting that personhood in that region is rather 'dividual' or relational. Recent research adds to this debate, noting a distinction between individuality and individualism (Cohen 1994:168), the coexistence of both individuality and dividuality, even in Marilyn Strathern's model (Rumsey 2006b:343), the existence of a concept of selfishness (LiPuma 1998:79) and the possibility of an individuation that is 'freed and enacted in particular circumstances' (Corin 1998:87).

Figure 7.1 Kiale Yokona at Hirane, March 2005.

Figure 7.2 Pati instructs in the creation of headdresses at Hirane, March 2005 (although he is somewhat obscured by the men he is instructing, Pati can be recognised at left of photograph by his distinctive white hat).

Photo by *Tim Scott*

Pati spoke about his role as teacher of traditions to Huli and Duna men, particularly as they pertained to dress and body adornment (he stated that he did not instruct in the manner of singing). When I asked him if he had any concern about a potential loss of traditions, he replied in his basic Tok Pisin:

> Ol laik kam long mi, mi lanim. Nau, ol i no toktok na ol i no kam long mi, mi lusim nau…ol i no kam, mi bai hat long tokim aut, ol i no harim tok bilong mi. Olsem na mi lusim.

> [If they all want to come to me, I'll teach them. Now they don't say (that they want to learn), and they don't come, so I leave it…(as) they don't come, it is hard to speak out, they don't listen to what I say. So I leave it.]

The next year, I conducted an interview with Duna man Hawai Pawiya in Mount Hagen, after he and his friend had performed a number of the ancestral song genres of *yekia* and *selepa* for me to record (see Figure 7.4). Of a similar age to Kiale, Hawai had been living in the town for some time. According to him, *yekia* and *selepa* are sung in the houses of Duna people who live in Mount Hagen.[6] Hawai expressed his belief that the ancestral (or 'tumbuna') way would not be lost to the people at home in the Southern Highlands or in Mount Hagen because it is 'inside the blood':

---

6 I was unable to witness such performances myself as it was considered unwise for a white person, or indeed any young woman, to walk around the town of Mount Hagen in the evening (advice offered by both Duna people and Australians).

Figure 7.3 Pati Kweria at Hirane, April 2005.

Dispela pasin bilong tumbuna em i pasin insait long blut. Em i stap yet. Em pasin tumbuna em, em kastom pasin hia na em bai yumi no inap lusim, em yumi holim, em yumi laikim, em bilong mipela. Em...Tasol 123 kam na ABC kam na ol sampela kain sios o lotu o kain samting, gutpela kain samting i kam nau, yumi olgeta manmeri i go long dispela hap na nau yumi i stat skul na lanim i go kam i stap. So pasin tumbuna bilong yumi em yumi ino lusim, em i pas long blut so dispela...yumi i stap yet. Bihain bihain tu bai yumi givim long pikinini bilong mipela yet.

[This ancestral way is the way that is inside the blood. It is still inside. The ancestral way, it is the custom way here and we will not be able to lose that, we hold it, we like it, it belongs to us. That it does...But (now) 123 (numeracy) comes and ABC (literacy) comes and some churches or religions or various other things, various good things come now, and we all (Duna) people go to that side and now we start school and learning. So the ancestral way we have we cannot lose, it runs in the blood so this...we will still remain. Much later too we will still give it to our children.] (Hawai Pawiya, Interview, 10 July 2006)

Hawai commented that he liked the 'tumbuna' way, it was good and it was better than any other way:

Mi laikim tumbuna pasin bilong mi. Tumbuna pasin em gutpela. Em i moa gutpela long olgeta samting—em gutpela. Em.

[I like the ways of my ancestors. The ancestral way, it is good. It is better than anything—it is good. That it is.]

The Duna as a group have expressed this 'tumbuna pasin' at public forums both within their 'place' and outside. These public displays, however, have as their primary goal a display of Duna identity, not necessarily the preservation of traditions, though it can be considered that this might be one outcome of the displays. The examples presented here are the performances accompanying election campaigns and the Duna and Mount Hagen Cultural Shows.

Figure 7.4 Hawai Pawiya showing his newly constructed pigpens at his place in Mount Hagen, July 2006.

Politics

Times of political activity, particularly times of campaigning preceding an election, are often also times of cultural performance for the Duna. Robinson (2002:143–4) writes that the 1997 national elections inspired the regular practising and performance of 'singsings' at Lake Kopiago. Although details of the musical practices incorporated are not given, it can be fairly safely assumed that the performances were of *mali* (as this is the only group singing, moving and playing available and used for celebratory occasions). Haley similarly writes that the 1997 elections were a forum for teaching and reinforcing Duna dress and behaviour—in particular, as opposed to the neighbouring Huli language group, who also had candidates in the election. She recounts:

> [In the] weeks, even months, leading up to the election there were regular dance contests at the Dilini market place, in which the supporters of each candidate, dressed in traditional dress, would compete against each other in order to demonstrate the worthiness of their candidate. These occasions also served as an opportunity for older men and women to instruct the younger ones on the true 'Duna' way to dress and conduct oneself. Individuals who were seen to be adopting or incorporating what were viewed to be Huli forms of dress were publicly chastised. (Haley 2002b:132)

Some scholars see occasions of politics as a way to 'misuse' culture. Ammann (2001:156) writes: 'There are many groups among [Pacific] islander populations who do not want, or who do not care about, the maintenance of Melanesian cultural values…Besides not caring about cultural values, or even rejecting their culture, people may deliberately misuse their culture, especially during political campaigns and debates.' It is not clear what Ammann means by 'misuse' here. It might be considered a 'misuse' when a cultural practice is being performed in a context different to that originally intended; however, a new context can be considered a creative adaptation rather than a misuse and could be the only context available for such traditional practices in a contemporary world.

In many cases, politics lies at the heart of the revival of traditional cultural practices. Another institution is equally, if not more, effective in Papua New Guinea, and this is the phenomenon of the cultural show.

The Duna and cultural shows

The cultural show in Papua New Guinea has been popular across the country for several decades, since the first shows were mounted in the Highlands centres of Goroka and Mount Hagen in the 1950s and held in alternate years. Crowdy describes the phenomenon as follows:

> These cultural shows usually consist of a performance arena for traditional dance groups, a stage for power bands and an arena for commercial displays. Based on Australian rural shows and instigated and supported by the Australian administration in the 1950s and 1960s they have become an important part of cultural production in PNG, with a considerable degree of kudos associated with participation, by both traditional and popular music groups, and results in their competitive sections. (Crowdy 2001:142–3)

It has been written that the cultural show in Papua New Guinea was established in the Highlands as 'a substitute for warfare' (Sullivan n.d.:15; see also Kunda 2006:40)—that is, to promote peace.[7] With opposing Highlands groups competing in the show context for prize money, however, the cultural show in this context can rather be seen as an extension of warfare in another guise. Due to the often violent consequences of such competition in the past, winning groups are still judged but the prize money—at the Mount Hagen Cultural Show at least—is now distributed equally among participants and in 2006 the amount given to each performer was K60 (Max Kumbamong, Chairman of the Mount Hagen Cultural Show, Email communication, 10 May 2007).[8]

Cultural shows are considered by Papua New Guineans to be vital to tourism and the preservation of culture. A Papua New Guinean newspaper article describing the revival of the Waghi Cultural Show declares that

> [p]reserving and promoting traditional culture is the only way to attract overseas tourists to flock into the country. Papua New Guinea is venturing into the modern way of life and our culture and traditions are slowly fading, with only a few people struggling to preserve it to bring in tourists. (Taime 2006)

---

7   The show was also said to have been initiated in order 'to assist in population censuses' (Kunda 2006:40).

8   In 2005 a system of grading participant groups was in place in which the best groups were paid K60 each, the regular groups K50 and the poorest groups K40. This grading was based on the level of authenticity of the groups' 'bilas' (their adornments and body decoration for the performance); K40 performers would be those who incorporated much non-traditional material into their outfit (for example, plastic bottles or grain bags). This grading scale was meant to encourage the use of traditional materials, but was not enforced in 2005; rather, all performers that year received K50 each. Although it was expressed that the committee wished to enforce this grading better in 2006, it appears from Kumbamong's correspondence above that the grading did not eventuate that year either (Don Niles, Email communication, 19 May 2007).

This same newspaper also featured a full-page advertisement entitled 'Reviving the Malagan Show' (Namuri 2006). Thus it seems that the idea of reviving culture through shows is prominent in contemporary Papua New Guinean consciousness, and actively encouraged.

The Duna first participated in a cultural show in Goroka in 1958, in a small group together with representatives of the Huli (Sinclair 1984:164–5). They were reportedly well received, described as 'the hit of the Show' and 'their arrogant bearing and unique wigs, far superior in design and execution to the pudding-basin and bullock-horn wigs of the Enga-speaking tribes of Wabag, aroused keen interest' (Sinclair 1984:165). It seems that the Southern Highlanders continued to be of interest in subsequent show appearances for the remoteness of their place of origin; in a description of the 1967 Mount Hagen show, the Duna from Kopiago were reported to be one of the groups that had travelled the furthest—193 km—in order to participate (Anonymous 1967:10).

Before the 2006 Mount Hagen Cultural Show, most Duna people in the town that I spoke to did not think that their culture would be represented at the show that year. One young woman said that there was too much fighting and too much disagreement among the Duna who lived in Mount Hagen for them to form a group (Jacqueline Jack, Personal communication, 11 August 2006). Richard Alo said the Duna living in Mount Hagen would not be able to participate in the show as they did not have the required bush materials at hand to make their costumes and body decorations and it was too difficult for Duna people living at home in the Southern Highlands to travel to Mount Hagen to perform, due to the inaccessibility of transport (Richard Alo, Personal communication, June 2006).

I was, therefore, quite surprised when moving about the arena at that year's show to hear my name being called out by one of the performers. Turning around, I saw my young Duna friend Oksi Mapu, whom I had met at Kopiago the previous year, and who had come to Mount Hagen to 'raun nating' (to just go around with nothing particular to do). With a group of other young men, he was painted quite unlike anything I had ever seen before, with black and white stripes across the body, reminiscent of the patterns of a football jersey (a favourite garment among Highlander men). The resemblance did not seem coincidental, with some men even having painted numbers on their backs. The only piece of clothing they wore was a pair of football shorts. The football motif can be extended further, too, when one considers the arena on which they were performing: normally a rugby league ground where, on the second and final day of the Hagen Cultural Show, performers had to make sure they left the arena early so that the regular game of rugby league could start on time at 3 pm.

One young Duna man had bamboo attached to his fingers and he led the group, which moved in a chain with their hands on the hips of the person in front (see Figure 7.5). The young men were in turn led by a slightly older man carrying a sign that read 'Kund Rot SS group', meant to identify their 'singsing' group. At intervals, the performers would stop their chain-like movement and pose for the cameras (see Figure 7.6).

At one of these breaks in their performance, I took the opportunity to question the leader about himself and his group. He gave his name as Henri Hiruma and his place of origin as Hirane on his mother's side (he said that his father came from Pori, which is on the border of the Duna and Huli-speaking areas of the Southern Highlands). The performers, he said, came from several settlement areas in Mount Hagen and the payment per participant was, he said, the motivation for their forming the group. Of the dance, Henri assured me that it was a traditional Duna dance form known as *ita khawua* (meaning 'wild pig'), which was performed during the daytime, by men only, to make the pigs come; the only vocals utilised in the dance were pig-like snorts, which is often the way Duna people call their pigs. The dance had been renamed the 'snek denis' (snake dance) after the group's distinct snake-like movements.

Figure 7.5 Duna performance at Mount Hagen Cultural Show, 19 August 2006 (note the painted number 9 on the man in the foreground).

The movements were certainly distinct. I had not seen anything like them and thought it odd that I had not seen or heard about this genre at Kopiago (admittedly, though, as there is no *ipakana* [singing] or *alima* [instruments] involved in the *ita khawua*, it could have been considered by the Duna people to be outside my research interests). So I turned to my companion at the show, Richard Alo, for further explanation.

Richard specified that the performance was a *khawua kohu*. It was something performed in times past, after the *yekia* ritual when the men and women wished to remove the *ipa siri* (water spirits) who had been with them inside the *yekianda*.[9] There was no particular body decoration for this chasing away of the *ipa siri*; despite Henri's statements to the contrary, Richard assured me that the body decorations I saw in front of me now were pure show creations. Similar body decoration (black and white painted stripes, bamboo finger attachments) can be seen in two photographs published by Rainier (1996:74–5), attributed to the Minj area in the Waghi Valley and to Chimbu Province, which suggests that this style of decoration is a pan-Highlands creation.

Figure 7.6 Duna performers at rest (Oksi Mapu faces camera at far left).

---

9   It should be remembered from the previous chapter that the *ipa siri* are said to have a role in bringing men and women together in courtship (in this way the *ipa siri* could be said to resemble the Cupid of the Western world).

It is worth noting that at the 2007 Mount Hagen Cultural Show another Duna group from the settlement was formed to present the 'snek denis'. Their movements and their body decorations were much the same, with the addition of a declaration of place on their backs: 'LK NANE' ('Lake Kopiago Boys') (see Figure 7.7).

Figure 7.7 Duna performers take a break at the 2007 Mount Hagen Cultural Show.

A second 'snek denis' group was also in attendance at the 2007 Mount Hagen Cultural Show. Their group sign declared them as the 'Warakala Snake Boys', and when I spoke to them after their performance they told me they were originally from Tari (Huli language speakers) but now lived in a settlement area near the Mount Hagen army barracks named after a small creek called Kala. The leader of the Warakala Snake Boys—that is, the boy at the front of the 'snake' line—had added to his costume a mask he had purchased at the local store, which was to represent the head of the snake (see Figure 7.8). This mask was none other than a replica of that used in the popular US horror film series *Scream*, which is of course based on the Norwegian expressionist painter Edvard Munch's famous work of 1893 entitled *The Scream* (see Figure 7.8).

Figure 7.8 Warakala Snake Boys.

The cultural show, then, in these cases does not seem to be very successful at all in the preservation of ancestral performance practices. Some elements of traditional practice might be revived for the context, but here it was heavily reinvented—recontextualised, re-dressed and even renamed. One might ask why an antral genre of display such as Duna *mali mapu* was not chosen to be performed. Perhaps, as Richard suspected, it was because of a lack of materials for the dress and body decoration. Perhaps the Duna people of Mount Hagen were unskilled in performing that genre and others were not able to travel the distance. Perhaps, though, the very prominent display by the Huli people of their *mali mbawa* at the show (and also at other shows in times past) dissuaded a presentation of a similar dance by the Duna, who would wish to assert their difference and deny resemblance in the name of identity (Harrison 2006).

During my fieldwork at Kopiago in 2005, there was continued talk of the impending Duna Cultural Show. The supposedly annual event had even been advertised on posters produced by the National Cultural Commission and on the Internet through the Papua New Guinea Tourism and Business Directory web site (as the 'DSPB Cultural Show' of 'Lake Koplage [sic] District', where it continues to be erroneously listed). The show, however, never happened. Various reasons were given for this, the most common being the lack of funds available (though from where, no-one was sure—some said the provincial government) and the limited (and seemingly variable) availability of the president of the Kopiago local government council, Paiele Elo, who was the organiser of the Duna Cultural Show but who lived predominantly in the provincial capital of Mendi.

Petros Kilapa described to me his experience of the Duna Cultural Show of times past. The seven language groups that make up the descendents of the Hela brothers (see Chapter 2 and the story of Mburulu Pango) and are believed to share the same ancestry (Bogaya, Sinali, Hewa, Duna, Oksi, Huli and Enga) were said to come together at this time and celebrate, and also to trade among themselves—for example, the Hewa would trade feathers with the Duna for modern items such as pots or other Kopiago store products. The different groups would display their ancestral performance genres, with the Duna showcasing *mali mapu*, *selepa* and *yekia*. Duna could even join in other groups' dancing if they dressed and decorated themselves in exactly the same way. Stringband competitions with their own compositions were held and church songs could also be sung (religion did play a part, as pastors opened the show). Other events included tug-of-war competitions for men, 'tanim rop' races for women (rolling string or wool as part of the preparations to make bags), fire-making and tree-felling races, and much selling of crafts (Petros Kilapa, Personal communication, 25 April 2005).

In 2005, however, none of these anticipated activities occurred; the Duna Cultural Show did not eventuate. Reportedly it had not been held for several years. So it seems that cultural shows held on a local level are not that successful in terms of 'preservation' for Duna music either—not because of a lack of ancestral genres performed, but simply because they rarely come to pass. Does this mean, then, that the Duna are not interested in cultural preservation?

It can be said that during the time of this research, Duna attitudes to the maintenance of their ancestral past were mixed. A few people (namely older people) expressed concern that certain traditions were no longer practised; however, the majority did not express an opinion on the matter or did not, in fact, seem to comprehend why I might ask such a question, when I looked explicitly for an opinion. This non-engagement with the issue can be interpreted in a number of ways and one of these is that many Duna did not perceive that there was a decline in ancestral practices, in particular as it applied to Duna song. I have argued throughout that continuity is present in the themes, functions and now the composition of Duna songs, so such an interpretation can be supported here. After all, '[p]eople act in the world in terms of the social beings they are, and it should not be forgotten that from their quotidian point of view it is the global system that is peripheral, not them' (Sahlins 1999:412).

Those Duna who expressed concern over a decline in past practices thought that educational institutions could be of service to this cause. Two individuals— Richard Alo and Sane Noma—cited contemporary and ancestral institutions and both stressed the need for such education to be funded by external first-world sources, particularly Australian ones.[10]

---

10   It is important to remember that these ideas were expressed in these terms to me, an Australian.

Education for preservation: the school and the *haroli palena*

In Papua New Guinea, as elsewhere, it is widely understood that schools are an important place for the teaching of culture (cf. Faik-Simet 2006). Duna people too have recognised this. Richard Alo once accounted to me his desire to introduce a program of cultural studies to Kopiago schools, in which traditional ways (he specified traditional dress and decoration) would be taught by the older people in the community. Such a program had been implemented on a small scale (Wednesday mornings only) and for a short period in 2005 by the Rewapi Elementary School in Hirane parish, whose teachers were supported financially by an Australian benefactor. Richard stressed, however, that he would need to be funded by a body such as the Australian Agency for International Development (AusAID), which manages the Australian government's overseas aid program, in order to implement such a program. When I asked why, he responded with another question: 'How else will I pay the teachers?' (Richard Alo, Personal communication, 4 August 2006). His express need for external funding for his project echoes the sentiments expressed by Sane Noma below.

As revealed in Chapter 2's overview of Duna ancestral musical practices, the *haroli palena* bachelor cult was in the past the most important space for the education of adolescent boys and younger men. The *mindimindi kão* spearheaded the music of this education process. As was described in Chapter 2, the *mindimindi kão* are spells that instruct and educate the *haroli palena* initiates. Example 7.1 is part of a *mindimindi kão* sung to me for recording. The first minute is translated below.

Example 7.1 (▶ Audio 52, 0:00–1:02) *Mindimindi kão.*

alupa kendata hunake ha nake	*alupa* head on pillow in deep sleep
paiyape kendata hunake ha nake	*paiyape* head on pillow in deep sleep
remeti kendata hunake ha nake	*remeti* head on pillow in deep sleep
hundu kendata hunake ha nake	*hundu* head on pillow in deep sleep
ili hinika kundale kundapa kunda yope yopa	clean with the leaves of the *ili* tree then go
rewaya hinika kundale kundapa kunda yope yopa	clean with the leaves of the *rewaya ili* tree then go
kayema hinika kundale kundapa kunda yope yopa	clean with the leaves of the *kayema ili* tree then go
kundale hinika kundale kundapa kunda yope yopa	clean with the leaves of the *kundale ili* tree then go
ipa kurukuta koko sopa heyana kepa kepa	(on the) saltwater, the light is coming down, look, look
ripu sopa heyana kepa kepa	the *ripu* light is coming down, look, look

ripai sopa heyana kepa kepa	the *ripai* light is coming down, look, look
ngoto ngototia wayarua wayarua	*ngoto* morning lights are coming, coming
ripu riputia wayarua wayarua	*ripu* morning lights are coming, coming
hongo kokotia wayarua wayarua	*hongo koko* morning lights are coming, coming
hambua kutiakutiatia wayarua wayarua	*hambua kutia* morning lights are coming, coming
rakutia rakutiatia wayarua wayarua	*raku* morning lights are coming, coming
rangoli rangolitia wayarua wayarua	*rangoli* morning lights are coming, coming
ripu riputia wayarua wayarua	*ripu* morning lights are coming, coming

The repetitive textual and melodic structure of this *mindimindi kão* instructs the *haroli palena* boys to sleep well and to clean themselves using a particular kind of leaf. Bachelor cult initiates are often depicted as having glowing skin, and the juxtaposition of the description of light shining on water and the dawning light with these instructions on how to sleep and clean oneself indicates how this desired result can be obtained.

Outside the *haroli palena, mindimindi kão* are not often heard, except when people such as myself ask about musical practices from the 'taim bipo' ('time before'). The oldest generations of Duna people are the ones who hold this knowledge from their time in the *haroli palena*. Men under the age of fifty years or so have to refer back to the elders of their clan in order to understand completely the texts and praise names of *mindimindi kão* and the messages conveyed by the sound of the instruments once used in the *haroli palena*. In other words, much of the creative expression within the *haroli palena* has not been adapted to the changing social context.

A former *haroli palena* leader, Sane Noma saw enormous cultural change for the Duna people over his lifetime. We met regularly over the course of my fieldwork in 2005 and at almost every meeting we had he expressed his concern for his people and for the future. One of the ideas he voiced was the re-establishment of the *haroli palena* in order to restore order in his community (which had recently been destabilised by the violent behaviour of a group of young men). The absence of the *haroli palena* is problematic for Duna men. Stürzenhofecker writes:

> The demise of the Palena cult may also be seen as having contributed to male anxiety. One thing the cult accomplished was the removal of boys from domestic life with their mothers and their institutionalized socialization into male personhood under the tutelage of ritually pure bachelors…This time of separation no longer exists, and in a sense boys pass in an unrecognized and amorphous period of limbo from boyhood to manhood without a context in which they are unambiguously taught

the proper way to be men. Many later filled this void by seeking work outside of the local area as laborers on coastal plantations or, more recently, on mining sites. (Stürzenhofecker 1998:171)

On my visit to Kopiago in 2005, Sane was keen to find out if there was any funding available for him to re-establish the *haroli palena*. Although in times past one would not have needed cash to do this, Sane said he needed the money to 'katim diwai na wokim haus' ('cut the trees and build the house')—that is, pay for the use of the local sawmill owned by one of the pastors to cut and shape timber and to source other building items such as nails and corrugated iron. Although Sane championed ancestral practices, he wished to gain financial support from visitors and benefit from the high social status that such support would bring. This process of combining the capitalist world with the pre-contact one could on the surface appear incongruous, but could rather be considered as 'the indigenization of modernity, [establishing] their own cultural space in the global scheme of things' (Sahlins 1999:410). A return to the *haroli palena*, however, does not on its own satisfy, as the following section reveals.

Being 'in the middle'

Many young Duna men are acutely aware of the lack of transmission between generations and what that means for their future and their identity.[11] Jeremiah Piero, Kipu Piero's brother, who was introduced in Chapters 3 and 4 and who was in his early twenties at the time of interview, explains the situation as he sees it:

> Sapos yumi i putim long skul tasol, na mi faul establishing kastom bilong mipela, em ol save holim nau, mi lus tingting na mi stap. Laki mama bilong mi i stap na mi askim. Na ol man i stap na mi askim. Sapos mama bilong mi i no stap na ol man i dai, na yupela kam olsem na askim mi, mi tok olsem 'mi no save' ya. Mi bai tok olsem tasol i go.

> [If I just go to school and don't learn the custom of my people, that which they know now, I'll forget everything. It's lucky that my mother is here and I can ask her. The old men are alive and I can ask them. But if my mother wasn't here and the old men were dead, and you people came and asked me (questions), I'd have to say 'I don't know'. I'd say that and then go.] (Jeremiah Piero, Interview, 2 April 2005)

---

11   An earlier version of this section first appeared within a conference presentation entitled '*Singsing i go we*?: the revival of traditional music practices in a Highlands Papua New Guinea community', International Council for Traditional Music 38th World Conference, Sheffield, England, 3–10 August 2005.

Jeremiah's generation, in grappling with a liminal state, often appeals to visitors to their community for guidance and ultimately assistance in their quest for identity. In the same interview, Jeremiah said to me:

Taim mi bin stap long skul, mi bin komparim ol pasin bilong wait man, na mi bin komparim ol pasin bilong tumbuna bilong mi. Na mi lukim olsem dispela pasin bilong waitman em i stap long we. Na pasin bilong tumbuna bilong em i stap long we. Mi stap [long] namel stret. Mi hat long go bek long kisim pasin bilong tumbuna. Na mi hat long go kisim pasin bilong ol waitman. Na dispela ask tasol mi laik askim long yu: sapos mi stap namel stret, mi lusim skul, na mi laik kisim pasin bilong waitman, em i hat na hat olgeta. Na mi laik kisim pasin bilong ol tumbuna bilong mi, em hat na hat olgeta. Na mi stap namel stret. Husait bai sapotim mi… Nau mipela i stap namel stret na mipela i float raun long hia. Yu gat we long helpim mipela long dispela o nogat?

[When I was at school (Mendi High School, located in the provincial capital), I compared the white man's ways with the ways of my ancestors. And I can see that the white man's ways are a long way away. And the ways of my ancestors are a long way away. I'm really in the middle. It's hard for me to go back and get the ways of my ancestors. And it's hard for me to go and get the ways of the white man. Now this question I'd like to ask you: if I'm in the middle, and I've left school but I would like to get the ways of the white man, it's really hard. And if I would like to get the ways of my ancestors it's really hard. Who will support me… Now we (young men) are stuck in the middle and just floating around here. Have you got a way to help us with this or not?

When I asked Jeremiah what he thought about going into a re-established *haroli palena* as a solution, he responded:

Sapos yumi putim olgeta pikinini i go bek long 'bachelor culture' bilong mipela…em husait bai lukautim ol pikinini bilong skul? Husait bai lukautim haus sik? Husait bai toktok wantaim ol waitman, 'interpreting'?…mipela no inap lusim edukesen, mipela i no inap lusim kastom. So this tupela wantaim, sapos yumi holim tupela wantaim, em bai 'balance'. Sapos yumi go bek long kastom bilong mipela, em bai 'unbalance' na 'unbalance'.

[If we put the boys back into the bachelor cult…who will look after the children at school? Who will look after the medical clinic? Who will talk with the white man, interpreting?…we can't leave education, (but) we can't leave custom. So these two together, if we can have the two together, it will be balanced. If we go back to (only) custom, it will be really unbalanced.]

A balance involving the *haroli palena*, it seems, would be very hard to achieve for Duna people in the face of a desired 'modernity'. A revival of the *haroli palena* now, in order to stabilise Duna society and guide young men as once before, and to maintain cultural practices of the past at this critical time, would be fraught with difficulties. The people implicate the researcher (and in particular the Australian researcher) in their efforts to forge an identity that is current in their new world.

Conclusion: preservation in the continuity of creativity

As people create music that is built partly on musical elements already established (which, as Liep makes evident, is an essential aspect of the creative process), a key result is the conservation or maintenance of these elements through their use in a new form. Of course, not all elements are conserved; otherwise there would not be creativity.

Staged efforts to display and, in effect, maintain traditions have generally not been successful for the Duna cause, being seen as at best irregular efforts (for example, the Duna Cultural Show) and, at worst, entirely unrepresentative of Duna genres (as was seen at the 2006 Mount Hagen Show). They are, however, sites for creativity, sites where, to paraphrase Sahlins, the modern is indigenised—or, rather, the indigenous is modernised.

Jeremiah Piero has provided the answer to his concerns: combining old and new ways will achieve balance. His generation is finding a way to continue traditions—at least musical traditions—in a creative way that acknowledges and integrates the past with the current context, using both old and new musical mediums. Perhaps, as Appadurai (1991:474) suggests, rather than reject these new musical expressions created by the Duna, scholars should instead consider that 'it may be the idea of a folk world in need of conservation that must be rejected, so that there can be a vigorous engagement with…the world we live in now'.

8. Conclusion

> [T]he history of music, and of culture in general, consists not
> merely of the evolution of overtly new genres and styles, but
> of the rearticulation of extant idioms to respond to new social
> circumstances. (Manuel 1994:277)

The Duna live in a physical environment of steep slopes (*mei konenia*) that
are sometimes difficult to traverse. A stick of bamboo (*sola*) used as a prop
goes a long way in assisting a struggling traveller. Similarly, the Duna live in
a social and cultural environment of steep slopes, where the path on which
they walk can be precarious and unpredictable. Songs, like the stick of
bamboo, assist the Duna in picking their way over this terrain by providing
a forum for them to process change as it is experienced, in relation to what
is already known.

The change that the Duna have experienced, and continue to experience,
is enormous, with colonisation occurring relatively recently—less than 50
years ago—followed by an intense period of missionisation, then a rapid
move to independence and the subsequent departure of Europeans almost
as quickly as they came. If social change is expressed and experienced
through music then there should be little wonder that such change for the
Duna would be manifest in an outpouring of song.

The number and variety of musical examples that have been presented here
are testimony to the importance of music, and song in particular, in Duna
lives. They are also testimony to Duna cultural resilience and creativity
in the face of this extraordinary and rapid social change. This research
has provided a wide-ranging account of Duna musical practice, describing
song, instrumental music and music accompanied by dance. Although it has
been as inclusive as possible regarding the various genres of Duna music,
the focus has been on Duna song. It is through the examination of Duna
song that the argument for continuity can be most clearly seen, and thus it
is on the analysis of songs that this research is based.

In Chapter 1, I engaged with some of the recent thinking in contemporary
anthropology regarding debates about binary oppositions, hybridity, the
dividual person and processes of translation and documentation of oral
traditions. Taking a step back from the ethnography at hand for a moment,
we could ask: what can we contribute to these anthropological debates by
focusing on music and on cultural production? In that same chapter, I cited

Bohlman (1992:132): 'Musical ethnography should represent the musical moment, the creator of that moment, and the indigenous meaning of that moment.' My own research has moved between musical ethnography and an anthropology of music, the latter of which 'brings to the study of music the concepts, methods, and concerns of anthropology' in order to consider 'the way music is a part of culture and social life' (Seeger 1987:xiii). An anthropology of music contextualises the musical moment, explaining what its place is in a historically situated socio-cultural trajectory. In doing this, it can be seen that the musical moment is multiply determined by relatively autonomous components such as the musical tools available and the dynamics of the social situation, and that these musical moments are components of events that are always enacted as part of a value-creation process—asserting identity, modernity, attachment to place, religion, tension and desire. The outcomes of musical ethnography are enriched when considered in conjunction with this anthropological approach.

In the light of Manuel's observation in the above epigraph, this publication has shown both how existing Duna song genres have responded to change and how more recently introduced genres can be seen to continue aspects of these more established forms of musical creativity. After the world of Duna ancestral music was described in Chapter 2, the next chapter explained the exogenous origins of new Duna music and demonstrated to the reader— through the first individual song analyses of the book—two of the most essential concepts of continuity in Duna song creation across the spectrum of styles: textual innovation and melodic recycling. It was shown that new compositions, for the church or for secular purposes, often take as their material pre-existing melodies—a process that is the essence of ancestral song composition as it was defined in Chapter 2. These songs also show the high level of importance that is placed on creativity in text, utilising the features of parallelism and word substitution, all of which is consistent with ancestral genres.

In Chapter 4, I took the specific ethnographic example of Wakili Akuri's death to reveal laments as a platform for intense creativity, and how one singer in particular composed her laments in a number of styles but with a marked continuity of text structure, content and melodic contour. The Duna's intimate and complex relationship to land was described in the next chapter, and we saw how continuity is apparent in the way Duna people sing about place, especially in the continued use of *kẽiyaka* across genres, in the way land could be praised or denigrated in order to attract a lover and in how people sang about their movements through the landscape. Chapter 6 revealed how Duna ancestral genres of *yekia*, *selepa* and *khene ipakana* can be sung with modified texts for new contexts such as contemporary politics, visiting white women and new forms of recreation—a perfect example of what Manuel describes regarding extant idioms. The chapter explored new courting practices, especially the guitar as a kind of substitute for the ancestral *alima*, played to woo a woman, and the disco as the new courting house or *yekianda*. One of the functions of courting songs, that of eliciting sympathy, was shown to continue across the spectrum of song, and continuity regarding particular listener reactions to songs—namely, self-mutilation and suicide—was also discussed.

In Chapter 7, there was less discussion of musical continuity and more discussion of change and the potential (and reality) of loss. I showed that there is little concern expressed by the Duna regarding a loss of ancestral musical traditions. This is in contrast with many other cultural groups around the world, including other Melanesian groups—for example, those of New Caledonia and Vanuatu, where the indigenous people continue to speak of the need to maintain what they identify as 'kastom' (Ammann 2001). Such a lack of preservationist rhetoric could be interpreted in two ways: there is no perceived loss of tradition or the Duna simply do not care if there is. I would like to propose an alternative interpretation of this situation, however, in the light of the analysis presented here: as it is obvious that some ancestral musical genres are not practised at all anymore, and most are not practised in their original context, a lack of rhetoric of loss suggests in itself that there is a certain continuity at play, whether the Duna are conscious of it or not.

Such continuity should not be surprising; after all, all cultural practices occur in an already existing cultural setting and relate to ideas and values that have gone before. It would be convenient to conceive of Duna music of indigenous and exogenous origin as two opposing forms of expression, but this is simplistic and ultimately misleading. In order to understand, and ultimately to respect, Duna contemporary song composition, it must be viewed in all its complexity, with its relations to the past and to the present.

I have argued against setting up dichotomies of the 'traditional' and 'modern' in music, and in doing so I have highlighted indigenous agency in creative forms of expression. It is hoped that this approach to music research will provide inspiration for a new way of viewing other musical cultures that might have a similar colonial or exogenous history to the Duna. This in turn should assist in elevating the status of what is often classified as 'popular music' and dismissed as insignificant.

As this is the first study of Duna music of its kind, more research is needed in order for all the issues surrounding Duna musical practice to be fully explored. In particular, a study into gender and contemporary song would yield valuable insights into Duna human relations and the changing dynamics between male and female spheres of being. For example, 30 years ago it was reported that 'Duna women do not really sing at all' (Modjeska 1977:332); however, my research has revealed a plethora of songs created and sung by women—many of which were clearly inspired by exogenous music. Duna women's participation in new cultural spheres such as the church could be facilitating a new era of expression for them, musically and otherwise, and research into this area of Duna life would be very rewarding.

In *The Interpretation of Cultures*, Geertz (1973:29) wrote: 'Cultural analysis is intrinsically incomplete.' And in Herndon's (1993:78) words, 'there is no definitive truth; we can only aspire to see a bit more clearly'. I acknowledge that this account is by no means the only way to see Duna music in all its variety; but I do hope that it will have contributed significantly to a clearer understanding of present musical practices.

As evoked in the title, 'Steep Slopes', the Duna exist in a very unstable present. The introduction of a monetary economy connected to wage labour means that the organisation of performance often requires cash, as I have shown with Sane Noma's comments on the revival of the *haroli palena* and in my discussion of the Duna's participation in cultural shows, where culture combines with tourism. The development of a formal system of education shows a shift in the value-creation process regarding learning: it is now accepted that certain things, if they are of value, should be taught in schools (by people who in turn receive monetary payment for their services). While this desire for an engagement with a monetary economy—and the world it represents—surges ahead, ironically in reality many Duna people's engagement with this external world seems to be retreating, as they sing of being isolated and without essential services. There is at the moment no clear trajectory for the Duna but rather a strong sense of being somewhere 'in the middle', as Jeremiah Piero described it. In such a context, the recursive and reflexive dimension of cultural process comes to the fore, and in this space the possibilities for finding a 'balance' can be explored through creative means. We cannot tell how Duna music will shape itself in the future. We can only imagine that their music will be as vital and as vivid as their songs of today.

Figure 8. A picture of continuity, 1964.

Photo by *David Hook*

Appendix 1

Musical examples

All audio recorded by the author unless otherwise indicated.

AUDIO	TITLE	PERFORMERS	FILE SOURCE	TIME
1	Example 2.6: *alima*	Sane Noma	2005 vol. 1, audio 16, 1:08–1:34	0:38
2	Example 2.7: *kuluparapu*	Sane Noma	2005 vol. 1, audio 15, 0:29–1:00	0:51
3	Example 2.8: *pilipe*	Kalupi Kuako (recorded by Lila San Roque)	Lila San Roque	0:56
4	Example 2.9: *luna*	Sane Noma	2005 vol. 1, audio 12, 0:00–1:04	1:06
5	Example 3.1: 'lotu' *yekia*	Petros Kilapa	2005 vol. 3(2), audio 6	0:20
6	Example 3.2: *Ten Little Indians*	Kipu Piero, Wakili Akuri, Justin Kenny	2004 DAT 2, audio 10	0:18
7	Example 3.4: '*nane* laip senis *nganda waya keina*'	Aisak Kalumba and friend (guitars), Jeremiah Piero (ukulele), children's chorus	2005 vol. 3(1), audio 5	2:27
8	Example 3.5: 'Memba *pi nakaya*'(campaign song)	Stanley Piero, Rodney Kenny, Justin Kenny, Manapol Kenny, Hupa Pepa	KG1-060401A&B (Marantz 1), audio 23	0:45

9	Example 3.6: *'Memba pi nakaya'*(Ben Peri)	Stanley Piero, Rodney Kenny, Justin Kenny, Manapol Kenny, Hupa Pepa	KG1-060401A&B (Marantz 1), audio 22	0:50
10	Example 3.7: *'Memba pi nakaya'*(Pita Pex)	Rodney Kenny (ukulele), Justin Kenny (guitar), Manapol Kenny, Hupa Pepa, Poni Tangi	2005 vol. 1, audio 3	0:38
11	Example 3.8: *'Memba pi nakaya'(Apa Ngote)*	Aisak Kalumba (guitar, vocals), Jeremiah Piero (ukulele), Kipu Piero, children's chorus	2005 vol. 3(1), audio 18	1:35
12	Example 4.1: Alo's descent	Alo Manki and mourners	2005 vol. 1, audio 22, 2:10–2:54	0:46
13	Example 4.2: Pokole's *khene ipakana yakaya*	Pokole Pora	2005 vol. 1, audio 25, 0:55–1:15	0:20
14	Example 4.3: Kipu's *khene ipakana yakaya*	Kipu Piero	2005 vol. 1, audio 24, 0.05–1.05	6:37
15	Example 4.5: Kepo's *khene ipakana yakay*a	Kepo Akuri and Kipu Piero	2005 vol. 1, audio 51, 0.18–2.10	6:34
16	Example 4.7: *khene ipakana* (with guitar accompaniment)	Kipu Piero	2005 vol. 2, audio 14	1:08
17	Example 4.8: Kipu's *khene ipakana* in Tok Pisin	Kipu Piero	2005 vol. 2, audio 18	2:03

18	Example 4.9: Kipu's *khene ipakana* based on Example 4.8, in Duna	Kipu Piero	2005 vol. 2, audio 20	1:19
19	Example 5.2: *yekia*	Jim Siape (solo), Kenny Kendoli, Jeremiah Piero (chorus)	2005 vol. 2, audio 3, 3.40–4:04	0:26
20	Example 5.3: '*mei konenia*'	Wakili Akuri, Kipu Piero, Janet Pando	KG1-060401A&B (Marantz 1), audio 14	0:56
21	Example 5.4: 'maunten wara bilong kalipopo'	Jim Siape (solo vocals, guitar), Jeremiah Piero (vocals, guitar), Sipik Yeru (vocals, ukulele), Stanley Piero and Kipu Piero (vocals)	2005 vol. 1, audio 60	2:37
22	Example 5.5: *yekia*	Jim Siape (solo), Kenny Kendoli, Jeremiah Piero (chorus)	2005 vol. 2, audio 3, 1.27–1:50	0:25
23	Example 5.6: *yekia*	Jim Siape (solo), Kenny Kendoli, Jeremiah Piero (chorus)	2005 vol. 2, audio 3, 4:05–4:30	0:27
24	Example 5.7: *selepa*	Jim Siape (solo), Kenny Kendoli, Jeremiah Piero (chorus)	2005 vol. 2, audio 5, 0:55–1:10	0:18

25	Example 5.8: *selepa*	Kenny Kendoli (solo), Jim Siape, Jeremiah Piero (chorus)	2005 vol. 2, audio 5, 1:11–1:27	0:18
26	Example 5.9: *pikono*	Pokole Pora	2005 vol. 2, audio 15, 0:06–0:36	0:34
27	Example 5.10: *'Yesu epo'*	Nelson Wakalo, Agnes Kamako, Jelin Siape	2005 vol. 5, audio 37	1:22
28	Example 5.11: *'kalipopo nane rokania'*	Kipu Piero	KG1-060402 (DAT 2), audio 12	0:32
29	Example 5.12: *pikono*	Kiale Yokona	2005 vol. 3(2), audio 1, 26:33–27:05	0:34
30	Example 5.13: *pikono*	Kiale Yokona	2005 vol. 3(2), audio 2, 4:16–4:55	0:40
31	Example 5.14: *'ipa sipi sayata'*	Wakili Akuri, Kipu Piero, Janet Pando, Marame, Polome Lone	NH1-060406B, audio 7, 2:20–3:59	1:41
32	Example 5.15: *'ipa ikili mbiteya'*	Rodney Kenny (ukulele), Justin Kenny (guitar), Manapol Kenny, Hupa Pepa, Poni Tangi	2005 vol. 1, audio 8	0:40
33	Example 5.16: *'akalu nene nene keno raroko'*	Stanley Piero, Rodney Kenny, Justin Kenny, Manapol Kenny, Hupa Pepa	KG1-060401A&B (Marantz 1), audio 24	0:40
34	Example 5.17: *'Kirsty Lila ne anene'*	Lepani Kendoli	2005 vol. 6, audio 14	1:45
35	Example 5.18: *'imane itupa pi'*	Rachel Hirari, Meri Kembou, Frida Hirari	2005 vol. 6, audio 13	1:07

36	Example 5.19: *'hewa Mande ngi'*	Rachel Hirari, Meri Kembou, Frida Hirari	2005 vol. 6, audio 7	1:44
37	Example 5.20: *'antia yo moni ndu ngi'*	Stanley Piero (vocals, guitar), Hupa Pepa, Rodney Kenny, Epeto Maki (vocals)	2005 vol. 2, audio 10	0:52
38	Example 5.21: *'no Mosbi ngata karoko'*	Deni Kilapa, Kenny Koaria, John Alo, Mark Yoke, Jiare Sakuwa, Markson Eric	2006 vol. 8, audio 5	4:49
39	Example 5.22: *'ipa auwi'*	Deni Kilapa, Kenny Koaria, John Alo, Mark Yoke, Jiare Sakuwa, Markson Eric	2006 vol. 8, audio 6	2:40
40	Example 6.1: *yekia*	Unidentified (recording by Modjeska)	2006 vol. 1, audio 2, 5:54–6:16	0:24
41	Example 6.2: *yekia*	Pokole Pora	2005 vol. 2, audio 16	0:21
42	Example 6.3: *yekia*	Lekari Lombaye	2006 vol. 5, audio 9, 0:31–0:52	0:23
43	Example 6.4: *yekia*	Lekari Lombaye (solo), Lepani Kendoli	2006 vol. 5, audio 9, 0:52–1:19	0:29
44	Example 6.5: *yekia*	Lekari Lombaye (solo), Lepani Kendoli	2006 vol. 5, audio 9, 4:30–5:04	0:30

45	Example 6.6: 'meri *suwaka*'	Jim Siape (solo vocals, guitar), Jeremiah Piero (vocals, guitar), Sipik Yeru (vocals, ukulele), Stanley Piero and Kipu Piero (vocals)	2005 vol. 1, audio 59	2:26
46	Example 6.7: '*sola alimbu leka suwano*'	Jim Siape (solo vocals, guitar), Jeremiah Piero (vocals, guitar), Sipik Yeru (vocals, ukulele), Stanley Piero and Kipu Piero (vocals)	2005 vol. 1, audio 63	1:11
47	Example 6.8: '*itape koke*'	Janet Pando (solo), Wakili Akuri, Kipu Piero, Marame, Polome Lone	NH1-060406, audio 8	0:36
48	Example 6.9: 'manki *pakura* pilaim gita'	Janet Pando (solo), Wakili Akuri, Kipu Piero, Marame, Polome Lone, Monika Kenny	NH1-060406B, audio 12	0:31
49	Example 6.10: '*imane ketele*'	Stanley Piero (vocals, guitar), Hupa Pepa, Rodney Kenny, Epeto Maki (vocals)	2005 vol. 2, audio 11	0:58

50	Example 6.11: *'no awa'*	Stanley Piero (vocals, guitar), Hupa Pepa, Rodney Kenny, Epeto Maki (vocals)	2005 vol. 2, audio 12	1:44
51	Example 6.12: *khene ipakana ('re lene keno')*	Kipu Piero	2005 vol. 4, audio 44, 0:22–1:09	0:49
52	Example 7.1: *mindimindi kão*	Raki Palako	2005 vol. 1, audio 54, 0:12–1:15	3:16

Appendix 2

Kipu's *khene ipakana yakaya*

Example 4.3 in full.

Translated with Lila San Roque, Kenny Kendoli and Kipu Piero

antia wali-o antia wali-a	mama mama oh mama mama ah	mother mother oh mother mother ah
aluarena kenaka aru awanana na panenope?	mitupela save lukautim ol yelogras, nau bai mi mekim wanem?	we two care for and cradle the blonde children, now what will I do?
antia wali-o	mama mama oh	mother mother oh
antia wali-o	mama mama oh	mother mother oh
keno wara wanpis kenaka aru awanana na panenope?	mitupela save lukautim *wara* wanpis, nau bai mi mekim wanem?	we two care for and cradle the lone *wara*, now what will I do?
antia wali-o	mama mama oh	mother mother oh
antia wali-o	mama mama oh	mother mother oh
keno warali wanpis kenaka aru awanana na panenope?	mitupela save lukautim *warali* wanpis, nau bai mi mekim wanem?	we two care for and cradle the lone *warali*, now what will I do?
antia wali-o	mama mama oh	mother mother oh
keno ayako wanpis kenaka aru awanana na panenope?	mitupela save lukautim *ayako* wanpis, nau bai mi mekim wanem?	we two care for and cradle the lone *ayako*, now what will I do?

0:30	*antia wali-a antia wali kone antia wali*	mama mama ah mama mama tru	mother mother ah mother true mother
		mama mama	mother mother
	antia wali-o	mama mama oh	mother mother oh
	na wara nendeke nangayana na panenope?	mi no save go pren wantaim ol arapela wara meri, nau bai mi mekim wanem?	I don't go and make friends with other *wara* women, now what will I do?
	no wali-a	mama bilong mi ah	my mother ah
	antia wali-o *ko warali koanina ko kono neyape? antia wali*	mama mama oh yu *warali* yangpela meri yet na yu no tingim na yu dai a? mama mama	mother mother oh you are just a young *warali* woman, weren't you thinking? mother mother
	antia wali-o *aya koanina ko kono neyape?*	mama mama oh yu *aya* yangpela meri yet na yu no tingim na yu dai a?	mother mother oh you are just a young *aya* woman, weren't you thinking?
	antia wali-a	mama mama ah	mother mother ah
	antia wali-a *na ayako wanpis na ko kono neyarape?*	mama mama ah mi *ayako* wanpis na yu no tingim mi a?	mother mother ah I'm a lone *ayako*, weren't you thinking?
	antia wali-a	mama mama ah	mother mother ah
1:00	*antia wali-o* *wara ai nendeke no ngoaepe?*	mama mama oh husait meri tru mi bai go stap wantaim em?	mother mother oh what *wara* woman can I go to as a friend?
	antia wali-a	mama mama ah	mother mother ah
	antia wali-a	mama mama ah	mother mother ah

aye kelo kota kata komopinia	mi ting olsem mi stap strong long yu	I think it's as though my *aye* strength came from you
antia wali-a	mama mama ah	mother mother ah
antia wali-o	mama mama oh	mother mother oh
aye kelo kota kata komoyerua	mi pilim olsem mi stap strong long yu	I feel it's as though my *aye* strength came from you
antia wali	mama mama	mother mother
antia wali	mama mama	mother mother
aye kelo kota kata komoyarua	mi pilim olsem mi stap strong long yu	I feel it's as though my *aye* strength came from you
antia wali-a	mama mama ah	mother mother ah
antia wali	mama mama	mother mother
ipili kelo kota kata komoyarua	mi yet mi pilim olsem mi stap strong long yu	I feel it's as though my *ipili* strength came from you
antia wali-o	mama mama oh	mother mother oh

1:28	*antia wali-o*	mama mama oh	mother mother oh
	aiyo no warali kelo kata komoyarua	aiyo mi meri pilim olsem mi stap strong long yu	aiyo I feel it's as though my *warali* strength came from you
	antia wali-o	mama mama oh	mother mother oh
	antia wali	mama mama	mother mother
	aiyo ipili kelo kota kata komoyarua	aiyo mi meri pilim olsem mi stap strong long yu	aiyo I feel it's as though my *ipili* strength came from you
	antia wali-o	mama mama oh	mother mother oh
	antia wali-o	mama mama oh	mother mother oh
	noya...	bilong mi...	my...

[1.40–1:55
unintelligible]

1:56   *antia wali-a*   mama mama ah   mother mother ah

antia wali-a	mama mama ah	mother mother ah
no <u>warali</u> kelo kota kata komoyarua	mi meri pilim olsem mi stap strong long yu	I feel it's as though my *warali* strength came from you
antia wali-o	mama mama oh	mother mother oh
<u>wara</u> wanpis nakarape aya kelo kota kata komoyarua	a ting mi wanpis meri, mi pilim olsem mi givim strong long yu na stap	maybe I'm a lone *wara*, I feel it's as though my *aye* strength came from you
antia wali-o	mama mama oh	mother mother oh
<u>warali</u> wanpis nakarape aya kelo kota kata komoyarua[a]	a ting mi wanpis meri, mi pilim olsem mi givim strong long yu na stap	maybe I'm a lone *warali*, I feel it's as though my *aye* strength came from you
antia wali-o	mama mama oh	mother mother oh
no <u>iki</u> wanpis nakarape ikiya kelo kota kata komoyarua	a ting mi wanpis meri, mi pilim olsem mi givim strong long yu na stap	maybe I'm a lone *iki*, I feel it's as though my *ikiya* strength came from you
antia wali-o antia wali-a	mama mama oh mama mama ah	mother mother oh mother mother ah
<u>ayako</u> kelo kota kata komoyarua	mi pilim olsem mi stap strong long yu	I feel it's as though my *ayako* strength came from you

2:27

antia wali-a	mama mama ah	mother mother ah
na <u>wara</u> nendeke ai reita nganope?	husait meri tru bai mi go stap wantaim em?	who will I want to go and sit with as a *wara* friend?

antia wali-o	mama mama oh	mother mother oh
<u>*warali*</u> *nendeke ai nendeke nganope?*	husait meri tru bai mi go stap wantaim em?	who will I want to go to as a *warali* friend?
antia wali-a	mama mama ah	mother mother ah
Waki Mbeta neya hatia ima yanenia	a ting em i no dispela Waki Mbeta em mas narapela meri dai	it can't be Waki Mbeta, it must be some other woman
antia wali-a antia wali kone antia wali kone	mama mama ah mama mama tru mama mama tru	mother mother ah mother mother true mother mother tru
ya no antia no antia antia wali-o antia wali-o	ya mama bilong mi mama mama mama bilong mi oh mama mama oh	ya my mother my mother mother mother oh mother mother oh
antia wali-a	mama mama ah	mother mother ah
<u>*warali*</u> *wanpis na kenaka aru awanana na paneno(pe)?*	Monika mitupela wantaim save holim nau bai mi mekim wanem?	we two care for and cradle the lone *warali*, now what will I do?
antia wali-a	mama mama ah	mother mother ah

3:00	*antia wali*	mama mama	mother mother
	kenaka wanpisna kenaka aru awanana na paneno(pe)?	Monika mitupela wantaim save holim nau bai mi mekim wanem?	we two care for and cradle the lone one, now what will I do?
	antia wali-o	mama mama oh	mother mother oh
	ya antia no antia no	ya mama mama bilong mi	ya mother my mother

warali _suni_
narayania ruwata
kenaka aru awanana
na panenope?

yu tok, mi no gat
las susa bilong mi,
na mitupela save
lukautim, nau bai
mi mekim wanem?

you said I had no lastborn
warali suni sister and we
two would care for and
cradle (my children), now
what will I do?

antia wali-o
ayako _suni_ narayania
ruwata na awanana
panenope?

mama mama oh
yu tok, mi no gat
las susa bilong mi,
na mitupela save
lukautim, nau bai
mi mekim wanem?

mother mother oh
you said I had no
lastborn _ayako suni_ sister,
you would cradle (my
children), now what will
I do?

ka Mokia ritana
hame wandape?

yu kolim Monika
ya, yu laik mekim
olsem a?

you call for Monika, is
that what you want?

yaka Mokia kua
ritana hame
wandape?
antia wali-a antia
wali-a

yu singautim
Monika, yu laik
mekim olsem a?
mama mama ah
mama mama ah

you call for Monika to
come, is that what you
want?
mother mother ah mother
mother ah

antia wali-a
ipi _suni_ narayanania
ka paneme pape?

antia wali-a

mama mama ah
mi no gat las susa
bilong mi, na yu
mekim wanem?

mama mama ah

mother mother ah
I have no lastborn _ipi_
suni sister, what are you
doing?

mother mother ah

3:34 _antia wali-o antia_
wali-o antia wali-o

antia wali
warali kelo kota
kata komoyarua ye
paneno(pe)? ruwa o

mama mama oh
mama mama oh
mama mama oh

mama mama
mi pilim olsem
strong bilong mi
stap wantaim yu,
yu tok, bai mekim
wanem?

mother mother oh mother
mother oh mother mother
oh

mother mother
I feel it's as though my
warali strength came from
you, tell me, what will I
do?

	antia wali-o	mama mama oh	mother mother oh
	no aya kelo kota kata komoyarua no ayako kelo kota komoyarua	mi pilim olsem strong bilong mi stap wantaim yu, mi pilim olsem strong bilong mi stap wantaim yu	I feel it's as though my *aya* strength came from you, I feel as though my *ayako* strength came from you
	antia wali antia wali-o	mama mama mama mama oh	mother mother oh mother mother oh
	no hakini suni ndu raruape kone ndokondokoya ranana ka konono	mi gat susa bilong mi stap a? mi save bihainim bihainim yu, yu tingim	what, do I have a lastborn *suni* sister? we would always stick together, think about it
3:58	*antia wali-o*	mama mama oh	mother mother oh
	no warali suni ndu raruape? na kone ndokondokoya ranana ka konono	mi gat warali susa bilong mi stap a? mi save bihainim bihainim yu, yu tingim	what, do I have a lastborn *warali suni* sister? you and I would always stick together, think about it
	antia wali-a antia wali-a	mama mama ah mama mama ah	mother mother ah mother mother ah
	ya antia-o ya antia-o	ya mama oh ya mama oh	ya mother oh ya mother oh
	na ai reira ai reira ngano?	mi bai go sindaun wantaim husait?	who will I go and stay with?
	antia wali-a	mama mama ah	mother mother ah
	ya antia wali-a ya antia wali-a antia wali-o	ya mama mama ah ya mama mama ah mama mama oh	ya mother mother ah ya mother mother ah mother mother oh
	ya antia antia Monika kampani koneya antia wali-a aki pora antia wali-a	ya mama mama tru wantok bilong Monika, nau yu mekim wanem?	ya mother mother Monika's true companion, what have you done?

4:28 *antia <u>warali</u> wanpis kenaka aru awanana*

mama warali wanpis yumitupela save lukautim em

oh mother, we two care for and cradle the lone *warali*

ye no antia <u>ipili</u> wanpis keno karu awana o

ya mama bilong mi ipili wanpis yumitupela save lukautim em

ya my mother, we two care for and cradle the lone *ipili*

antia wali-o antia wali-o
yo ya

mama mama oh mama mama oh
yo ya

mother mother oh mother mother oh
yo ya

antia wali
ya papu hutia noae ndu ngutia antia wali-o

mama mama
yu givim sori long mi na yu go aiyo mama

mother mother
you gave me this sorrow to stomach and I watched you go

antia wali-a
no ipapu hutia noae ndu ngutia antia wali-a

mama mama ah
yu givim sori long mi na yu go aiyo mama

mother mother ah
you gave me this sorrow to stomach and I watched you go

antia wali-a
na aki waipe? antia wali-a antia wali-a

mama mama ah
bai mi mekim wanem?

mother mother ah
what can I do?

antia wali-a
nota o kutiana aki watape? nota o kutiana aki watape?

mama mama ah
yu trikim mi olsem wanem? yu trikim mi olsem wanem?

mother mother ah
how did you fool me? how did you fool me?

4:59 *antia wali-a*
nota o kutiana aki watape?

mama mama ah
yu trikim mi olsem wanem?

mother mother ah
how did you fool me?

antia wali-o

mama mama oh

mother mother oh

ya antia-o	ya mama oh	ya mother oh
Waki Mbeta antia kone antia wali-a	Waki Mbeta mama tru mama mama ah	Waki Mbeta mother true mother mother ah
antia wali	mama mama	mother mother
no <u>warali</u> <u>suni</u> narayana ko konorape konda kora?	mi no gat las susa bilong mi, yu save o yu lus tingting?	I have no lastborn *warali suni* sister, do you remember or have you forgotten?
antia wali-o antia wali	mama mama oh mama mama	mother mother oh mother mother
na ai nendeke kanape? ka konopa	mi save stap wantaim husait? yu tingim	who would I be close to? think about it
antia wali-o	mama mama oh	mother mother
<u>warali</u> ai nendeke kanape? ka konopa	*warali* mi save stap wantaim husait? yu tingim	what *warali* would I be close to? think about it

5:32	*antia wali-o*	mama mama oh	mother mother oh
	<u>ayako</u> ai nendeke kanape? ka konopa	*ayako* mi save stap wantaim husait? yu tingim	what *ayako* would I be close to? think about it
	ya antia-o	ya mama oh	ya mother oh
	na hakini <u>suni</u> pi ndu raora ngoaepe? ya antia-o ya antia-o	mi gat las susa bilong mi i stap na bai mi go stap wantaim em a?	do I have a lastborn *suni* sister that I can go to?
	ya antia-o ya antia-o	ya mama oh ya mama oh	ya mother oh ya mother oh
	ya antiali antia wane ya antiali antia wane kone	ya dia mama mama mama ya dia mama mama tru	ya dear mother mother daughter ya dear mother daughter true

ya antia wane kone	ya mama mama tru	ya mother daughter true
antia Waki Mbeta	mama Waki Mbeta	mother Waki Mbeta
antia wane kone	mama mama tru	mother daughter true
antia wane kone	mama mama tru	mother daughter true
hakini yo		sister yo

6:03   *Wakili antia wane*   Wakili mother daughter

         kone antia wali kone   true mother mother

         antia wane kone   true mother mother true

         antia wali kone   mother mother true

[6:14 translation
ends]

Appendix 3

Pronunciation guide

The table below is a pronunciation guide for the Duna alphabet prepared by Lila San Roque, representing the sounds using the International Phonetic Alphabet (IPA) and showing correspondence (or near correspondence) with the sounds of (Australian) English. It follows the Duna orthography used in San Roque (2008), which is based largely on the system devised and used by missionaries in the translation of the New Testament and in early Duna literacy programs (see Cochrane and Cochrane 1966; Giles n.d.).

LETTER	TYPICAL DUNA PRONUNCIATION(S) (IPA)	CLOSE MATCH(ES) IN AUSTRALIAN ENGLISH
a	a	as in father
e	E	as in net
h	h ·	as in hot
i	i	as 'ee' in sheep
k	k g	as 'k' in skip or 'g' in get
kh	kH X	as in key
l	‰ Ò	as in colour
m	m	as in mint
mb	…b	as in amber
n	n	as in net
nd	<d	as in under
ng	'g	as in finger
o	ç	as 'or' in corn
p	p b	as 'p' in spot or 'b' in bib
ph	pH ∏	as 'p' in pot or 'f' in fit
r	R d	as 'tt' in butter in fast speech
s	s ts t5H	as 's' in see, 'ts' in hits, or 't' in talk
t	t5 d5 L5	as 't' in stop or 'd' in did
u	u	as 'oo' in boot
w	w	as in wood
y	j	as in yellow

233

Notes

Palatalisation

Some consonants are *palatalised* when they occur in between the vowel 'i' and the vowel 'a'. For example, the written sequence 'ina' can be pronounced to sound like *inya* and the written sequence 'ita' pronounced to sound like *itya*. Consonants that can undergo palatalisation in between 'i' and 'a' include k, l, n, nd, ng, r and t. The consonant 't' can also undergo palatalisation in between 'u' and 'a' (so that 'uta' can sound like *utya*).

Labialisation

Some consonants are *labialised* when they occur in between the vowels 'u' or 'o' and the vowel 'a'. For example, the written sequence 'una' can be pronounced to sound like *unwa* and the written sequence 'oka' pronounced to sound like *okwa*. Consonants that can undergo labialisation in between 'u' and 'a' include k, n, nd, ng and r.

Transition vowels

When the vowel *a* precedes a glide *w* or *y* there is typically an additional 'transitional' vowel pronounced that matches features of the glide. For example, the written sequence 'aw' can sound like *auw* and the written sequence 'ay' can sound like *aiy*. This can also be the case for 'e' preceding 'y' (that is, 'ey' can sound like *eiy*).

Bibliography

Allen, Bryant 2005, Poor people or poor places?, Paper read at Papua New Guinea: 30 Years of Independence, The Australian National University, Canberra, 13 September 2005.

Allen, Bryant and Frankel, Stephen 1991, 'Across the Tari Furoro', in E. L. Schieffelin and R. Crittenden (eds), *Like People You See in a Dream: First contact in six Papuan societies*, Stanford University Press, California.

Alexeyeff, Kalissa 2004, 'Sea breeze: globalisation and Cook Islands popular music', *The Asia Pacific Journal of Anthropology*, vol. 5, no. 2, pp. 145–58.

Ammann, Raymond 1998, 'How Kanak is Kaneka music?: the use of traditional instruments in the modern music of the Melanesians in New Caledonia', *World of Music*, vol. 40, no. 2, pp. 9–27.

Ammann, Raymond 2001, 'Using ethnomusicology to assist in the maintenance of *kastom*, with special reference to New Caledonia and Vanuatu', in H. R. Lawrence and D. Niles (eds), *Traditionalism and Modernity in the Music and Dance of Oceania: Essays in honour of Barbara B. Smith*, University of Sydney, New South Wales.

Ammann, Raymond 2004, *Karum Nupu: Basket of songs*, [Film], VKS-Productions, Port Vila, Vanuatu.

Anonymous 1967, 'Spectacle, colour, pageantry—and thousands of glistening warriors', *Qantas Airways Australia*, vol. 33, no. 11, pp. 6–13.

Appadurai, Arjun 1991, 'Afterword', in A. Appadurai, F. J. Korom and M. A. Mills (eds), *Gender, Genre, and Power in South Asian Expressive Traditions*, University of Pennsylvania Press, Philadelphia.

Appadurai, Arjun, Korom, Frank J. and Mills, Margaret A. 1991, 'Introduction', in A. Appadurai, F. J. Korom and M. A. Mills (eds), *Gender, Genre, and Power in South Asian Expressive Traditions*, University of Pennsylvania Press, Philadelphia.

Armitage, Ian 1969, 'Gospel recordings in one of New Guinea's remotest areas', *The Treasury*, June.

Barwick, Linda 1990, 'Central Australian women's ritual music: knowing through analysis versus knowing through performance', *Yearbook for Traditional Music*, vol. 22, pp. 60–79.

Barz, Gregory F. and Cooley, Timothy J. (eds) 1997, *Shadows in the Field: New perspectives of fieldwork in ethnomusicology*, Oxford University Press, New York and Oxford.

Basso, Keith H. 1996, 'Wisdom sits in places: notes on a Western Apache landscape', in S. Feld and K. H. Basso (eds), *Senses of Place*, School of American Research Press, Santa Fe, New Mexico.

Bhabha, Homi K. 1994, *The Location of Culture*, Routledge, London.

Bilby, Kenneth 1999, '"Roots explosion": indigenization and cosmopolitanism in contemporary Surinamese popular music', *Ethnomusicology*, vol. 43, no. 2, pp. 256–96.

Blacking, John 1977, 'Some problems of theory and method in the study of musical change', *Yearbook of the International Folk Music Council*, vol. 9, pp. 1–26.

Bohlman, Philip V. 1992, 'Ethnomusicology's challenge to the canon; the canon's challenge to ethnomusicology', in K. Bergeron and P. V. Bohlman (eds), *Disciplining Music: Musicology and its canons*, University of Chicago Press, Chicago and London.

Born, Georgina and Hesmondhalgh, David 2000, 'Introduction: on difference, representation and appropriation in music', in G. Born and D. Hesmondhalgh (eds), *Western Music and its Others: Difference, representation, and appropriation in music*, University of California Press, Berkeley.

Brutti, Lorenzo 2000, 'Afek's last son: integrating change in a Papua New Guinean cosmology', *Ethnohistory*, vol. 47, no. 1, pp. 101–11.

Cesara, Manda 1982, *Reflections of a Woman Anthropologist: No hiding place*, Academic Press, London and New York.

Chenoweth, Vida 1969, 'An investigation of the singing styles of the Dunas', *Oceania*, vol. 39, no. 3, pp. 218–30.

Chenoweth, Vida 2000, *Sing-Sing: Communal singing and dancing of Papua New Guinea*, Macmillan Brown Centre for Pacific Studies, Christchurch, New Zealand.

Chenoweth, Vida and Bee, Darlene 1971, 'Comparative-generative models of a New Guinea melodic structure', *American Anthropologist*, vol. 73, no. 3, pp. 773–82.

Clifford, James 1986, 'Introduction: partial truths', in J. Clifford and G. E. Marcus, *Writing Culture: The poetics and politics of ethnography*, University of California Press, Berkeley.

Cochrane, Dennis and Cochrane, Nancy 1966, Duna essentials for translation, Manuscript submitted to the Grammar Department, Summer Institute of Linguistics, Papua New Guinea Branch.

Cohen, Anthony P. 1994, *Self Consciousness: An alternative anthropology of identity*, Routledge, London and New York.

Cooke, Peter n.d., 'Heterophony', in L. Macy (ed.), *GroveMusic Online*, viewed 28 March 2006, <http://www.grovemusic.com>

Corin, Ellen 1998, 'Refiguring the person: the dynamics of affects and symbols in an African spirit possession cult', in M. Lambek and A. Strathern (eds), *Bodies and Persons: Comparative perspectives from Africa and Melanesia*, Cambridge University Press, Cambridge.

Corn, Aaron 2002, Dreamtime wisdom, modern-time vision: tradition and innovation in the popular band movement of Arnhem Land, Australia, PhD dissertation, University of Melbourne, Victoria.

Corn, Aaron with Gumbula, Neparrnga 2002, 'Nurturing the sacred through Yolngu popular song', *Cultural Survival*, vol. 26, no. 2, viewed 29 October 2007, <http://www.cs.org/publications/csq/csq-article.cfm?id=1550>

Crowdy, Denis 1998, 'Creativity and independence: Sanguma, music education and the development of the PNG contemporary style', *Perfect Beat*, vol. 3, no. 4, pp. 13–25.

Crowdy, Denis 2001, 'The guitar cultures of Papua New Guinea: regional, social and stylistic diversity', in A. Bennett and K. Dawe (eds), *Guitar Cultures*, Berg, New York and Oxford.

Crowdy, Denis 2005, *Guitar Style, Open Tunings, and Stringband Music in Papua New Guinea*, Institute of Papua New Guinea Studies, Boroko.

Day-O'Connell, Jeremy n.d., 'Pentatonic', in L. Macy (ed.), *Grove Music Online*, viewed 12 April 2007, <http://www.grovemusic.com>

Denoon, Donald 2005, *A Trial Separation: Australia and the decolonisation of Papua New Guinea*, Pandanus Books, Canberra.

Doherty, Peter 1995, Burning the bark of the areca palms: a study of the changing use of metaphor in song lyrics of the Kewa of the Southern Highlands Province, Papua New Guinea, Masters dissertation, Department of Music, University of New South Wales, Sydney.

Donohue, Mark 1997, 'Tone systems in New Guinea', *Linguistic Typology*, vol. 1, pp. 347–86.

Dunbar-Hall, Peter and Gibson, Chris 2004, *Deadly Sounds, Deadly Places: Contemporary Aboriginal music in Australia*, University of New South Wales Press, Sydney.

Ellis, Catherine J. 1994, 'Music', in D. Horton (ed.), *The Encyclopaedia of Aboriginal Australia: Aboriginal and Torres Strait Islander history, society and culture*, Aboriginal Studies Press for the Australian Institute of Aboriginal and Torres Strait Islander Studies, Canberra.

Ellis, Catherine J. 1995, 'Response: whose truth?', in L. Barwick, A. Marett and G. Tunstill (eds), *The Essence of Singing and the Substance of Song: Recent responses to the Aboriginal performing arts and other essays in honour of Catherine Ellis*, University of Sydney, New South Wales.

England, Nicholas M., Garfias, Robert, Kolinski, Mieczyslaw, List, George, Rhodes, Willard and Seeger, Charles 1964, 'Symposium on transcription and analysis: a Hukwe song with musical bow', *Ethnomusicology*, vol. 8, no. 3, pp. 223–77.

Faik-Simet, Naomi 2006, 'Singsing Mendek', *The National*, Friday 4 August, p. 8.

Fearon, W. Jon (ed.) 1980, Inanaga ibagana: *Local language songs of Papua New Guinea*, Dauli Teachers' College, Tari, Papua New Guinea.

Feld, Steven 1982, *Sound and Sentiment: Birds, weeping, poetics and song in Kaluli expression*, University of Pennsylvania Press, Philadelphia.

Feld, Steven 1984, 'Sound structure as social structure', *Ethnomusicology*, vol. 28, no. 3, pp. 383–409.

Feld, Steven 1988 'Aesthetics as iconicity of style, or "lift-up-over sounding": getting into the Kaluli groove', *Yearbook for Traditional Music*, vol. 20, pp. 74–113.

Feld, Steven 1995, 'Wept thoughts: the voicing of Kaluli memories', in Ruth Finnegan and Margaret Orbell (eds), *South Pacific Oral Traditions*, Indiana University Press, Bloomington.

Feld, Steven 1996, 'Waterfalls of song: an acoustemology of place resounding in Bosavi, Papua New Guinea', in S. Feld and K. H. Basso (eds), *Senses of Place*, School of American Research Press, Santa Fe, New Mexico.

Feld, Steven 2001, *Bosavi: Rainforest music from Papua New Guinea*, [Recording], Smithsonian Folkways Recordings SFW CD 40487.

Feld, Steven and Brenneis, Donald 2004, 'Doing anthropology in sound', *American Ethnologist*, vol. 31, no. 4, pp. 461–74.

Feld, Steven and Crowdy, Denis 2002, 'Papua New Guinean music and the politics of sound recording', *Perfect Beat*, vol. 5, no. 4, pp. 78–85.

Feld, Steven and Fox, Aaron A. 1994, 'Music and language', *Annual Review of Anthropology*, vol. 23, pp. 25–53.

Firth, Stewart 1997, 'Colonial administration and the invention of the native', in D. Denoon (ed.), *The Cambridge History of the Pacific Islanders*, Cambridge University Press, Cambridge and New York.

Flora, Reis W. 2006, A view of ethnomusicology, Paper read at Graduate Student Symposium, The School of Music, The Australian National University, Canberra, 23 June 2006.

Foster, Robert J. 1995, 'Introduction: the work of nation making', in Robert J. Foster (ed.), *Nation Making: Emergent identities in postcolonial Melanesia*, University of Michigan Press, Ann Arbor.

Friedrich, Paul 1986, *The Language Parallax: Linguistic relativism and poetic indeterminacy*, University of Texas Press, Austin.

Gammage, Bill 1998, *The Sky Travellers: Journeys in New Guinea 1938–1939*, Melbourne University Press, Carlton.

Geertz, Clifford 1973, *The Interpretation of Cultures*, Basic Books, New York.

Giles, Glenda n.d., A guide to the pronunciation of Duna, Unpublished manuscript held at Summer Institute of Linguistics Library, Ukarumpa, Papua New Guinea.

Gillespie, Kirsty 2007a, '"Laip senis": music and encounter in a Papua New Guinean community', in R. Moyle (ed.), *Oceanic Music Encounters: The print resource and the human resource—essays in honour of Mervyn McLean*, Department of Anthropology, University of Auckland.

Gillespie, Kirsty 2007b, 'Moving', *SEM Newsletter*, vol. 41, no. 4, pp. 3, 28.

Gillespie, Kirsty 2008, 'Na Kkai Taku: Taku's musical fables/guitar style, open tunings, and stringband music in Papua New Guinea', *Ethnomusicology*, vol. 52, no. 1.

Gillespie, Kirsty 2009, '"Behind every tree"?: Ethnomusicology in Papua New Guinea', in E. Mackinlay, B-L Bartleet and K. Barney (eds), *Musical Islands: Exploring connections between music, place and research*. Cambridge Scholars Press, Cambridge.

Gillespie, Kirsty and San Roque, Lila (forthcoming), 'Music and language in Duna pikono', in A. Rumsey (ed.), *Sung Tales from the Papua New Guinea Highlands*, ANU E Press, Canberra.

Goddard, Michael 2000, 'Village court system of Papua New Guinea', in B. V. Lal and K. Fortune (eds), *The Pacific Islands: An encyclopedia*, University of Hawai'i Press, Honolulu.

Goddard, Michael 2001, 'From rolling thunder to reggae: imagining squatter settlements in Papua New Guinea', *The Contemporary Pacific*, vol. 13, no. 1, pp. 1–32.

Goldsworthy, David 1998, 'Indigenization and socio-political identity in the *kaneka* music of New Caledonia', in P. Hayward (eds), *Sound Alliances: Indigenous peoples, cultural politics and popular music in the Pacific*, Cassell, London and New York.

Green, Lucy 2003, 'Music education, cultural capital, and social group identity', in M. Clayton, T. Herbert and R. Middleton (eds), *The Cultural Study of Music: A critical introduction*, Routledge, New York and London.

Haley, Nicole 1996, 'Revisioning the past, remembering the future: Duna accounts of the world's end', *Oceania*, vol. 66, no. 4, pp. 278–85.

Haley, Nicole 2002a, *Ipakana yakaiya*: mapping landscapes, mapping lives: contemporary land politics among the Duna, PhD dissertation, The Australian National University, Canberra.

Haley, Nicole 2002b, 'Election fraud on a grand scale: the case of the Koroba-Kopiago open electorate', in R. J. May and R. Anere (eds), *Maintaining Democracy: The 1997 elections in Papua New Guinea*, University of Papua New Guinea, Boroko.

Haley, Nicole 2008, 'Sung adornment: changing masculinities at Lake Kopiago, Papua New Guinea', *The Australian Journal of Anthropology*, vol. 19, no. 2, pp. 213–29.

Halvaksz, Jamon 2003, 'Singing about the land among the Biangai', *Oceania*, vol. 73, no. 3, pp. 153–69.

Hannerz, Ulf 1997, '*Fluxos, frontieras, hibridos: Palavras-chave da antropologia transnacional* [Flows, boundaries and hybrids: keywords in transnational anthropology]', *Mana*, vol. 3, no. 1, pp. 7–39.

Hanson, L. W., Allen, B. J., Bourke, R. M. and McCarthy, T. J. 2001, *Papua New Guinea Rural Development Handbook*, The Australian National University, Canberra.

Harrison, Simon 2006, *Fracturing Resemblances: Identity and mimetic conflict in Melanesia and the West*, Berghahn Books, New York and Oxford.

Hau'ofa, Epeli 1993, 'Our sea of islands', in E. Waddell, V. Naidu and E. Hau'ofa, *A New Oceania: Rediscovering our sea of islands*, School of Social and Economic Development, The University of the South Pacific, in association with Bleake House, Suva.

Herndon, Marcia 1993, 'Insiders, outsiders: knowing our limits, limiting our knowing', *The World of Music*, vol. 35, no. 1, pp. 63–80.

Herndon, Marcia and McLeod, Norma 1983, *Field Manual for Ethnomusicology*, Norwood Editions, Norwood, Pennsylvania.

Herndon, Marcia and Ziegler, Susanne 1990, 'Preface', in M. Herndon and S. Ziegler (eds), *Music, Gender, and Culture*, Noetzel, Wilhelmshaven.

Hobsbawm, Eric and Ranger, Terence (eds) 1983, *The Invention of Tradition*, Cambridge University Press, Cambridge and New York.

Hogbin, H. I. and Wedgwood, C. H. 1953, 'Local grouping in Melanesia', *Oceania*, vol. 23, no. 4, pp. 241–76.

Hughes, Philip 2000, *Issues of governance in Papua New Guinea: building roads and bridges*, State, Society and Governance in Melanesia Discussion Paper Series, Research School of Pacific and Asian Studies, The Australian National University, Canberra.

Ingemann, Frances 1968, The linguistic structure of an Ipili-Paiyala song type, Paper read at VIIIth International Congress of Anthropological and Ethnological Sciences, Tokyo.

Jebens, Holger 1997, 'Catholics, Seventh-Day Adventists and the impact of tradition in Pairundu (Southern Highlands Province, Papua New Guinea)', in T. Otto and A. Borsboom (eds), *Cultural Dynamics of Religious Change in Oceania*, KITLV Press, Leiden.

Jolly, Margaret 1992, 'Specters of inauthenticity', *The Contemporary Pacific*, vol. 4, no. 1, pp. 49–72.

Jones, Jennifer J. 2004, *The Theory and Practice of the Music in the Seventh-Day Adventist Church in Papua New Guinea*, Institute of Papua New Guinea Studies and Pacific Adventist University, Boroko.

Jorgensen, Dan 2004, Hinterland history: mining and its cultural consequences in Telefolmin.

Kaeppler, Adrienne L. 1998, 'Music and gender', in A. L. Kaeppler and J. W. Love (eds), *The Garland Encyclopedia of World Music. Volume 9*, Garland, New York.

Kahn, Miriam 1996, 'Your place and mine: sharing emotional landscapes in Wamira, Papua New Guinea', in S. Feld and K. H. Basso (eds), *Senses of Place*, School of American Research Press, Santa Fe, New Mexico.

Kaiabe, Alfred 2006, 'Why a Hela province!', *Post-Courier*, Tuesday 14 November, viewed 29 October 2007, <http://www.postcourier.com.pg/20061114/focus. htm>

Kartomi, Margaret J. 1981, 'The process and results of musical culture contact: a discussion of terminology and concepts', *Ethnomusicology*, vol. 25, no. 2, pp. 227–49.

Kartomi, Margaret J. 1990, Problems of the intercultural reception and methods of describing and analysing musical rhythm, Paper read at Symposium of the International Musicological Society, Osaka, Japan.

Keil, Charles 1979, *Tiv Song*, University of Chicago Press, Ill.

Keesing, Roger M. 1982, 'Kastom in Melanesia: an overview', *Mankind*, vol. 13, no. 4, pp. 297–301.

Kemoi, Nixon 1996, 'The history of the bamboo band in Bougainville', *Kulele*, no. 2, pp. 31–7.

Kendoli, Kenny (forthcoming), 'Yuna pikono', in A. Rumsey (ed.), *Sung Tales from the Papua New Guinea Highlands*, ANU E Press, Canberra.

Kidula, Jean 1995, 'The appropriation of Western derived music styles into Kenyan traditions: case study of some Nairobi Christian musics', *Pacific Review of Ethnomusicology*, vol. 7, pp. 1–16.

Kidula, Jean 1999, Where is your tradition?: on the problematics of an African ethnomusicologist research on Christian musics, Paper read at Southeastern Regional Seminar in African Studies (SERSAS) Fall Conference, Savannah, Georgia, 15–16 October 1999.

Knopoff, Steven 2003, 'What is music analysis?: problems and prospects for understanding Aboriginal songs and performance', *Australian Aboriginal Studies*, vol. 1, pp. 39–51.

Knopoff, Steven 2004, 'Intrusions and delusions: considering the impact of recording technology on the subject matter of ethnomusicological research', in M. Ewans, R. Halton and J. A. Phillips (eds), *Music Research: New directions for a new century*, Cambridge Scholars Press, London.

Koskoff, Ellen 1989, 'An introduction to women, music, and culture', in E. Koskoff (ed.), *Women and Music in Cross-Cultural Perspective*, University of Illinois Press, Urbana.

Koskoff, Ellen 1998, 'Gender and music', in A. L. Kaeppler and J. W. Love (eds), *The Garland Encyclopedia of World Music. Volume 8*, Garland, New York.

Kubik, Gerhard 1986, 'Stability and change in African musical traditions', *The World of Music*, vol. 28, no. 1, pp. 44–68.

Kunda, Elias (ed.) 2006, Coca-Cola Mt Hagen Show 2006, Unpublished booklet.

Lawrence, Helen Reeves 1995, 'Death of a singer', in L. Barwick, A. Marett and G. Tunstill (eds), *The Essence of Singing and the Substance of Song: Recent responses to the Aboriginal performing arts and other essays in honour of Catherine Ellis*, University of Sydney, NSW.

Lawrence, Helen Reeves and Niles, Don (eds) 2001, *Traditionalism and Modernity in the Music and Dance of Oceania: Essays in honour of Barbara B. Smith*, University of Sydney, NSW.

Lawson, Mary Elizabeth 1989, Tradition, change and meaning in Kiribati performance: an ethnography of music and dance in a Micronesian society, PhD dissertation, Department of Music, Brown University, Providence, RI.

Leahy, Michael J. 1967, 'Discovering Mount Hagen', *Walkabout*, vol. 33, no. 5, pp. 26–9.

Leavitt, John 2006, 'Thick translation: three soundings', in C. O'Neil, M. Scoggin and K. Tuite (eds), *Language, Culture and the Individual: A tribute to Paul Friedrich*, Lincom, Munich.

Lewellen, Ted C. 2002, *The Anthropology of Globalization: Cultural anthropology enters the 21st century*, Bergin & Garvey, Westport, Conn., and London.

Liep, John 2001, 'Introduction', in J. Liep (ed.), *Locating Cultural Creativity*, Pluto Press, London and Sterling.

Linkels, Ad 1992, *Sounds of Change in Tonga: Dance, music and cultural dynamics in a Polynesian kingdom*, Friendly Islands Book Shop, Nuku'alofa, Tonga.

LiPuma, Edward 1998, 'Modernity and forms of personhood in Melanesia', in M. Lambek and A. Strathern (ed.), *Bodies and Persons: Comparative perspectives from Africa and Melanesia*, Cambridge University Press, Cambridge.

List, George 1974, 'The reliability of transcription', *Ethnomusicology*, vol. 18, no. 3, pp. 353–77.

Litteral, Robert 1999, *Four decades of language policy in Papua New Guinea: the move towards the vernacular*, SIL Electronic Working Papers, 1999-001 (February), Summer Institute of Linguistics, viewed 15 February 2007, <http://www.sil.org/silewp/1999/001/silewp1999-001.html>

Love, J. W. 1998, 'Metaphor and symbolism', in A. L. Kaeppler and J. W. Love (eds), *The Garland Encyclopedia of World Music.Volume 9*, Garland, New York.

Lutkehaus, Nancy C. 1998, 'Gender in New Guinean music', in A. L. Kaeppler and J. W. Love (eds), *The Garland Encyclopedia of World Music.Volume 9*, Garland, New York.

McLean, Mervyn 1986, 'Towards a typology of musical change: missionaries and adjustive response in Oceania', *The World of Music*, vol. 28, no. 1, pp. 29–42.

McLeod, Norma 1974, 'Ethnomusicological research and anthropology', *Annual Review of Anthropology*, vol. 3, pp. 99–115.

Magowan, Fiona 1994a, Melodies of mourning: a study of form and meaning in Yolngu women's music and dance in traditional and Christian contexts, PhD dissertation, Oxford University, Oxford.

Magowan, Fiona 1994b, '"The land is our *märr* (essence), it stays forever": the *yothu-yindi* relationship in Australian Aboriginal traditional and popular musics', in M. Stokes (ed.), *Ethnicity, Identity and Music: The musical construction of place*, Berg, Oxford, UK, and Providence, Rhode Island.

Magowan, Fiona 2001, 'Shadows of song: exploring research and performance strategies in Yolngu women's crying-songs', *Oceania*, vol. 72, no. 2, pp. 89–104.

Magowan, Fiona 2005, 'Dancing into film: exploring Yolngu motion, ritual and cosmology in the Yirrkala Film Project', in F. Magowan and K. Neuenfeldt (eds), *Landscapes of Indigenous Performance: Music, song and dance of the Torres Strait and Arnhem Land*, Aboriginal Studies Press, Canberra.

Magowan, Fiona 2007, *Melodies of Mourning: Music and emotion in Northern Australia*, James Currey, Oxford, UK.

Manuel, Peter 1994, 'Puerto Rican music and cultural identity: creative appropriation of Cuban sources from *danza* to salsa', *Ethnomusicology*, vol. 38, no. 2, pp. 249–80.

May, R. J. (ed.) 1977, *Change and Movement: Readings on internal migration in Papua New Guinea*, ANU Press, Canberra.

Merlan, Francesca and Rumsey, Alan 1986, 'A marriage dispute in the Nebilyer Valley (Western Highlands Province, Papua New Guinea)', in S. A. Wurm (ed.), *Papers in New Guinea Linguistics. Volume 25*, Pacific Linguistics, Canberra.

Merriam, Alan Parkhurst 1964, *The Anthropology of Music*, Northwestern University Press, Evanston, Illinois.

Mihalic, F. 1971, *The Jacaranda Dictionary and Grammar of Melanesian Pidgin*, The Jacaranda Press, Milton, Qld.

Modjeska, Charles Nicholas 1977, Production among the Duna: aspects of horticultural intensification in Central New Guinea, PhD dissertation, The Australian National University, Canberra.

Modjeska, Charles Nicholas 1982, 'Production and inequality: perspectives from central New Guinea', in A. Strathern (ed.), *Inequality in New Guinea Highlands Societies*, Cambridge University Press, Cambridge.

Modjeska, Charles Nicholas 1983, Place and town: party music of the Kopiago people of Southern Highlands Province, Unpublished manuscript, Institute of Papua New Guinea Studies, Port Moresby.

Morphy, Howard 1991, *Ancestral Connections: Art and an aboriginal system of knowledge*, University of Chicago Press, Ill.

Moyle, Alice Marshall 1961, Letter, 27 November, Sydney.

Moyle, Alice Marshall 1992, *Music and Dance of Aboriginal Australia and the South Pacific: The effects of documentation on the living tradition. Papers and discussions of the Colloquium of the International Council for Traditional Music held in Townsville, Queensland, Australia, 1988*, University of Sydney, NSW.

Munn, Nancy 1986, *The Fame of Gawa: A symbolic study of value transformation in a Massim (Papua New Guinea) society*, Cambridge University Press, Cambridge and New York.

Myers, Fred R. 1986, *Pintupi Country, Pintupi Self: Sentiment, place, and politics among Western Desert Aborigines*, University of California Press, Berkeley.

Myers, Helen 1993, 'Indian, East Indian, and West Indian music in Felicity, Trinidad', in S. Blum, P. V. Bohlman and D. M. Neuman (eds), *Ethnomusicology and Modern Music History*, University of Illinois Press, Urbana.

Namuri, Ethel 2006, 'Reviving the Malagan Show', *Post-Courier*, Friday 16 June, p. 43.

Nettl, Bruno 1983, *The Study of Ethnomusicology: Twenty-nine issues and concepts*, University of Illinois Press, Urbana.

Neuenfeldt, Karl and Costigan, Lyn 2004, 'Negotiating and enacting musical innovation and continuity: how some Torres Strait Islander songwriters incorporate traditional dance chants within contemporary songs', *The Asia Pacific Journal of Anthropology*, vol. 5, no. 2, pp. 113–28.

Niles, Don 2001, '"Local" and "foreign" ethnomusicological writings in Papua New Guinea', in H. R. Lawrence and D. Niles (ed.), *Traditionalism and Modernity in the Music and Dance of Oceania: Essays in honour of Barbara B. Smith*, University of Sydney, NSW.

Niles, Don 2005, '*Susap*, Papua New Guinea', in T. E. Miller and A. C. Shahriari (eds), *World Music: A global journey*, Routledge, New York.

Niles, Don 2006, 'Drums', in P. Peltier and F. Morin (eds), *Shadows of New Guinea: Art from the great island of Oceania in the Barbier-Mueller Collections*, Somogy éditions d'art, Paris, and Musée Barbier-Mueller, Geneva.

Niles, Don 2007, 'Sonic structure in *tom yaya kange*: Ku Waru sung narratives from Papua New Guinea', in R. Moyle (ed.), *Oceanic Music Encounters: The print resource and the human resource. Essays in honour of Mervyn McLean*, Department of Anthropology, University of Auckland.

Niles, Don and Webb, Michael 1987, *Papua New Guinea Music Collection*, Institute of Papua New Guinea Studies, Port Moresby.

Noll, William 1997, 'Selecting partners: questions of personal choice and problems of history in fieldwork and its interpretation', in G. F. Barz and T. J. Cooley (eds), *Shadows in the Field: New perspectives of fieldwork in ethnomusicology*, Oxford University Press, New York and Oxford.

O'Hanlon, Michael 1993, *Paradise: Portraying the New Guinea Highlands*, British Museum Press, London.

Okole, Henry 2005, 'Papua New Guinea's brand of Westminster: democratic traditions overlaying Melanesian cultures', in H. Patapan, J. Wanna and P. Weller (eds), *Westminster Legacies: Democracy and responsible government in Asia and the Pacific*, UNSW Press, Sydney.

Papua New Guinea Tourism and Business Directory, viewed 11 May 2007, <http://www.pngbd.com/travel/tourism_guide_tpa>

Pesaps n.d., *Souths Ame. Volume 1*, [Recording], CHM Supersound Studios, CHMCD196.

Petrovic, Ankica 1990, 'Women in the music creation process in the Dinaric cultural zone of Yugoslavia', in M. Herndon and S. Ziegler (eds), *Music, Gender, and Culture*, Noetzel, Wilhelmshaven.

Pugh-Kitingan, Jacqueline 1977, 'Huli language and instrumental performance', *Ethnomusicology*, vol. 21, no. 2, pp. 205–32.

Pugh-Kitingan, Jacqueline 1981, An ethnomusicological study of the Huli of the Southern Highlands, Papua New Guinea, PhD dissertation, University of Queensland, St Lucia.

Pugh-Kitingan, Jacqueline 1982, 'Language communication and instrumental music in Papua New Guinea; comments on the Huli and Samberigi cases', *Musicology*, vol. 7, pp. 104–19.

Pugh-Kitingan, Jacqueline 1984, 'Speech-tone realisation in Huli music', in J. C. Kassler and J. Stubington (eds), *Problems and Solutions: Occasional essays in musicology presented to Alice M. Moyle*, Hale & Iremonger, Sydney.

Pugh-Kitingan, Jacqueline 1998, 'Southern Highlands Province: Huli', in A. L. Kaeppler and J. W. Love (eds), *The Garland Encyclopedia of World Music. Volume 9*, Garland, New York.

Rainier, Chris 1996, *Where Masks Still Dance: New Guinea*, Little, Brown, Boston.

Rice, Timothy 1997, 'Toward a meditation of field methods and field experience in ethnomusicology', in G. F. Barz and T. J. Cooley (eds), *Shadows in the Field: New perspectives of fieldwork in ethnomusicology*, Oxford University Press, Oxford.

Robbins, Joel 2004, *Becoming Sinners: Christianity and moral torment in a Papua New Guinea society*, University of California Press, Berkeley.

Robbins, Joel 2005, 'Introduction: humiliation and transformation: Marshall Sahlins and the study of cultural change in Melanesia', in J. Robbins and H. Wardlow (eds), *The Making of Global and Local Modernities in Melanesia: Humiliation, transformation, and the nature of cultural change*, Ashgate, Burlington, Vermont.

Robinson, Rebecca 2002, 'Koroba-Lake Kopiago open: "the final election"', in R. J. May and R. Anere (eds), *Maintaining Democracy: The 1997 elections in Papua New Guinea*, University of Papua New Guinea, Boroko.

Rumsey, Alan 2006a, 'The articulation of indigenous and exgenous orders in Highland New Guinea and beyond', *The Australian Journal of Anthropology*, vol. 17, no. 1, pp. 47–69.

Rumsey, Alan 2006b, 'Verbal art, politics, and personal style in Highland New Guinea and beyond', in C. O'Neil, M. Scoggin and K. Tuite (eds), *Language, Culture and the Individual: A tribute to Paul Friedrich*, Lincom, Munich.

Rumsey, Alan and Weiner, James (eds) 2001, *Emplaced Myth: Space, narrative, and knowledge in Aboriginal Australia and Papua New Guinea*, University of Hawai'i Press, Honolulu.

Rumsey, Alan and Weiner, James (eds) 2004, *Mining and Indigenous Lifeworlds in Australia and Papua New Guinea*, Sean Kingston, Oxford.

Sahlins, Marshall 1999, 'Two or three things that I know about culture', *Journal of the Royal Anthropological Institute*, vol. 5, no. 3, pp. 399–421.

Sahlins, Marshall 2000, *Culture in Practice: Selected essays*, Zone Books, New York.

Said, Edward 1991, *Musical Elaborations*, Chatto & Windus, London.

San Roque, Lila 2004, Falling about: coming to terms with working on a tonal language, Unpublished manuscript.

San Roque, Lila 2008, An introduction to Duna grammar, PhD dissertation, The Australian National University, Canberra.

Sanders, Ernest H. n.d., 'Hocket', in L. Macy (ed.), *GroveMusic Online*, viewed 20 April 2006, <http://www.grovemusic.com>

Schieffelin, Edward L. 1976, *The Sorrow of the Lonely and the Burning of the Dancers*, St Martin's Press, New York.

Schieffelin, Edward L. 1991, 'Introduction', in E. L. Schieffelin and R. Crittenden (eds), *Like People You See in a Dream: First contact in six Papuan societies*, Stanford University Press, California.

Schieffelin, Edward L. and Crittenden, Robert 1991, 'Preface', in E. L. Schieffelin and R. Crittenden (eds), *Like People You See in a Dream: First contact in six Papuan societies*, Stanford University Press, Calif.

Schieffelin, Edward L., Crittenden, Robert, Allen, Bryant, Frankel, Stephen, Sillitoe, Paul, Josephides, Lisette and Schiltz, Marc 1991, 'The historical impact: Southern Highlands epilogue', in E. L. Schieffelin and R. Crittenden (eds), *Like People You See in a Dream: First contact in six Papuan societies*, Stanford University Press, Calif.

Schneider, Arnd 2003, 'On "appropriation". A critical reappraisal of the concept and its application in global art practices', *Social Anthropology*, vol. 11, no. 2, pp. 215–29.

Seeger, Anthony 1987, *Why Suyá Sing: A musical anthropology of an Amazonian people*, Cambridge University Press, Cambridge and New York.

Sewald, Ronda L. 2005, 'Sound recordings and ethnomusicology: theoretical barriers to the use of archival collections', *Resound: A quarterly of the Archives of Traditional Music*, vol. 24, nos 1–2, pp. 1–12.

Shelemay, Kay Kaufman 1991, *A Song of Longing: An Ethiopian journey*, University of Illinois Press, Urbana.

Shils, Edward 1971, 'Tradition', *Comparative Studies in Society and History*, vol. 13, pp. 122–59.

Shiner, Larry 2003, 'Western and non-Western concepts of art: universality and authenticity', in S. Davies and A. C. Sukla (eds), *Art and Essence*, Praeger, Westport, Connecticut., and London.

Sinclair, James 1984, *Kiap: Australia's patrol officers in Papua New Guinea*, Robert Brown and Associates, Bathurst, NSW.

Slawek, Stephen M. 1993, 'Ravi Shankar as mediator between a traditional music and modernity', in S. Blum, P. V. Bohlman and D. M. Neuman (eds), *Ethnomusicology and Modern Music History*, University of Illinois Press, Urbana.

Society for Ethnomusicology 1994, *A Manual for Documentation, Fieldwork, and Preservation for Ethnomusicologists*, Society for Ethnomusicology, Bloomington, Indiana.

Sollis, Michael 2007, Musical–lingual interplay in a Papua New Guinea sung story, Honours dissertation, The Australian National University, Canberra.

Sollis, Michael 2010, 'Tune-tone relationships in sung Duna *pikono*', *Australian Journal of Linguistics*, vol. 20, no. 1, pp. 67-80.

Sounds of Hela 2004, *Sounds of Hela.Volume 1*, [Recording], CHM Supersound Studios, CHMCD1780.

Spearitt, Gordon D. 1984, 'Problems in transcription: drum rhythms and flute music of Papua New Guinea', in J. C. Kassler and J. Stubington (eds), *Problems and Solutions: Occasional essays in musicology presented to Alice M. Moyle*, Hale & Iremonger, Sydney.

Stewart, Pamela J. and Strathern, Andrew 2000a, 'Naming places: Duna evocations of landscape in Papua New Guinea', *People and Culture in Oceania*, vol. 16, pp. 87–107.

Stewart, Pamela J. and Strathern, Andrew 2000b, *Speaking for life and death: warfare and compensation among the Duna of Papua New Guinea*, Senri Ethnological Reports 13, National Museum of Ethnology, Osaka.

Stewart, Pamela J. and Strathern, Andrew 2002a, *Gender, Song, and Sensibility: Folktales and folksongs in the highlands of New Guinea*, Praeger, Westport, Connecticut.

Stewart, Pamela J. and Strathern, Andrew 2002b, *Remaking the World: Myth, mining, and ritual change among the Duna of Papua New Guinea*, Smithsonian Institution Press, Washington, DC.

Stewart, Pamela J. and Strathern, Andrew 2004, 'Indigenous knowledge confronts development among the Duna of Papua New Guinea', in A. Bicker, P. Sillitoe and J. Pottier (eds), *Development and Local Knowledge: New approaches to issues in natural resources management, conservation and agriculture*, Routledge, London and New York.

Stewart, Pamela J. and Strathern, Andrew 2005, 'Duna *pikono*: a popular contemporary genre in the Papua New Guinea Highlands', in P. J. Stewart and A. Strathern (eds), *Expressive Genres and Historical Change: Indonesia, Papua New Guinea and Taiwan*, Ashgate Publications, Aldershot, UK.

Stock, Jonathon 2001, 'Ethnomusicology and the individual', *The World of Music*, vol. 43, no. 1, pp. 5–19.

Strathern, Andrew 1974, *Melpa amb kenan: Courting songs of the Melpa people*, Institute of Papua New Guinea Studies, Boroko.

Strathern, Andrew 1979, '"It's his affair": a note on the individual and the group in New Guinea Highlands societies', *Canberra Anthropology*, vol. 2, no. 1, pp. 98–113.

Strathern, Andrew 1984, *A Line of Power*, Tavistock, London and New York.

Strathern, Andrew 1991, '"Company" in Kopiago', in A. Pawley (ed.), *Man and a Half: Essays in Pacific anthropology and ethnobiology in honour of Ralph Bulmer*, The Polynesian Society, Auckland.

Strathern, Andrew and Stewart, Pamela J. 2004, *Empowering the Past, Confronting the Future: The Duna people of Papua New Guinea*, Palgrave Macmillan, New York.

Strathern, Andrew and Stewart, Pamela J. 2005, 'Introduction', in P. J. Stewart and A. Strathern (eds), *Expressive Genres and Historical Change: Indonesia, Papua New Guinea and Taiwan*, Ashgate Publications, Aldersot, UK.

Strathern, Andrew and Stewart, Pamela J. 2009, 'History, conversion and politics: three case studies from Papua New Guinea', in P. J. Stewart and A. Strathern (eds), *Religious and Ritual Change: Cosmologies and histories*, Carolina Academic Press, Durham, NC.

Strathern, Marilyn 1988, *The Gender of the Gift: Problems with women and problems with society in Melanesia*, University of California Press, Berkeley.

Stürzenhofecker, Gabriele 1993, Times enmeshed: gender, space, and history among the Duna, PhD dissertation, University of Pittsburgh, Pennsylvania.

Stürzenhofecker, Gabriele 1998, *Times Enmeshed: Gender, space, and history among the Duna of Papua New Guinea*, Stanford University Press, California.

Sullivan, Nancy n.d., 'Sing-sings and self-decoration', *A Brief Introduction to the History, Culture and Ecology of Papua New Guinea*, Trans Niugini Tours, Mount Hagen.

Summer Institute of Linguistics and Christian Missions in Many Lands 2006, Organised phonology data: Duna (Yuna) language, Unpublished manuscript, viewed 27 September 2009, <http://www.sil.org/pacific/png/abstract.asp?id=48959>

Suwa, Jun'ichiro 2001a, 'Representing sorrow in stringband laments in the Madang area, Papua New Guinea', *People and Culture in Oceania*, vol. 17, pp. 47–66.

Suwa, Jun'ichiro 2001b, 'Ownership and authenticity of indigenous and modern music in Papua New Guinea', in H. R. Lawrence and D. Niles (eds), *Traditionalism and Modernity in the Music and Dance of Oceania: Essays in honour of Barbara B. Smith*, University of Sydney, NSW.

Taime, Mal 2006, 'Reviving the Wahgi cultural show', *Post-Courier*, Friday 16 June, p. 36.

The Oxford English Dictionary 1989, 'Syncretism', *The Oxford English Dictionary*, Second edition, *OED Online*, Oxford University Press, viewed 6 December 2007, <http://dictionary.oed.com/cgi/entry/50245315>

Titon, Jeff Todd 2003, 'Textual analysis or thick description?', in M. Clayton, T. Herbert and R. Middleton (eds), *The Cultural Study of Music: A critical introduction*, Routledge, New York and London.

Tolbert, Elizabeth 1990, 'Magico-religious power and gender in the Karelian lament', in M. Herndon and S. Ziegler (eds), *Music, Gender, and Culture*, Noetzel, Wilhelmshaven.

Toner, Peter G. 2003, 'Melody and the musical articulation of Yolngu identities', *Yearbook for Traditional Music*, vol. 35, pp. 69–95.

Toner, Peter G. and Wild, Stephen A. 2004, 'Introduction—world music: politics, production and pedagogy', *The Asia Pacific Journal of Anthropology*, vol. 5, no. 2, pp. 95–112.

Toynbee, Jason 2003, 'Music, culture, and creativity', in M. Clayton, T. Herbert and R. Middleton (eds), *The Cultural Study of Music: A critical introduction*, Routledge, New York and London.

Toyoda, Yukio 2006, 'Art and national identity: a case of Papua New Guinea', in M. Yamamoto (ed.), *Art and Identity in the Pacific: Festival of Pacific Arts*, The Japan Center for Area Studies, Osaka.

Tunstill, Guy 1995, 'Learning Pitjantjatjara songs', in L. Barwick, A. Marett and G. Tunstill (eds), *The Essence of Singing and the Substance of Song: Recent responses to the Aboriginal performing arts and other essays in honour of Catherine Ellis*, University of Sydney, NSW.

Umezaki, Masahiro and Ohtsuka, Ryutaro 2003, 'Adaptive strategies of highlands-origin migrant settlers in Port Moresby, Papua New Guinea', *Human Ecology*, vol. 31, no. 1, pp. 3–25.

Urban, Greg 1988, 'Ritual wailing in Amerindian Brazil', *American Anthropologist*, vol. 90, no. 2, pp. 385–400.

Wagner, Roy 1977, 'Scientific and indigenous Papuan conceptualizations of the innate: a semiotic critique of the ecological perspective', in T. P. Bayliss-Smith and R. G. Feachem (eds), *Subsistence and Survival: Rural ecology in the Pacific*, Academic Press, London.

Waterman, Christopher A. 1990, '"Our tradition is a very modern tradition": popular music and the construction of pan-Yoruba identity', *Ethnomusicology*, vol. 34, no. 3, pp. 367–79.

Webb, Michael 1993, *Lokal Musik: Lingua franca song and identity in Papua New Guinea*, Institute of Papua New Guinea Studies, Boroko.

Webb, Michael 1995, 'Pipal bilong music tru'/a truly musical people: musical culture, colonialism, and identity in northeast New Britain, Papua New Guinea, after 1875, PhD dissertation, Wesleyan University, Middletown, Connecticut.

Webb, Michael 1998, 'Popular music: Papua New Guinea', in A. L. Kaeppler and J. W. Love (eds), *The Garland Encyclopedia of World Music. Volume 9*, Garland, New York.

Webb, Michael and Niles, Don 1987, 'Periods in Papua New Guinea music history', *Bikmaus: A journal of Papua New Guinea affairs, ideas and the arts*, vol. 7, no. 1, pp. 50–62.

Were, Eric 1968, *Perilous Paradise: Photo story of New Guinea and its emerging people*, Pacific Press, Mountain View, California.

Weiner, James 1991, *The Empty Place: Poetry, space, and being among the Foi of Papua New Guinea*, Indiana University Press, Bloomington.

Wierzbicka, Anna 1997, *Understanding Cultures Through Their Key Words*, Oxford University Press, New York and Oxford.

Wolffram, Paul 2006, '"He's not a white man, he's a small bird like you and me": learning to dance and becoming human in southern New Ireland', *Yearbook for Traditional Music*, vol. 38, pp. 109–32.

Yampolsky, Philip 2001, 'Can the traditional arts survive, and should they?', *Indonesia*, no. 71, pp. 175–85.

Zagala, Stephen 2003, 'Michel Tuffery: aesthetic archipelagoes', in C. Turner and N. Sever (eds), *Witnessing to Silence: Art and human rights*, The Australian National University, Canberra.

www.ingramcontent.com/pod-product-compliance
Lightning Source LLC
Chambersburg PA
CBHW061244270326
41928CB00041B/3402